"So, I hate my job. You hate your job. We all
hate our jobs. Big deal. But for Daniel Levine, work
is more than a daily, eight-hour annoyance,
more than the ultimate four-letter word. It is
his pet cause, and the impetus for one of the most successful
Web cyberzines to come about of late, *Disgruntled*."
—*Long Island Voice*

*More praise for the Web site that's brought fast,
effective relief to thousands of workers . . .*

"With humor and irreverence, *Disgruntled* seeks out the sources of
the malaise—and skewers them. The sharpest barbs are aimed at
corporate V.I.P.s, a collection of penny-pinchers, bumblers, and
martinets described in detail—usually anonymously—by their
unfortunate subordinates, readers who write of their personal
experiences in the workplace."

—*The New York Times CyberTimes*

"This cyberpublication provides comic relief and sound advice to the
malcontent worker. . . . The Dilbert generation (as opposed to the
'Man in the Gray Flannel Suit' set) will appreciate this funny,
revealing and useful look at the real working world."

—*Lycos*

"*Disgruntled* is pervaded with a mordant sense of humor. . . . But
there is also a no-nonsense aspect to *Disgruntled* found in features
that inform readers on current and ongoing labor issues and a
resource list of dozens of organizations addressing various
workplace concerns."

—*Newsday*

"This 'zine is must reading for anyone who has ever updated their
resumé out of frustration."

—*Internet Underground*

DISGRUNTLED

THE DARKER SIDE OF THE WORLD OF WORK

Daniel S. Levine

Berkley Boulevard Books, New York

DISGRUNTLED: THE DARKER SIDE OF THE WORLD OF WORK

A Berkley Boulevard Book / published by arrangement with
the author

PRINTING HISTORY
Berkley Boulevard trade paperback edition / September 1998

DISGRUNTLED can be found on the World Wide Web at
www.disgruntled.com

The Penguin Putnam Inc. World Wide Web site address is
http://www.penguinputnam.com

ISBN: 0-425-16507-8

BERKLEY BOULEVARD
Berkley Boulevard Books are published by The Berkley Publishing Group,
a member of Penguin Putnam Inc., 200 Madison Avenue,
New York, New York 10016.
BERKLEY BOULEVARD and its logo
are trademarks belonging to Berkley Publishing Corporation.

PRINTED IN THE UNITED STATES OF AMERICA

10 9 8 7 6 5 4 3 2 1

For Jonah, Julian and Kaiya
for teaching me there is more to life than work
and to Cherie
for being my classmate in their classroom

"One of the symptoms of approaching nervous breakdown is the belief that one's work is terribly important. If I were a medical man, I should prescribe a holiday to any patient who considered his work important."

—BERTRAND RUSSELL
The Autobiography of Bertrand Russell

Contents

A Memo from the Boss

ONE SUMMER DAY in a newsroom where I worked—probably while I was stewing because an editor couldn't get it through his thick skull why some brilliant story idea I was proposing was so brilliant—I was overwhelmed with a thought: I should start a publication called "DISGRUNTLED." It would be "The Business Magazine For People Who Work For A Living." I just blurted it out from somewhere deep in my subconscious, unaware of the thought until it came out of my mouth. But once out, it would not go away.

I had initially envisioned *DISGRUNTLED* as a conventional print publication, but there were financial realities to consider. I turned to the Internet as a low-cost alternative to see if the readership I was confident existed really did. A small investment in a book that explained how to create web pages, an account with an Internet service provider and an easy-to-remember domain name (disgruntled.com) and suddenly I was an international publisher. The first issue of *DISGRUNTLED* was officially launched on-line on November 9, 1995.

One of the unexpected benefits of publishing on the web was that it allowed readers to share their experiences from the workplace with each other. Initially there was a single section called "Around the Water Cooler" for these stories, but it quickly expanded into more than a dozen sections. Several reader stories appear throughout this book as sidebars. My own stories from work do not.

When reporters interview me about *DISGRUNTLED,* one of the first questions I am asked is why I started it. The presumption is that I must have had some really bad experience in the workplace. I've been fairly fortunate in my job history, although when I say that, my wife is quick to remind me that there was no job I had that I didn't relish bitching about. (She's one to talk.)

For the curious, my work history, starting in high school, has included stints as a janitor at a pool and at a temple, where I mopped floors and cleaned bathrooms; working in a Chinese takeout, where I ran the cash register, took orders and did light prep work in the kitchen; a few weeks at a construction site, where I dug dirt for eight hours a day to lower a foundation; several jobs making cold calls for various companies, including an insurance company and Time-Life Books; five years as a stockbroker (through the 1987 crash); and the last ten years or so as a journalist.

My reason for creating *DISGRUNTLED* grew out of my frustration with journalism in general. As a business reporter, I found publications I worked for were concerned with stories written from a CEO's perspective, an investor's perspective, an entrepreneur's perspective or a consumer's perspective. What editors generally didn't want were stories written from an employee's perspective. This always struck me as rather strange, since most of us are employees. I had become a journalist to afflict the comfortable and comfort the afflicted, but I found more often I was comforting the comfortable and afflicting the afflicted. On those rare occasions when newspapers do spill a little ink on employees, it is often about such pressing issues as what to wear on "Casual Day," rather than the daily assault on civil liberties in the workplace.

I have found a perception among business editors that people who work for a living don't read the business page. Why should they if there is nothing there that speaks to them? But even if they do, they're not the readers newspapers want. There is an economic reality. Newspapers want an attractive demographic to be able to sell advertising. They want an audience that buys portable computers and cellular phones, not work boots and beer.

As this frustration was growing within me I noticed that the people I interviewed increasingly expressed their frustration with work to me. In casual conversation with me, people at various levels of the corporate ladder would express their feelings that they were working longer and harder than they would like to be, getting less financial and psychic rewards than they believed they deserved and that work pulled them away from things more important to them, such as their families.

There are many people I'd like to thank for their encouragement, support, advice and assistance in this project. At the top of this list is Cliff Palefsky, an attorney in San Francisco who has made a career out of fighting for the rights of employees and who generously shared his expertise, counsel and library.

John Kaufman, Jerry Sullivan and Marcy Burstiner were helpful during the early stages of *DISGRUNTLED* in small but critical ways. Mike Consol, Mary Huss and Ray Shaw's trust in me helped limit the financial sacrifice necessary to make the publication a reality by sparing me the uncomfortable choice between my job and my soul.

Along the way Mindy Pines joined as a volunteer assistant editor and spent a year helping improve the content and appearance of *DISGRUNTLED*. Nell Arzab and Hugh Donovan joined later and helped carry the publication further.

Martin Sprouse, James Howard, Paul Tobias, Josh Levine, Steve Symanovich, Michael Levy and Ethan Winning all offered ongoing guidance and assistance in their own ways. The faith of my agent, Bonnie Nadell, and editor, Elizabeth Beier, made this book a possibility.

My wife, Cherie, deserves a special acknowledgment here for the unusual self-control, restraint and patience she exhibited during the writing of this book, despite the creeping sea of paper that began spilling off my desk and out into other parts of our home. She also provided a fresh pair of eyes that proofread the completed manuscript.

Last, I would like to thank my father for his unwavering support and encouragement, even though he thought I was being too negative in this book, and my mother, who didn't, because she works for my father.

PART 1

Minimum Rage

Why Work Sucks

"They say hard work never hurt anybody, but I figure why take the chance."

—RONALD REAGAN

BOBBY **NORTHINGTON HAD** nothing to lose but his chains. A \$5.50-an-hour production worker at Hambleton-Hill Publishing in Nashville, Tennessee, Northington had been on the job three days. Early on the afternoon of July 12, 1995, he rose from his seat, walked about ten feet to a colleague to give her a piece of chewing gum and immediately returned to his workstation. His supervisor then approached him with a chain and padlocked him to his desk. Amused, she laughed and said that she should now finally be able to get some production out of him. He was kept that way for forty minutes, a fitting image of life on the job today.

Northington worked the rest of the day, then resigned and filed suit against his company and supervisor for false imprisonment, outrageous conduct and creating an extreme and abusive work environment. Some people just don't have a sense of humor. In response to the allegations, Hambleton-Hill Publishing denied any wrongdoing. The company said it immediately checked into the charges and found conflicting reports. The company said that as a matter of policy it does not approve of the activity alleged in the suit—at least not without the supervisor's completing all of the requisite forms in triplicate.

Welcome to the wonderful world of work. From the moment God threw Adam's sorry ass out of Eden and told him to go work for a living, we have toiled to get our bread from the sweat of our brows. For many of us, the hot sun may have been replaced by the harsh glow of fluorescent bulbs, the green fields by gray cubicles and the physical strain by that unique brand of torment that could only come from working for someone stupider than ourselves, but it's work just the same.

If the existentialists are right—that action defines being—then we are what we do and what we do is work. It defines us and consumes us. When we are not at work, we are driving to it or escaping from it, doing it at home or preparing for it. If our struggle for the legal tender has put us a bit on edge these days so that we go home and yell at the kids or kick the dog now and then, that's too bad. It's part of making a living and they probably deserve it anyway.

The daily routine may vary, but it's essentially the same for all of us. The body lies motionless. While the left eye stays buried deep in the pillow, the right eyelid slowly rolls its way upward, like a window shade being raised carefully so as not to make any noise that might stir its owner. Slowly the red digital output from the clock radio comes into focus and the calculations and negotiations begin as if it is the first time and not the same routine over and over each day. As time keeps marching forward, a high standard of personal hygiene moves dangerously close to being traded away for a few more precious minutes of sleep. "If I don't shower . . . If I don't shave . . . If I don't brush my teeth . . . ," the thinking goes in the final moments before full consciousness kicks in with a yawn of the adrenal gland. No time for coffee, so a portable breakfast is this morning's fare—a can of warm diet Coke to swill in the car.

Once the car engine is fired up, the drive begins. The steering wheel not only controls the car, but acts as a perfect rest against which to balance the morning paper. A tilt of the rearview mirror, and

Bagging the Job

I am 18 years old. I live in South Carolina. I am happily (currently) employed in the produce department of a grocery store. It's a part-time job while I attend school. This isn't my first job in the grocery business. So let me tell you why my former employer can kiss my ass.

I started working at a major grocery chain the summer after I turned 16. I wanted money so I could save for college and get a car. I started at $4.35 per hour—minimum wage at the time.

I was a bagger. I quickly became the best bagger there—not that bagging requires skill. I would make customers laugh by juggling cans, cracking jokes and poking friendly fun at the cashiers. Customers, cashiers and baggers all loved me. I figured I'd get a raise soon.

After a year, I began to realize that my raise wasn't coming. I began to ask the boss where my raise was. "You're up for one now," he said. "You'll get it in the next month."

After a month, I asked him again. "I put you in for a raise," he said with a smug grin. "How much?" I asked. "To $4.50," he said, grinning smugly. I waited. My paycheck came, with no raise. I bugged the boss every two weeks about my raise. I always got the answer, "It'll be on your next paycheck."

I went job hunting. I had produce experience, and I landed a job at another grocery store. I told nobody except the produce manager at the store that I was quitting. The last Sunday I worked there, I said goodbye to everyone and told them where I was going. The boss was in a meeting with managers from all the other stores in the chain in the area. Everyone but him knew what was coming.

When he came up front, I clocked out. As I walked out the door, he said goodbye, and that he'd see me later. "No you won't," was my reply. I didn't turn around. "What?" he said, confusion in his voice. "Shove my job up your ass," I said. "Right along with that raise I never got."

This, I did in front of about six store managers. They most likely all wanted explanations as to why I was so pissed.

I returned two weeks later to pick up my paycheck. I was greeted with cheers from my ex-fellow employees. I did what they all wanted to do. My new employer appreciates me. I've been there nine months, and I've had two raises. I get to make my own schedule, I'm up for another raise and I'm training to be a produce manager.

My former employer—kiss my ass.

Crowley

not only can traffic behind the vehicle be monitored, but lipstick or
an electric shaver can be guided to insure no spot is missed. By using
the knees to hold the steering wheel on a long straightaway, acces-
sories such as a necktie or earrings can be put into place. The accidents this nearly causes, along with a honk of the horn and a
good-morning flip of the bird to a fellow commuter, release the additional adrenaline needed to make up for any shortage of caffeine.

It is in this relaxed way that the new workday begins. A day
filled with rancid coffee, angry clients, drawn-out staff meetings,
grouchy supervisors, incompetent coworkers, lecherous bosses, un-
reliable equipment, relentless faxes, incessant voice mail and enough
"Dear Colleague" memos to move the acid production in the stom-
ach into high gear.

If it seems we are working harder and longer for less, that's because we are. The economic data paint a grim statistical portrait of
what lies behind the amorphous mix of grief and anxiety that has
caused many of us to develop sudden cravings for Hamburger
Helper. For more than twenty years there has been a steady slide in
real wages (wages adjusted for inflation) and a recent blip upward
has done little to reverse the trend. In fact, about the only economic
indicators that are setting records these days are corporate profits
and executive compensation. These increases are not being driven
by faster growth of productivity, but instead came about from a
squeeze on wages in the 1990s, according to the Economic Policy
Institute, a liberal think tank in Washington, D.C. So for the boss,
it's a lifestyle of the rich and famous, while for everyone else it's
jeopardy.

The debate gets framed in many ways. Critics talk about the
widening gap between rich and poor, between workers and CEOs,
but what really eats away at people and demoralizes them is their
failed expectation of fairness in the workplace. For some reason they
expect hard work to be rewarded, think those rewards should be pro-
portional to the contributions made to an enterprise and feel everyone should be treated the same. The workplace has never been fair.

Like they used to say in ancient Egypt, "You don't get promoted to Pharaoh by working hard on a pyramid."

Executive compensation is a glaring example of the inequity that is the rule rather than the exception in the workplace. At a time when wages for workers in the U.S. creep at a petty pace, executive pay packages at the nation's largest corporations continue to reach staggering heights. "There is no reason why they need to be paid this sort of money. They could use that money to lower the cost of products, give workers raises or give shareholders more profits," said executive compensation expert Graef Crystal. "These guys are pigs."

Crystal did offer a modest proposal for reining in executive pay packages. Taking a cue from executives who shut down plants here for cheaper labor overseas, he suggested hiring British executives to run American companies. "They get a quarter of what American executives get paid," he said, "and they speak better English than we do."

What has made these pay packages particularly harsh to swallow these days is that they have come at a time not only of stagnant wages, but of massive downsizing—often at the very companies that have showered their fearless leaders with enough money to make anyone fearless. Consider AT&T's former CEO Robert Allen, who aimed the corporate ax at the necks of some forty thousand AT&T employees who were slated to lose their jobs through a massive downsizing plan. For leading the telecommunications giant to a point where such drastic steps needed to be taken, Allen saw his compensation package rise in value to $16 million in 1995 from $6.7 million the year before.

The total number of announced corporate layoffs since 1989 now exceeds 3 million. The staggering figures caused the outplacement firm Challenger, Gray & Christmas to say that one of the greatest challenges facing managers these days is rebuilding and redefining the employer-employee relationship and getting employees more committed to their jobs and their company. "Ongoing layoffs and restructurings combined with the blinding speed of

Hacking It in the 21st Century

U.S. Secretary of Labor, Robert Reich offered a set of rules workers will need to follow if they want to succeed in the new economy of the 21st century. Reich says:

Rule 1: Get computer literate, regardless of the type of work you do.

Rule 2: Education will give you an edge, but you must continuously build new knowledge and skills.

Rule 3: Don't think of your career in a linear way. Plan on advancing because of skills, not seniority.

Rule 4: Be aggressive about networking. Information is the key to advancement.

Rule 5: There is no "I" in Team. People will work in teams, though team members may be dispersed and connected by technology. Enhance your value by learning to play all the positions.

Grunty noticed that the secretary left a few things off his list and thought he would offer some additional rules for cutting it in the new millennium.

Rule 6: Bosses will always know less about how the equipment in their office works than employees do. Use this to your advantage and grind things to a halt if you are tired or aggravated.

Rule 7: If your employer pays for training, take a course that will get you a better job.

Rule 8: Forget about climbing the corporate ladder. Instead, use company time and resources to develop a new product, write a screenplay or launch a business.

Rule 9: Information is the key to advancement. Find out who your boss is sleeping with and get compromising photographs.

Rule 10: You can't spell "Stupid Son of a Bitch" without "B-O-S-S." Don't take crap. There is always another job.

technological changes are wearing down the 'soul' of organizations and creating upheaval, confusion and anxiety in the workplace," said John Challenger, executive vice president of the firm. "Management is making a major effort to refocus workers on what their role is at the company and to create a sense of meaning and purpose at work. By doing this, management is demonstrating how much they value the people who work for them."

Some of those employees already know how valued they are, such as one controller in Wisconsin who was asked to prepare a two-year cash projection, a revised budget and a suggested plan for lay-offs and department eliminations. He was told to have it in by Friday at 4 P.M. Forty-five minutes after meeting his deadline he was handed a pink slip and told his services were no longer needed. Among his final duties was to type his own severance agreement. So, Mr. Challenger's friends have a daunting task for themselves. They need to build trust and commitment from employees—employees who have regularly seen the rewards of loyalty.

Having created an environment of fear and loathing, employers react with puzzlement when employees raid the supply cabinet for their personal use, make long-distance phone calls to friends from the office or doctor their expense reports to edge themselves just a little closer toward the salaries they deserve. The real way to build loyalty—the only way to build loyalty—is to demonstrate loyalty. Executives can throw away all of their management best-sellers with their five steps, six rules and seven qualities to achieve the win-win situation of virtually reengineered team empowerment they all seem to want. Would life on a slave ship be much better if the galley-master first asked the rowers to help write a mission statement? What employers need to come to terms with is the economic, cultural and societal benefits of being loyal to their employees. If they don't, eventually their abuses will bite them on the ass.

Ichiro Oshima took a fleshy nibble on his employer's bottom, even though he seemed like just another hapless victim of work. Oshima killed himself at the age of twenty-four, just seventeen months

Copyright Out of There

I used to work for the information systems division of a company in Northern California. I did data entry eight hours a day. If you got up to use the restroom too much, you were called into a meeting and reprimanded. If your 15 minute break took 15 minutes and 10 seconds, you were "talked to" (seriously!).

They have a group of self-important, no-life scumbags known as the "Secret Police" that tell your boss every time you fart, breathe wrong or look cross-eyed. I suffered through this shit for two years with the promise that when a better internal opening came along, I would have first shot at it. Bullshit!! Every time I applied for a different position they would find a "problem" with my work, attitude, experience or something else that would hold me back. They'd tell me that maybe next time things would "work out."

I finally got canned when my boss loaned me some software to take home for my PC, then fired me for copyright violations. They can all kiss my ass now. A little more than a year after my dismissal I am the manager of a large corporation's technology group. I guess things did "work out" after all.

Mike G.

after joining Dentsu, Japan's largest advertising agency. During that time he worked seven days a week without taking a single day off. Because of the exhaustive hours he put in on the job, he survived on between thirty minutes and two and a half hours of sleep each night, according to press accounts. Security logs from Dentsu's building showed that Oshima had worked until 2 A.M. on sixty-six occasions. In the month of August alone, he worked around the clock six times and burned the oil until 6:30 A.M. once every three nights. Being a good employee, he had waited until he had completed a major project he was working on before taking his own life. In the United States, going into advertising will cost you your soul, but everything is more expensive in Japan.

The Japanese call it *karoshi*—a term meaning "death from overwork." The Japanese Labor Ministry reported there were at least sixty-three cases of karoshi through the first eleven months of 1995. Oshima could have been just another sorry corpse tucked away in the catacombs of one corporation's dirty little history, but instead his story offers some inspiration for us all. Five years after he killed himself, he reached from beyond the grave to remind us it's never too late to get even with an employer.

In 1996, a Japanese court found Dentsu liable in his death and ordered the company to pay Oshima's family $1.2 million. Japan's highest court upheld the decision but reduced the damages to $738,000. The case was unusual because even though allegations of death from overwork had been made in lawsuits before, those instances involved death by so-called natural causes such as heart attacks and strokes. The Oshima case was the first one involving suicide. Dentsu argued that Oshima's personal problems, and not work, had caused him to kill himself. The judge disagreed and said that the company knew about his long hours and worsening health, but failed to do anything about them.

For those who might think the Oshima case is uniquely Japanese, fret not. The Japanese may have turned *karoshi* into a commercial success, but like the automobile, color TV and VCR, we

Armed, Dangerous and Plain Fuckin' Dumb

Armed gunmen who threatened to kill employees of TCI Cablevision of Tulsa, Oklahoma during a 1993 robbery turned out to be part of a "security seminar" set up by the company, the *Washington Post* reported.

Traumatized workers, who thought it was real, were not amused. Five employees later sued the company charging TCI and the security company it retained with assault with a deadly weapon and intentional infliction of emotional distress.

"It was my son's seventeenth birthday and I believed that I was never going to see him again," said one employee. "I was standing there with my hands over my head shaking and I came to the realization that I was going to die."

It's a good thing they never got around to their plans for a fire drill.

1/30/97

invented it first and still work ourselves to death as well as anyone else today.

Why does work suck? If it didn't, it wouldn't be called work. Sure, there are a few misguided souls who profess a sincere love of their work, just as there are those people who have been told by their dogs to worship Satan, have had devices planted in their brains so their thoughts can be monitored by the CIA and have been anally probed by visitors from outer space. Except for those people who lack the imagination to do something more in the absence of work than sit around picking lint from their belly buttons as they watch the *Jerry Springer Show,* it's hard to believe that we don't all have better things to do. We work because we need food, shelter, clothing and anything that numbs the pain of work itself. If it weren't for the fact that the only thing that sucks worse than work is having to look for it, who'd do it?

If we are ever to improve the situation, we need to begin talking about work in an honest way. We need to break the seal that says "sanitized for your protection" and get down to the dirty business of confronting our creation. We have so embraced our Ward Cleaver illusions of the workplace that when we are faced with harsh reality, we have come to question reality rather than the illusion. We make excuses for our boss's childish outbursts. We talk about our "careers" because "jobs" remind us our hands might get dirty. And, we delude ourselves into thinking that all those overtime hours for which we are not getting paid will hold a bigger reward of a promotion and raise because we are dedicated and loyal servants, not a bunch of saps who are being cheated out of our due.

A few years back when I was reporting on the advertising industry I wrote a story about a new campaign from the California State Lottery. I had a chance to talk to the brain trust at the advertising agency that put this together. The flack for the agency, beaming with pride over the new campaign, explained to me that the ads showed the actual thoughts that went through the minds of lottery winners when it finally sunk in that they had won all of this money. One moron, rolling a cart down a grocery store aisle, pronounces that

It Came from Outer Space

For the last four years, I have worked for a major housing authority. I handle the graphic design and word processing for one department. Everything was going along just great for two and one-half years until my old (halfway decent) boss quit and a new one was hired.

Well, this gal's body is on Earth, but her mind is somewhere in the cosmos. She constantly rambles on and on about aliens, synergy and how liberal she is. This, of course, means that she is a total loon.

The day she began work, she decided that I did not merit the little cubicle I occupied since we moved into the building and that I needed to not only operate a computer, but be a receptionist as well. Never mind that we have a clerk-typist and an administrative assistant, both of whom are qualified to act as receptionist. Also, I type all kinds of confidential material which is not confidential anymore because anyone can read it.

This 51/50 (police lingo for a loony tune) woman also insisted that I was out to sabotage her authority. She constantly harassed, watched and bothered me about trivial matters like personal phone calls, which I don't make.

I finally had to take three months of disability leave because my blood pressure zoomed up due to stress. The day I returned from disability, she informed me that the temporary worker would keep my cubicle. I could not have my computer, nor could I use anyone else's. There are a lot more incidents of this nature, but it would take a tome to catalogue them all. Needless to say, I have complained about this sorry excuse for a human being for a looooong time!

The tide has finally turned and my complaints have been heard by the right people. One of our contractors sued, other coworkers are complaining about her and she talks more and more about the solar flares that are causing such strife in the workplace. I am happily ensconced in another department with a much better computer, desk and boss with the opportunity to be promoted. I truly hope this harpie rots in hell, or whatever her interpretation of it is!

McCorm

it finally hit him when he stopped in the dairy section. "I said, 'Hey, I could buy all this cheeeeeese.'"

Another commercial featured a giggling couple brushing their teeth in a bathroom newly outfitted with gold sinks. The camera

Punchy Dialogue with the Boss

I worked as a service manager for a small x-ray company for about seven years. I was salaried and worked about 55 to 60 hours, drove about 1,000 miles per week and spent almost three weeks each month out of town.

I never felt appreciated as my employer was always ready to show fault and place blame. I came in one Tuesday morning at about 8:45 A.M. The boss was instantly in my face, saying, "We start at 8:30 here!"

My reply was simple and to the point. "Fuck you, Tom!" to which he replied, "No, fuck you!" I went out to my company vehicle and came back in with a film transport rack from a Kodak film processor.

Slamming the newly rebuilt rack on the service desk, I interjected into his face, "While you were home last night watching reruns of *Roseanne,* I spent three hours rebuilding this. So, fuck you."

We argued. He attacked me while I was crouched down. As I fell backward with his hands on my throat, I got in three well aimed wallops to the side of his face. He choked me and ripped a bunch of hair out. We settled it and went about our jobs.

He sent me to a bordering city to pick up a part from a large x-ray company. They grabbed me when I came in and offered me the service manager job there. I haven't got into fights lately, and that poor lame-o was stuck with undertrained people and a butt load of work.

A lady I met at a clinic one day summed it all up. She had been filling in for the regular x-ray technician. We talked. As she was leaving for lunch, she stuck her head into the room and said, "One day you're going to realize there is more to life than being stuck in a corner, working on an x-ray machine." Then she walked off.

It woke me up big time!

Dale D.

spared us a view of the toilet, but how could anyone with any taste mix porcelain with that beautiful gold that we would all surely hope to be able to spit and rinse in someday? Maybe the ads spoke well to people who had already won the lottery, but they didn't speak to me. The thought of having my very own gold crapper is not exactly going to make me go out and spend a hard-earned, after-tax dollar on a one-in-a-gazillion chance to win the lottery. What would do it, though, is seeing some schlump who told me that after he won the lottery he bought the company where he spent the last umpteen years slaving away and fired the fat, no-good, son-of-a-bitch to whom he had answered all that time.

I think of Charlton Heston in *Planet of the Apes* where he wakes up after a long space voyage to find himself in a nightmarish world where talking apes rule and men are dumb creatures hunted and exploited. Heston, who has been muted by an injury he suffered when captured by the apes, lets out his first astonishing words to his new masters, who are shocked to learn a human has the intelligence to form words and communicate through language. As he turns to one of his captors, he says in a tone that would make Clint Eastwood tremble, "Get your stinking paws off me, you damn dirty apes."

Many people in the workplace today are like Heston. They find themselves in an unreal world surrounded by their ape masters, unable to speak for whatever reason. I hope there will be comfort here until you are able to form those words and triumphantly tell your boss to get his stinking ape paws off you. Of course, don't be surprised if the startled beast offers back two words of its own: "You're fired." But don't worry, at least you'd finally get a day off.

2

Pounding the Pavement

"I don't think McDonald's is necessarily a bad place to work, but I wouldn't say that's the only alternative for people who are trained in banking."

—PAUL HAZEN
Chairman of Wells Fargo & Co., responding at a press conference to a question as to whether the bank would provide retraining for thousands of fired employees so they could avoid fast-food jobs following a merger
—The Wall Street Journal, *October 9, 1996*

WHEN **S**IBI **S**OROKA applied to Target Stores for a job as a security guard in Pleasanton, California, he wasn't prepared for all of the questions the employer had for him. It wasn't that Target wanted to know what he thought his biggest weaknesses were or what he saw himself doing in five years. Rather, the retailer gave him a list of more than seven hundred true-and-false questions about himself, ranging from possible bad thoughts in his head to any problems he might have controlling his bowels. These included such questions as:

- ❖ I feel that I am strongly attracted to members of my own sex.
- ❖ I have never indulged in unusual sexual practices.
- ❖ I have had difficulty holding my urine.
- ❖ I feel there is only one true religion.
- ❖ I believe in the second coming of Christ.

Such questions might be appropriate for someone applying for a job as a priest at a scandal-shy church without plumbing, but would seem to cross the line for a job guarding housewares, toys and junk food.

The questions make up a test known as the Minnesota Multiphasic Personality Indicator—a test designed to help psychologists assess personality disorders, but later embraced by employers as a way to weed out undesirable job applicants. Soroka thought the questions went a tad too far and violated his privacy rights. In 1989, he filed a class-action suit against the company. "This was for store security people—unarmed individuals who are trying to see if people are stealing pens," said Brad Seligman, a civil rights attorney who represented the plaintiffs in the lawsuit against Target. "They have no right to use a weapon. No right to arrest a citizen. They are not police officers. They do not have the same safety consideration." The company settled the case by establishing a $1.3 million fund for an estimated twenty-five hundred job applicants and $60,000 each for Soroka and three other named plaintiffs. Target had said it chose to settle the suit to avoid costly litigation. Seligman said since the case, the establishment of the Americans with Disabilities Act has prohibited the use of such tests for preemployment screening.

Nevertheless, as employers try to get to know their job applicants up close and personal, other kinds of testing continues. Some seem to have as dubious a place in the hiring process as the Minnesota multiphasic test. Seligman is currently litigating a case filed in San Francisco Superior Court in 1994 that also involved job applicants for positions as security guards. His client, Mel Thompson, applied for a job with the security firm Burns International in 1993. He believed the interview for the job went well and the interviewer, according to the civil complaint, told him he was impressed with his experience and employment history in the security field. When he was done, the interviewer handed him a written test called the "P.A.S.S.-III SURVEY," which consisted of a hundred questions in the form of a statement that the test-taker had to answer "yes," "no," or "?" Among the statements the applicant was told to respond to on the test were:

- ❖ Workers' rights usually come last as far as most companies are concerned.
- ❖ Most companies make too much profit.
- ❖ Most employers demand too much for too little pay.
- ❖ The drinking age should be lowered.
- ❖ Marijuana smoking once or twice a day doesn't hurt anyone.

According to the suit, the tests were scored on the basis of "correct" responses and were used to determine the "risk" levels of job applicants. Cutoff scores were used to make hiring decisions.

The class-action suit against Burns International Security Services and Borg-Warner Protective Services Corporation charged that the company's preemployment screening discriminated in hiring on the basis of political views concerning corporations, workers' rights and drug and alcohol laws. The test also measured a candidate's riskiness in relation to indices of "alienation," "trustworthiness" and "drug attitudes." "The 'alienation' index of the test purports to measure whether an applicant believes in 'traditional' values, such as 'free enterprise' or whether the applicant identifies with 'antiestablishment (counterculture)' opinions; the 'drug attitude' index does not measure drug use or propensity for drug use or abuse; rather, it is intended to measure attitudes about drug and alcohol; a person scored 'low risk' as to this factor is claimed to have a 'conservative view of drug use'; and a person scoring 'high risk' on this index is said to be characterized by 'creativity, individualism and non-conformity,' " the suit said. It went on to charge that the test was designed to screen out people with moderate, liberal or progressive political beliefs and to identify those candidates whose political beliefs and affiliations conform to the company's. The company contended that the test was used to measure attitude, not politics.

Such tests are just part of the indignities some job seekers must endure as they shine their shoes, freeze a smile on their faces and try to take on the rosy outlook of Mister Rogers while they go knocking on doors in their neighborhood in search of a paycheck. Technology is making the search for job openings easier through the Internet— making it easier for people to network and use job search sites—but it is also changing the way companies hire. Increasingly computers and not hiring managers filter out resumes to find appropriate candidates, and database services provide intimate details about a candidate. And, as with the job listings, all of this information can be obtained over the Internet.

Routinely and for often what amounts to nominal fees, employers tap into available databases to examine applicants' motor vehicle records, discover if applicants have ever sued past employers, check their credit history, research if they have any kind of criminal record and see if they have ever filed a workers' compensation claim. In many cases the employee doesn't consent to such background checks, and he is usually unaware if they are made. The one exception is credit reports, which are covered by the Fair Credit Reporting Act. And, if a litigation search turns up that an applicant is divorced, an employer can saunter down to the courthouse and rummage through the dirty laundry and find out what accusations were made, what the applicant's assets were and all of the ugliness right down to who got the parakeet. Employers aren't just nosy. Some have fears that employees they hire might lie, cheat and steal (in ways other than they are paid to do). Others don't want to find out too late that they have put other employees or customers at risk because they didn't properly screen their new employees, such as in hiring a known child molester to run a day care center. In recent years there have been a handful of employers who found themselves on the wrong side of costly "negligent hiring" lawsuits. Courts have found that employers who disregarded relevant information or failed to take reasonable steps to discover such information about an employee's past could be found liable.

Handling the Tough Interview Questions

A lot of people know how to write a resume and talk their way into an interview. But when they get into the make-or-break dialogue, they stumble upon tough questions. Below, Grunty offers some advice on approaching the hard questions that interviewers like to throw at job applicants:

Why did you leave your last job?
Real answer: It sucked.
What you should say: I felt my talents and abilities were underutilized.

What are your biggest weaknesses?
Real answer: I can't concentrate for more than five minutes, hate all forms of authority and tend to fall asleep at my desk.
What you should say: I'm a workaholic. I just don't know when to put down my work.

You don't hold on to jobs long. Why should we think you'll be here any longer than at your last job?
Real answer: My employers have always had a hang-up about keeping only competent employees.
What you should say: I'm at a point in my career where I am tired of moving around. I really want to feel part of a team, a long-term enterprise, where I can make a contribution.

What does the word "success" mean to you?
Real answer: It means that I don't have to drag my sorry ass out of bed to kiss yours.
What you should say: Success, for me, would be knowing I am making a difference working with a team of people to make a more profitable enterprise.

Do you ever get angry with coworkers?
Real answer: I don't get angry, I get even.
What you should say: Nothing angers me more than to see a coworker not pulling his weight, goofing off or stealing. Yes, sometimes I do get angry with coworkers.

What does the word "failure" mean to you?
Real answer: It means I continue to collect unemployment insurance.
What you should say: Failure? I'm sorry, I don't know what you mean. That word is not in my vocabulary.

Job applicants have been known to stretch the truth a little too, listing a degree in their educational background for which they might not have quite completed the coursework. Some list colleges they never attended, concoct Social Security numbers, report jobs they never held and misreport the amount of time they were at a job so they don't have to explain a two-year gap when they worked in the metal shop at the state penitentiary. According to KTI, a Battlefield, Missouri, private investigation firm that provides background checks on job applicants, one-third of job applications contain fraudulent information. "There are people out there that won't check references and previous employers. They don't want to spend the money," said a representative of KTI. "They are taking a chance. Thirty years ago that might have been okay, but not today."

Once upon a time it was a lot easier to catch applicants in a lie through the use of polygraphs. While the Employee Polygraph Protection Act essentially eliminated the use of lie detector tests in almost all employment settings, written honesty exams have risen in their place. In these tests, people are required to answer "true" or "false" to a series of statements. The answers are compared with answers from a baseline of people deemed honest and dishonest. Diane Arthur, author of *Workplace Testing: An Employer's Guide to Policies and Practices,* said that while test publishers have performed research to support the predictive value of their tests, the Office of Technology Assessment questioned this value in a 1990 study. "At best, the OTA considered publisher claims to be unsubstantiated," she said. The office found in one instance that between 18 and 29 percent of the people test results identified as "counterproductive" were categorized erroneously. In another instance, the OTA found a test incorrectly identified 29 percent of the subjects as "counterproductive."

To highlight the flaws of such a test, Rebecca Locketz, legal director of the American Civil Liberties Union's National Task Force on Civil Liberties in the Workplace, points to the story of an "extremely honest nun." The nun took a pencil honesty test and was refused employment when she answered "true" to a statement that

Unwanted Career Advice

Some time ago, I was approached by a representative of a headhunting firm who saw my mini-resume, which was published in a directory by a local job hunting group.

When I went down for an interview after I sent her a copy of my full resume, she began chewing me out for my lack of experience.

She lambasted me for not having a degree in computer programming, and the fact that I had little real experience in the field. She suggested that I stay in the library field even though on top of a master's degree in library science with an emphasis on library automation, I had considerable training in programming.

This woman probably only had a bachelor's degree. She was also considerably younger than I was. What right did she have to question my decision to change from being a librarian to a computer programmer, especially when the market for librarians is so badly depressed that a librarian with more experience than I have with a Ph.D. or Ed.D. is competing for an entry-level library job?

It's stuff like this that makes me wonder how a person is supposed to move ahead in life when an employer questions an applicant about his or her career choices.

Robert L.

read, "I have stolen things from a workplace." She had answered "true" because she recalled an instance when she had inadvertently walked out with a pencil and some paper clips from an office. She was later able to straighten out the situation and was hired for the job.

The problem with all this, say critics of today's hiring process, is that employers have become so concerned with not making mistakes that they fail to fully and fairly evaluate the candidates before them. "It's gotten real mechanical. People have become real data-driven," said David W. Foerster, Jr., executive director of the Resource Center in Atlanta, which provides crisis mediation and counseling to employers. "They don't try to find out what a person's skills or gifts might be, but data about how a person pays their bills or whether there is a criminal record. We tend to look for reasons to exclude rather than focus on the attributes that would want us to include.

Until we get inclusionary, I don't think we will get the best people in the workplace."

As an example, Foerster pointed to the case of one attorney in the Southeast who found himself looking for a job after the firm where he worked decided to break up. The attorney was being considered for a position as a partner with a new firm, but was rejected after a credit check showed that he'd had tax problems ten years earlier. Even though the tax problems had been resolved long ago and the attorney was considered among the best in the region in his area of specialty, he was not hired. "There was an issue of appearance and some concern that if he handled his personal financial matters that

Unemployed You

I am a former police officer who is currently between jobs. I applied to the local university as a public safety officer. When I applied it was clear that the university was looking for a full-time officer and that I was looking for full-time work only.

I passed all the tests with very high scores and passed the background investigation. The background investigator told me that I was the only candidate and that he found no negative information. His last words were "I look forward to working with you. The chief should be calling you within a couple of weeks with an offer."

Nine days passed and the chief called me in for what I thought would be an offer for full-time employment. I arrived 15 minutes early and he was a few minutes late. When we started to talk, he went over my background and then offered me an on-call position. I told him that I was under the impression that the job was for full-time. He then said, "I want the department to reflect the student population which is 60 percent female. So right now I want to hire a female instead of a male."

He went on to tell me that the female candidate was still going through the background check and if she did not make it that I was still a candidate for the job. He also told me that she had no street experience and that her certifications were less than mine were.

I sensed that there was something wrong with this chief when during our first interview, he asked me how I am registered to vote and how did I vote for prop 209. I was very disappointed, especially since I spent almost $350.00 getting extra certifications at their request. Is this the way for a private university to conduct its business?

Kenji

Will Work for School

I'm twenty years old and in my third year of college. I need two more years to get my B.A., and I plan on getting a master's degree as well.

My problem? I have to work to be able to afford to go to school and still eat. But I can't get anyone to work around my class schedule. I know more about computers than many people twice my age do. I have good references and a good personality. However, in a town full of students just like me, that doesn't help much.

I'd like to get enough financial aid to quit working and finish school, but I don't qualify because of what my parents make. Even though I've been living on my own and supporting myself for almost three years, I'm not considered independent by the rules of financial aid until I'm 24. I've gotten some loans, but again, they won't give me the full amount I need because I'm under 24. No grants, no scholarships although I make fairly good grades.

I'm white and from a middle-class background, so it's automatically assumed my parents should pay for everything. I don't think they should have to: I'm an adult, and they can't really afford it, anyway. Because of this, there's really no solution for me but to take some time off from my lifelong dream of a degree to work until I reach the age of officially being recognized for what I've been for three years—a poor, financially independent adult who wants to learn.

M.C.

way he would make the same mistakes in his firm matters. I think the real reason is that they feared it might make them look bad," said Foerster. "The best people often have some difficulty in the past that is measured in some way by some reporting agency. To rule them out because of something that happened ten years ago is real foolish. We are robbing ourselves."

Though antidiscrimination laws are supposed to protect job applicants from the misuse of all of this information, human resource professionals say employers often disqualify candidates solely on the basis of revelations in such data banks and cover themselves by simply telling the candidate they found someone more qualified. "They'll find a reason," said Michael Rankin, who used to perform background checks for employers. "One of the biggest things that can scare an employer nowadays is someone who has filed for workers' comp." Among the more creative maneuvers employers use to find out about job candidates, according to Rankin, is to give them a piece of plain, unruled paper and ask them to write out their goals for the next five years. This is done not because they want to hire someone with direction, but because they want to perform handwriting analysis. "They don't care about your goals," said Rankin.

As if the humiliation that can go hand in hand with a job search were not enough, some people may find their efforts to find employment are being sabotaged by some not so mysterious forces. Rankin has switched sides and today is chief service officer for Documented Reference Check, a Diamond Bar, California, company that helps employees find out what their former employers are saying about them. Though the service's representatives never lie to the people they call—the company has several corporate names it legally uses when it calls employers—the employers believe they are talking to

Bargain Shoppers

Recently I read, for the 14,000th time, a type of "help wanted" ad that made me finally blow my stack. It contained the poisonous phrase, "send salary requirements."

I'd rather eat nails than work for a company who wore their bargain-hunting mentality on their sleeve like this! "Hey, stupid," I felt like saying, "how can I tell how much to ask for if I haven't even interviewed yet to find out what the job's about? Or is this your 'primary sort' criteria?"

"Hmmm," thinks the human resources representative, "let's go through the stack...wants too much, shitcan...wants too much, shitcan..." And so the trash fills up until he finds a willing slave who'll work cheaper than anyone else in the stack.

I finally got so sick of this bull I actually called the company up, got a hold of human resources, told them why I wasn't applying and wished them luck trying to find a "blue light special" slave.

Up the system. Poop on corporate culture!

Name withheld

someone looking for information about a job candidate. "We never state that we are hiring this person," said Rankin. "The only thing we do state is that we are doing a reference check."

Documented Reference Check essentially duplicates what a personnel director would do in checking out a candidate for a job. Using one of its many names, it calls its client's previous employer and conducts a thorough interview. The big difference, though, is that everything that is said is written down in a report and then delivered to the former employee. Because the reports can wind up as evidence in court, Documented Reference Check doesn't ask any extraordinary questions, just the type a typical personnel director would ask. Since it has no stake in the answers—it gets paid the same $79 whether the report is negative or positive—its reports have proved valuable in litigation.

Though employers don't particularly like Documented Reference Check and have tried to get its reports thrown out when they show up in official proceedings, the reports have consistently held up in courtrooms and administrative hearings. "Employers are the ones with the money and the private investigators snooping into people's privacy. They spy on their employees," said Don D. Sessions, an employee rights attorney in Mission Viejo, California, who has used the service for his clients. "They get very unsettled whenever we do anything to find out what they do." Usually, confronted with incriminating reports, employers know they have been caught red-handed and quickly try to settle matters.

In one case in Maine, a worker who was fired after filing a workers' compensation claim called on Documented Reference Check. His attorney suspected he had been wrongfully terminated and was now being blacklisted by his former employer. During a deposition, his employer denied saying negative things about the worker or making reference to the workers' compensation claim that the worker had filed. Then the attorney produced a transcript of the call from Documented Reference Check showing that the employer had said the employee was a problem had got rid of him because he filed a workers'

Radioactive Dating Methods

I am a registered technologist, certified in both x-ray and radiation therapy. I have given up on the radiation therapy, mostly because the last employer I interviewed with lied to me. I was told one thing at the interview and three months later he did a complete 180-degree turn around.

I decided to get into something else and selected ultrasound. I found out that my state has no certified ultrasound programs. I had to go out of state to get it. I got into a six-month program and did well. In order to sit for the boards, I need to complete six more months of clinical work. To absolutely no avail, I have written to hospitals, clinics, doctors' offices and others.

I have no way to prove it, but I strongly suspect I have not been able to find a spot anywhere because of my age. Facilities will say it was for any other number of reasons, but I believe it was age discrimination.

Mark M.

compensation claim. The case was settled without ever going to trial. "They cut their losses immediately and offered him his job back," said David Beneman, a partner with Levenson, Vickerson, & Beneman in Portland, Maine. "If I can get something that proves I'm right, usually, if there are any brains on the other side of the matter, we can get a resolution."

Because of potential legal liabilities, many lawyers advise employers to stick to the basics and just give name, rank and serial number on reference checks. But even if that is a company's policy, the individual getting the reference call will often go beyond that. The laws affecting reference checks vary from state to state. Essentially employers are allowed to share information as long as the information is true, it is pertinent to the position for which the person is applying and the person receiving the information has a corresponding right to know. While most laws provide civil remedies against slander and libel, about half the states have laws on the books that make it criminal for a former employer to blacklist or defame a former employee. In some cases these laws prohibit employers from volunteering information about an employee.

Consider the case of one airplane mechanic in Southern California who repeatedly complained to his employer that the company failed to comply with Federal Aviation Administration regulations in its work and documentation. He was considered a good worker, but had protested to his employer that the company wasn't following government regulations in its repairs and failed to complete proper paperwork. The employer told him to quit his complaining and just get the product out the door. When he and his employer parted ways, he had difficulty finding a new job. Eventually he discovered his former employer would tell people who called to check on his background that although he was a good worker, he was not a "team player" and slowed down the whole operation. The case is now being litigated.

Microbiologist Discovers Small Brains

I got laid off in March. The company had been bought and the budget had been cut. Of course, we must lay off the folks who do the work while we keep the high paid idiots who sit on their asses and take all the credit.

I have a B.S. in Biology and have worked in microbiology for five years. I hate to inform the medical field, but micro is micro. The only difference between industrial micro and clinical micro is that an industrial lab rat will get the bugs out of food, water or raw materials. A clinical lab rat will get them out of shit and piss. The techniques and precautions are the same.

But do the hospitals, doctors' offices, clinics and other medical establishments believe this? No! We all know dabbling about in a patient's piss and poop is much more difficult than doing the same damn thing in rotten meat and moldy candy!

So, I don't have a job yet. Unemployment insurance runs out in a month. My only real prospects are Wal-Mart, Kmart, and Target. We will not even discuss the fast food places. I used to test the food there and am mortally afraid of them. Yes, the places one can go with a degree and $5,000 worth of student loans.

Lorri R.

Adding to the frustrations of the job search for many people have been the circumstances under which they find themselves looking for work. According to a survey from the U.S. Bureau of Labor Statistics, from January 1993 through December 1995, a total of 4.2 million workers twenty years or older lost or left jobs they had held for three years or more because their company or plant closed, the company moved, there was insufficient work or their position was eliminated. Many of these so-called displaced workers long thought their good work was enough security for them to not have to worry about want ads, resumes and interviews.

In addition, another 5.2 million workers who had been in their positions for less than three years also found themselves displaced during the same time. The increasingly common experience of losing a job through no fault of one's own is helping to color these displaced workers' search for a new job, say those who assist them in their hunt. "They are more cynical about the process," said John Challenger, executive vice president of the Chicago-based outplacement firm Challenger, Gray & Christmas. "They are less trusting of employers, more cynical about a company's ability to provide security. They are looking at smaller companies today than they used to and have fewer expectations about the long term."

According to the Bureau of Labor Statistics' survey of displaced workers conducted in February 1996, workers who became displaced between January 1993 and December 1995 had mixed results when they found new work. Though nearly half of the workers who had lost full-time wage and salary jobs earned as much or more in their new jobs, one-third of those workers suffered a cut in wages of 20 percent or more. Those were the lucky ones. Of the 2.7 million full-time workers who lost their job after three years or more, four hundred thousand were either holding part-time jobs, were self-employed or were working as unpaid workers in family businesses.

The Clinton administration laid out its case for the good job news in a 1996 report from the Council of Economic Advisors called

What Do You Expect with a Journalism Degree

As with so many other educated Americans, I am just about to give up on the "American dream." All through college I remember my older and "wiser" brother telling me, "Once you get your degrees, a lot of doors will open and you'll never make less than your first salary."

Bull! I worked my fingers off to earn two B.A.s in both journalism and political science. I had a solid work ethic and history. My problem? I'm male, Caucasian and a disabled vet.

The government paid for career counseling after graduation in which any prospective employer would earn a significant federal tax credit as well as salary reimbursement for my first six months of employment in addition to the nominal disability "quota" thing. I couldn't even get an interview.

It's been more than two years since graduation and I've had to exist on the paltry wages offered by the local temp agencies. Why? Because companies are "rightsizing" to increase profits for the fickle stock holders who want a big return. We live in the age of disposable workers. If they're not your employees, you don't have to pay benefits or give raises. Things are going to get a lot worse. You may hold "quotas" and temps in contempt, but it ain't easy out there for anyone. You need all the angles you can to squirm into the front door. Don't give up, and don't give in!

Michael K.

Job Creation and Employment Opportunities: The United States Labor Market, 1993–1996. The report came out as Bill Clinton was trying to avoid becoming another middle-aged white guy who found himself out of work as his career was peaking. It found that contrary to the widespread anxiety that Americans seem to have about the job market, 8.5 million new jobs had been created since January 1993. While naysayers might suggest looking at the quality and not the quantity of these new positions, the report said the bulk of the jobs created hadn't been for hamburger-flippers, but well-paying jobs. In fact, hamburger-flippers didn't fare too well on the job creation front. The report noted that between 1994 and 1995 employment in the food service industry actually fell. Two-thirds of the net growth in full-time jobs between February 1994 and February 1996 occurred in industry and occupation groups paying above-median wages. That, however, is not to say those jobs actually paid more than the median wage, only that those industries in which they were created did so on average.

But even the upbeat report had to acknowledge the disquieting rumble below the surface. The share of permanent dismissals as opposed to temporary layoffs had increased, particularly from 1980 to 1993. As a result, more and more workers who lose their jobs today don't expect to get them back. This has made many people feel less secure about their job prospects. More revealing is a noticeable change in who is being laid off. The percentage of workers with three or more years on their current job who were displaced fell to 3.8 percent in the 1991–1992 period, down from 3.9 percent a decade before. Not much of an improvement, but things were not getting

Having a Fit to Print

Trouble in getting a job? You bet!

Since 1987, I've been looking for a long-term, permanent position in the printing field. Think I could get one? Not on a bet to save your ass!

Why? The people doing the hiring don't have a clue about what they are doing—that and discrimination. My people have been discriminated against for the past 2,500 to 3,000 years in every way imaginable. So when employers get a chance to keep one of us down, they do.

I have college and practical work-related experience. The problem, as I see it, is not only that personnel agents don't know what they are doing, they're afraid that I may take over their jobs. Plus, they feel threatened by someone who knows what they are doing; is innovative and creative; can work unsupervised and can truly make a contribution to the company.

I understand why people resort to crime. I have been steadily losing my motivation to gain employment and am seriously considering a life of crime. As soon as I can figure out how to be a computer hacker, I'll be all set! In the meantime, all job offers will be considered.

John M.

worse. The situation for blue-collar workers improved, as the percentage of displaced workers fell to 5.2 percent from 7.3 percent during the same period. That was a noticeable improvement. But the percentage of white-collar workers being displaced rose to 3.6 percent from 2.6 percent during that period. "These changes in the incidence of job displacement may be a reason for the reports of heightened anxiety regarding job loss," the report said. "Although blue-collar and less educated workers remain more likely to be displaced than others, displacement rates have clearly risen among those workers who had previously been largely immune from the threat of job dislocation."

Though losing a job is easy for no one in a society in which iden-

Not Encouraged

I am a white male in my mid-20's. I am having a heck of a time finding a job.

I was laid off four months ago from an Internet service provider. Every Sunday and Wednesday I have looked in the newspaper as these are the days with the most job listings.

Every time I find a job in a position I like, the ad says, "Women and minorities are encouraged to apply."

This really means: "White men can't get a job here." I have applied for about 30 of them, only to get one interview. The rest automatically got "filled," although I was almost over-qualified for the jobs.

I have experience in four programming languages. I can find my way around a computer better than anyone I know can. I am well experienced in computer programming and design. But, I can't get a job.

Employers are doing things differently now than they have done in the past. They consider part-time work to be 30 to 38 hours, and only hire part-time so they do not have to provide benefits. They hire people that fit the "racial" and "gender"-specific quota, regardless of the compatibility of the position. They create outrageous policies and laws about what employees do after hours.

                                                            Rick R.

tity and work are so closely intertwined, whether people who lose
their jobs land on their feet or their ass may depend on whether they
are gently moved out the door or just thrown out. While lower-level
employees who get downsized may be offered some group counseling about job search techniques, resume writing and interview skills,
middle and upper management often get the services of an outplacement firm for as long as a year. This provides these out-of-work individuals with a base of operation and personalized counseling to
help them land a new job.

Nevertheless, they often need to overcome emotional issues attached to losing a job that they may have held for a long time and in
which they performed well. Amidst frustrations about their situation
and anxiety about their financial future, they must turn around and
sell themselves. "They are not used to the humiliation that looking
for a job brings," said outplacement expert Challenger. "They are not
used to tooting their own horn—not used to asking for something.
You are doing the asking and getting rejected. It could be very
shame-producing to tell people you've been let go."

Still, for someone unexpectedly thrown into the job market or
entering it for the first time, it would seem to be a good time. The unemployment figures indicate the job market right now is about as
good as it gets. In May of 1997, unemployment fell to 4.8 percent,
its lowest level since 1973. But the numbers didn't tell the whole
story. The labor market was tight for people with the right skills; for
others, it was just as difficult to get a job as always. "It is especially
tight for talent," said Barry Lawrence, spokesman for the Society for
Human Resource Management. "Many people need jobs, but there
are few people with talents employers need, such as technology
skills, direct customer skills, political or corporate kinds of skills.
Those are things that are very hard to teach. You can't just read up
on it and apply."

The other problem with the unemployment figure is that it doesn't
tell the whole story. It undercounts the true unemployment rate because it does not include all people who are not working and want to

work. The unemployment figure only counts those people who have actively sought work during the past four weeks. The "underemployment" number includes "discouraged" workers who have sought work in the past twelve months but not in the last four weeks; the "marginally attached," people who want work but are unable to look for it for some reason, such as caring for an ill relative; and "involuntary part-time workers," who have some work, but not as much as they would like. In fact, the number of people who would like to work full-time is nearly twice as great as the number who do.

In addition, hidden below the surface of the rosy unemployment

Sidelined in the Rat Race

Being a divorced mom, it took me 12 years to complete college. I had several part-time jobs. I performed bookkeeping, accounting, catering, waitressing and card dealing. I taught high school history for two years part-time, while attending college to obtain a special education credential and a masters in media technology.

I remarried five years ago at the ripe age of 44, still searching for a career. I have a computer at home and have applied at temporary agencies for work. I have mounds of work and management experience, a good education and I am computer literate. I was never sent on a single job. My husband got laid off from his job (another horror story in itself). I was desperate. I figured that waitressing had always seen me through, so I set out applying for work.

I can't seem to get hired anywhere. Yet wherever I go, I find someone working with the public who can't even speak English. It's especially pleasant when you need some important information over the phone, like insurance, and can't understand a word the person says.

My husband finally found work as a delivery person for a deli, after having a management job for a huge drug rehabilitation facility.

We don't know what to do. I work at a swap meet for six dollars an hour, two days a week. I work on my web site about 60 hours a week.

My computer payments are $30/month for the rest of my life. Is it like this everywhere?

Truly Disgruntled Deborah D.

figure is an uneven rate of joblessness when it is broken down by race, sex and age. While unemployment stood at just 3.8 percent for adult men and 4.5 percent for adult women in May 1997, the unemployment rate hovered at 15.6 percent for teens and at 33.2 percent for black teens. During the same period, the unemployment rate for whites dropped to 4 percent, but the unemployment rate for blacks was more than two and a half times that, at 10.3, and it was 7.4 percent for Hispanics.

These disparities exist at a time when the government has an ambitious plan to reform welfare, moving those living off the government's checkbook into the job market—a job market in inner cities that already suffers from high unemployment and falling wages. "Here we are basically talking about recession-level or depression-level unemployment for black America when we are at the peak of the business cycle," said John Schmitt, an economist with the Economic Policy Institute. "What are we going to be talking about in two to three years?"

Of course, the problem with the poor is nothing more than a lack of imagination. Applying for jobs that provide wages that barely allow them to get by means they'll continue to struggle to keep up in the hamster wheel. All it really takes is a wish upon a star. The only jobs to take are the ones at the top. They pay better, and when you get fired, they don't just give you two weeks' severance. Disney's Mike Ovitz set the bar high for everyone. After a little more than a year as president of The Ultimate Mickey Mouse organization, Ovitz was given the E-ticket of severance packages. Ovitz walked away with a package of cash and stock valued at as much as $90 million. For Rick Otey, it would take 2,045 years at his current wages—longer than it's been since Jesus walked the earth—to make that.

Q and Pain in the A

Employers are restricted from asking job applicants certain information because of antidiscrimination laws.

Among the things employers are not supposed to ask a job applicant about are race, sexual orientation, age, religion, national origin, color, pregnancy or disabilities.

Beware crafty employers who try to elicit this information during a job interview through indirect questions.

There are exceptions when a specific job-related issue is involved, such as work in an industry that maintains age restrictions for certain jobs.

When an employer seeks inappropriate information, it can get sticky. Refusing to answer a question can mean kissing the job good-bye and lying about an answer is usually grounds for rejection or, if discovered later, dismissal.

Try to find out why the information is being sought in a friendly, respectful manner. If it seems that the employer is overstepping the bounds of the law, casually mention that it was your understanding that such questions are not allowed under the law and then offer an answer if they still want it.

If they still insist on the information, have no justification for it and have acted like such assholes that you realize you would rather go homeless than work for them, tell them to go fuck themselves.

3

Minimum Rage

"In the end, the argument comes down to a matter of elementary economics: when a working stiff demands a pay raise, it causes inflation and threatens the nation's prosperity. When a CEO gets a raise ten thousand times as large, it rewards enterprise and assures all our futures. The two phenomena, obviously, are entirely separate. Only a fool or a journalist could confuse them."

—JOHN CASSIDY
The New Yorker, *April 21, 1997*

RICK OTEY HAS what by most people's standards would be considered a good job. The forty-seven-year-old parts order-filler for Caterpillar, Inc., the maker of giant earthmoving machinery, earned about $44,000 in 1996, considerably more than the $25,480 median wage of American salaried workers. A father of four with one child already out of the house and a second in college, he lives in a three-bedroom home in what he calls the "sleepy" rural town of Tremont, Illinois, near the company's headquarters in Peoria. Each day he rises at 4:50 A.M. and after his morning ritual climbs into his 1988 Ford Aerostar with 155,000 miles on it and drives 10 miles north to the Caterpillar parts warehouse in Morton, Illinois, to start his shift. He makes a good living, but not quite as good a living as he used to make. Though he's been with the company for twenty-nine years, Otey has worked without a raise since 1991.

Caterpillar had been involved in a long-standing labor dispute with the United Auto Workers, which represents 13,000 of Caterpillar's 54,000 employees. Ironically, Otey works at the one facility that did not walk out, because of a no-strike clause in his unit's contract. So, when the company imposed conditions on the workers after negotiations failed to produce a contract, other UAW-represented employees received modest increases. At Otey's facility, though, employees continued to work under the terms of their expired contract.

Otey says that even though the contract called for an annual cost-of-living increase until a new contract was instituted, Caterpillar had a different reading. Otey made the same $16.24 an hour he did six years ago. Had he gotten the cost-of-living increases, he'd be earning an additional $2.35 an hour. That might offer him a little more breathing room, but in actuality would just put him where he was in real terms six years ago. "We've had to do without. My kids come to me and want a certain thing that maybe an office worker's kid can get and I can't give it to them," said Otey. "But I'm a Christian and I believe in God and he meets my needs without Caterpillar." A new six-year contract was approved in 1998, which provides for between a 2 and 4 percent increase and 3 percent lump sum payments every other year beginning in 1999.

Otey and his family get by, but they do feel financial pressure. His wife, Mary Ann, said that instead of replacing a dilapidated sofa in their family room, they have had to live with it. It's been eight years since the last "real" family vacation, which was a trip to the Grand Canyon. These days vacations consist of taking an extended weekend to visit relatives in the southern part of the state or neighboring Wisconsin. Their dryer is broken, but they don't feel they can afford the $120 it would take to fix it. For now, the family is drying its laundry on a clothesline outdoors. The roof on the house could use replacing—actually, Rick would like to move to a newer house. Those are just some of the things they have been forced to put off.

To help out, Mary Ann has started a day care service in their home, which brings in about $10,000 a year. In the past, she worked as an elementary school teacher's assistant. Though she is making more now, her responsibilities add two hours a day, or ten hours a week, to her work schedule. Unlike the school job, which offered plenty of time off, she now works a fifty-two-week year, taking only an occasional day off here and there. She said the work is necessary with one child already in college and another starting in September. "I just knew without that job, we couldn't send my son to college."

Donald Fites also works at Caterpillar, although he's doing considerably better these days than Otey. Instead of living with a wage freeze, Fites, chairman and CEO of the company, took home a 47 percent increase in 1996, with $2.3 million in salary and bonus, according to a Standard & Poor's Compustat study for *Business Week* magazine. But that wasn't all. Fites pocketed total direct compensation of $3.3 million. How Fites's pay package plays in Peoria might depend on who is asked. No doubt some people would say Fites earned it. Caterpillar's $16.5 billion in sales and $1.36 billion profit in 1996 set records for the company. And compared with some of his CEO brethren feeding alongside him at the trough, Fites looks like a lightweight.

While poor ol' Fites had to get by on his meager $3.3 million, Lawrence Coss, CEO of Green Tree Financial, took home the largest total compensation package in 1996, valued at $102.4 million. Andrew Grove of Intel with $97.6 million and Sanford Weil of Travelers Group with $94.2 million took silver and bronze in the '96 payday Olympics. Their hefty compensation packages came thanks largely to generous stock option grants from their boards and a raging bull market. Why do CEOs make so much money? Well, it's a little like the old joke about why dogs lick their balls: Because they can.

Ellen Tenity, program director for the Berkeley, California–based nonprofit Just Economics, an educational organization aimed at helping people better understand and become involved in public policy debates, likes to tell a story about a trip she made to Mexico in the late 1980s. While traveling, Tenity arranged a tour of a shoe factory in Michoacán, Mexico. The factory owner proudly led Tenity through the plant. As they entered one room where a hundred workers were hunched over shoes, busily stitching away, he paused. With great pride, the owner gestured across the room and said, "I feed one hundred families." As one worker stopped the owner to ask him a question, another pulled Tenity aside to correct the record. The worker said, "It takes one hundred of us to feed his family."

How someone views the economics of the working world depends in part on where he stands in it. Of course, these days lots of us feel like we are standing in— or more accurately have stepped in—something. The 1990s has been a time of seeming contradictions. It has combined the excesses of the 1980s with all of the fear, pain and insecurity of the 1930s. The stock market has set astounding records, corporate profits are at all-time highs and both inflation and interest rates have been kept in check. That allowed Bill Clinton to boast in his 1996 State of the Union address that the "economy is the healthiest it has been in three decades."

Nevertheless, many working people have not shared in the good times. Real wages—wages adjusted for inflation—remained stag-

The American Way

Don't you hate the way America allows CEOs to rape every company around? They elect each other to their boards of directors and vote each other huge raises and even bigger bonuses.

The union at our company got a 1 percent raise. Meanwhile the CEO got a 14 percent raise. Ugh!

To top it off, one division in my company had a terrible year. So, instead of getting rid of the responsible supervisors, they just played musical chairs.

These assholes probably would just rotate their tires if they got a flat on the way home from work.

Sun King

nant from the 1970s through the early 1990s. During the 1980s, married couples offset their deteriorating family incomes by turning stay-at-home wives into second wage earners. At the end of the decade, the average wife worked 314 hours more than she did in 1979, a 35.8 percent increase, according to the Economic Policy Institute. As a coping mechanism, that only went so far. By the time the 1990s rolled around, families were working just about as hard as they could and were no longer able to offset their income losses by working more. The Institute said that between 1989 and 1994 the income of the bottom 60 percent of married-couple families fell as the bottom 95 percent of these families saw the real wages of the husband drop.

So while Bill Clinton could extol the economic victories of his administration, a more somber and sober Labor Secretary Robert Reich could say in a 1995 Labor Day speech that "the earnings of most American workers are either stuck in the mud or sinking. Profits are up. Paychecks are not." Employees at the very bottom did manage to get a raise in 1996 when Congress boosted the minimum wage 90 cents to $5.15 (this was done in two installments, with the last 40 cents kicking in during September of 1997). It was, however, a small consolation for the 10 million workers who would directly benefit from the increase. The raise, the first in five years, left the minimum wage in real terms still lagging where it stood in April 1991.

Of course, not everyone has done poorly. As wages have stagnated for workers, CEO pay has skyrocketed. Between 1980 and 1995, factory wages rose 70 percent, trailing inflation, which climbed 85 percent. But during the same time corporate profits rose 145 percent and CEO compensation soared nearly 500 percent, according to the AFL-CIO's Executive Pay Watch project. The growth in pay has helped widen the gap between those at the top and the rest of the workforce. By 1995, CEO compensation rose to more than two hundred times the compensation of the average factory worker, up from about forty-five times three decades before, the AFL-CIO said.

It's Enough to Make You Sick

I am a dispatch supervisor for an ambulance company. I'm on salary. If I work more than forty hours a week, I only get paid for forty hours. If I work less than forty hours a week, it's deducted from my check. If you work a 24-hour shift, you only get paid for thirteen hours of it unless you get less than five hours sleep a night due to calls.

We do all the paperwork by hand. My boss doesn't know anything about computers and won't get us one because then she wouldn't know what we were doing. This is a family owned business. We've got four bosses and each of them are always telling us how to do something differently, so we are always caught in the middle of how to do a certain procedure.

There are no benefits whatsoever, not even disability. Starting wages, even for emergency medical technicians, are a little above minimum wage. They nitpick about every penny. We've even had to buy our own toilet paper in the past because they thought we were using too much of it.

All our phone conversations are monitored, even on the nonemergency line. They don't trust any of us, even those of us who have been there three or four years. There're only a couple of us that have been there for more than three years.

Employees do have a high turnover rate. I can't imagine why! Can you? There are no paid vacations per say. However, in all fairness to my employer, I do get one week paid vacation every year now. If I take two weeks, I take it with one week of no pay.

Disgruntled in Texas

Though people are starting to see their wages edge up, there continues to be a dramatic difference in wage increases between the top CEOs and their workers. In 1996, wages and benefits overall grew by just 3 percent, up from 2.8 percent the previous year, according to compensation consultant William M. Mercer, Inc., in a study for the *Wall Street Journal*. At the same time, total compensation for CEOs rose 18 percent to just less than $2.4 million, breaking the $2 million mark for the first time since the *Journal* began its surveys in 1989. The *Journal* survey, which examined pay at the 350 largest firms in the United States, found that fifty-nine of the CEOs owned more than $100 million worth of their companies' stock and options. Of those, forty-six were

A Scrooge in Santa's Clothing

Instead of getting some extra cash, some chocolate covered espresso beans or any sort of mindless but still O.K. gift, we all got one coupon for 25% off something in the store—not valid after Dec. 31—and a nice generalized fax saying happy holidays.

That's about the extent of it. I don't really know if that's the worst you've heard, but it still SUCKS!

KiWiMaN

neither founders nor descendants of founders of the company at which they worked.

Executive compensation expert Graef Crystal offers a concise history of the genesis of excess in compensation. The use of stock options to compensate executives started to take hold in the 1960s when Congress passed laws that gave favorable tax treatment to this form of compensation. In the 1970s, companies started granting their CEOs bigger and bigger options in order to make up for the languishing stock market, which remained sprawled on its ass. The attitude corporate boards took, said Crystal, was that there was something wrong with the stock market, "not our company." The reality, he said, was that corporate profits, when adjusted for inflation, were declining.

Around that time the fraternity of compensation consultants, of which Crystal had been a proud member, started to flourish. With new technology that could analyze how a given CEO's pay package compared with those of his peers in industry, time became compressed, and the feedback executives received on the pay packages of others accelerated the trend. No longer did a report take six months to calculate, mimeograph and distribute. The desktop PC allowed instantaneous and sophisticated computations that would have previously required a mainframe computer to perform. Today, as soon as a proxy statement is filed, a CEO with a Bloomberg terminal or Internet connection can find out how fat the cat next door is getting and call his compensation committee on the phone and start meowing for more.

It's hard to blame CEOs for today's obscene pay packages. They are doing what they are supposed to be doing in a free market. They negotiate the best deals they can for themselves. Instead, look to their friends who make up their boards of directors for the culprits. The huge options grants driving the bloat comes from a twisted attempt at so-called pay for performance. The idea is simple enough. Change the mixture of the compensation package so that the CEO's own financial interest is aligned with that of the stockholders. If the stock rises, the CEO benefits directly. If it falls, then he is penalized.

But that's hardly been the case. The options grants have been so large in many cases that even poor performers reap huge rewards. That leaves many people to wonder what incentive really exists. Because most stock options are exercisable at the price of a company's stock at the time the grant is made, even CEOs with lackluster performances have been able to ride the rising tide of the stock market. Though Crystal long supported the concept of pay for performance, he said the way it has been instituted by corporations has turned the notion on its head. He likens the effort to taking a percentage of a CEO's pay package and making it performance-based to a home

---

When the Date Book Says It's Time to Move On

I used to work at a place where every year for Christmas we got a crappy little date book that cost my employer a whole two dollars or so. We did, however, get the week off between Christmas and New Year's as a gift from our union, the only people who seemed happy that we were working at the college.

One year we all got a memo, about 2000 pieces of paper used up, telling us they could no longer afford to give us our Christmas gifts due to fiscal restraints. This was the same year our president went to Japan three times, first class naturally, to check out our useless, but prestigious satellite college campus.

I am so glad to be out of that place. Now I have a job and I can afford to buy myself an even nicer date book.

Beaner

owner with a three-thousand-square-foot house calling in a contractor to remodel a spare bedroom and turning it into the "pay-for-
performance room." The problem with that approach, said Crystal, is
that to do it right would involve taking something away from a
CEO—a process he describes as roughly equivalent to removing a
piece of prime filet from the jaws of a Doberman that hasn't eaten in
a week. Showing their ability to think outside the box, the business
community instead devised an ingenious approach. "They called in a
contractor and added a thirty-thousand-square-foot wing to the
house," said Crystal. "And then with a clear conscience they said 90-
some percent of our pay package is pay-for-performance-oriented."

So when the rise in H. J. Heinz stock moves at the speed of its
ketchup—11 percent in 1996, making it an underperformer against
both the Standard & Poor's 500 and other food companies—CEO
Anthony F. J. O'Reilly still gets plenty of gravy. In light of his $64.2
million pay package (a 39 percent increase from 1995) O'Reilly
shamelessly told *Business Week* that "there can be no more honorable
or fairer way" than stock options to compensate a CEO. O'Reilly's
compensation is not an isolated case of pay outstripping performance.
When Crystal examined compensation packages at the largest corporations in a 1996 study, he isolated the 47 CEOs in the group who
had been in their positions for at least three years. While the average
stock price for those companies had risen 31 percent since 1992, the
median value of stock options granted during the same period rose a
whopping 125 percent.

There have been efforts to rein in CEO pay. Shareholder ac-
tivists, pension funds, religious groups and unions routinely intro-
duce resolutions at annual meetings attacking CEO pay, but at best
they offer some momentary embarrassment that causes the CEO to
blush all the way to the bank. Even companies that try to do the right
thing find it is difficult to practice what they preach given the nature
of the market. Ben & Jerry's Homemade, Inc., in South Burlington,
Vermont, imposed a compensation ratio limit on itself that restricted
the pay of any executive to no more than seven times the lowest-paid

worker at the firm. Though it was one of the long-standing progressive tenets of the firm, it was scrapped in 1994 when the company went shopping for a new CEO.

"What we had to do was sacrifice one progressive symbol to keep the company viable, which in turn would save a number of other progressive elements," said Rob Michalak, spokesman for the company. In 1996, the top executive at Ben & Jerry's took home $353,600 in total compensation, compared with $22,934 for an entry-level worker at the firm, a ratio of 15.4 to 1. Though that's more than twice the limit the company used to live by, it still is a far more reasonable relationship than found at other companies. Michalak said that when the company operated under the pay ratio limit, it helped to create a sense of linkage between the employees at the bottom and those at the top, giving the enterprise some sense of "connectedess and singularity of mission." He noted, "That was stronger in the days of the ratio. It's still part of our internal culture, but it's not as strong now."

Grunty Fun Fact

About 6.2 percent of the workforce held more than one job in 1996, up from about 5.2 percent in 1970, according to the U.S. Bureau of Labor Statistics. Of those, 3.8 million had one full-time job and 244,000 had two full-time jobs.

The biggest challenge in recent years to high CEO pay hasn't come from fund managers or protesters, but from the bean counters. The Financial Accounting Standards Board didn't really want to cut CEO pay, but only to see that the cost of stock options was reflected on the corporate balance sheet. The independent rule-making body, which establishes the accounting practices for publicly held companies, had proposed a rule that would have required companies that compensate executives and other employees with stock options to take a charge against earnings for the value of the options they grant. Corporations take no such charge, which means they can give an executive as many options as they like without reducing their earnings.

The proposed rule set off an unprecedented lobbying effort in 1994, with companies in Silicon Valley leading the charge. Younger technology firms that don't have the cash necessary to lure top talent to their ventures rely heavily upon stock options to attract the executives they need. The corporate outcry succeeded in turning the screws by bringing congressional pressure to bear on the rule-making body. The board felt had it not backed off it would have risked having legislators determine the accounting rules in the future. Instead of taking a charge against earnings, companies today have to merely report in a footnote to their annual report what effect their options grants would have had on their earnings if they had taken such a charge.

The end result is that even though CEOs benefit significantly from these options, corporate boards continue to maintain the illusion that they cost the company nothing to issue. But such largesse is not without its consequences. "I'm not an economist, but I know you can't put ten pounds of shit in a five-pound bag. If they are not screwing the workers, they are screwing the shareholders, and if they are not screwing the shareholders, they are screwing consumers," said Crystal. "The truth may be it's a little of everybody. It becomes an added cost, like anything else."

Conservatives such as Mark Wilson, the Lukens Fellow in Labor Policy at the Heritage Foundation, have argued that the reason workers suffered stagnant wages from 1973 to 1994 was not because of money-grubbing CEOs and corporations unwilling to share their profits with their workers. In an April 1996 article, "Wages, Profits, and Income: Politics vs. Reality," he writes, "The slow growth in take-home pay is not the result of corporate greed or trade deficits. It is the result of a slowdown in the growth of productivity caused in part by the expansion of government regulation, which in turn reduces the net value of workers' output and contributes to slower wage growth. Further, an ever-larger share of workers' total pay

No Insurance for This

I work for a major life insurance company that is downsizing. I'd like to relate two stories of what heartless bastards they are.

My coworker's son went into a coma. When she called her supervisor to request time off, the lady had the nerve to ask her how she would be making up the time. (We have no sick days.)

Another woman on our floor had the same type of incident happen. Her mother had a stroke and she left the office. The next day when she returned she had been marked with an unauthorized absence.

When we recently lost our underwriting facilities, which had the highest paying jobs and required the least amount of actual work, the people were moved into positions they were not qualified for at the same pay rate. Meanwhile, the rest of us can't even get a cost of living raise.

Disgruntled? You bet!

Chris

(wages and benefits) is beyond their control, consumed by mandated benefits and taxes." Despite that, he argues that workers are actually better off today because their real compensation, including pension and health benefits, has continued to grow.

Productivity and taxes have indeed been issues in the wilting of the American paycheck. Productivity since 1973 has grown at a slower pace than it did in the period following World War II. Nevertheless, the Economic Policy Institute's report on the state of working America found that productivity between 1975 and 1993 still grew 25 percent, "enough of an increase in the size of the economic pie that should have allowed all income groups to experience real income gains." The report refutes any suggestion that a growth in benefits has offset wage declines suffered by workers. Rising health insurance costs did help drive the value of benefits up 1 percent annually between 1979 and 1994, but hourly compensation, including benefits, grew just .5 percent during the same period, .1 percent more than wages alone. That's because benefits account for just 19 percent of the total compensation for the average worker. So, while health insurance rose 45 cents an hour between 1979 and 1994, wages dropped 75 cents for the median worker and $2.04 for the median male worker.

There are those who think that corporate profits and CEO pay packages have not come at the expense of workers, but the numbers suggest otherwise. During the 1990s, corporate profits jumped significantly, even though there was not a corresponding jump in productivity growth. "If profitability had returned to rates comparable to those of earlier decades, there would have been significantly more room for compensation growth," the Institute's report said. "There has been, therefore, a profit squeeze on wages in the 1990s."

John Schmitt, an economist with the Economic Policy Institute and one of the coauthors of the *State of Working America* report, said the real problem is not taxes and productivity, but that the bargaining power of workers—union and nonunion, blue- and white-collar—has weakened dramatically because of deregulation of industries, globalization of the economy and the shift to low-wage service industries. "What we need are some policies that can shift the tide and level the playing field and put workers back on a more even footing when they negotiate with employers," said Schmitt. "Until the economic situation is such that workers feel they have bargaining power, you're not going to see a change."

It's not just stagnant wages, but longer hours that have been taking their toll on workers. While data from the Bureau of Labor Statistics show only a slight increase to the median of the American workweek—to 39.3 hours a week in 1996 versus 38.5 hours in 1980—other researchers argue that on an annual basis, the number of hours people are working has grown significantly. Juliet Schor, director of women's studies and senior lecturer in economics at Harvard University, examined the growing hours of work Americans subject themselves to in her 1991 book *The Overworked American*. Though her findings spark controversy among some academics, Schor argues that by 1987, the average American was working an additional 163 hours a year more than in 1969—an extra month of work.

In 1990, she found that a quarter of all full-time workers spent 49 or more hours on the job each week and that nearly half of them worked 60 hours or more. She attributed the extra hours to several factors, including the effects of moonlighting, overtime and shrinking vacations. She sees the problem in the organization of work itself. "We have a workplace structure where hours are set by firms and not by individuals. In order to succeed in a job, people have to work long hours, particularly as they move up the ladder," said Schor. "Moving into a salaried position means a person has to work 100 to 150 hours a year more. They work longer than they expected, longer than they would like to, but they have very little flexibility in their job to reduce hours. For the most part, if you want to reduce your hours you have to change your job, or change your career."

Longer hours and eroding pay is affecting employees in all kinds of jobs. As companies have downsized, employees who have remained with their jobs intact have found that their days have been upsized and their job responsibilities expanded. The pressure to wring additional profit out of businesses by having employees do things cheaper, faster and in greater volume has known no boundaries. Even highly skilled professionals such as doctors, who hold what have long been considered the cream-of-the-crop jobs, have not been immunized against the disease.

When John Asarian graduated from the University of California at San Francisco's Medical School in 1971, doctors still had Wednesdays off to play golf. After completing a residency in pediatrics at Stanford University Hospital and a stint at a low-income medical clinic, Asarian headed north to Mendocino, a coastal enclave known for its community of artists. He opened a practice in nearby Fort Bragg and became one of only two pediatricians serving the blue-collar town. The largest employer was Georgia Pacific, which ran a mill there. Asarian charged $15 for an office visit, $13.50 if you paid at the time of the visit. He worked three and a half days in the office

Give Me a Break

Workers in some parts of the world enjoy vacation allowances that are three times as much as in the United States, according to a study by the benefits consulting firm Hewitt Associates.

That's because length of service is the primary determinant of how much vacation time an employee is accorded in the United States, where it is used as a carrot to get employees to stay with a company. Typically, U.S. employers offer two weeks of vacation after the first year, three weeks after the fifth year and four weeks after fifteen years.

"Once an employee reaches twenty or more years of service, vacation allowances are comparable to those mandated by government agencies in other countries," said Inga Harris, a consultant and specialist in international benefit practices for Hewitt.

In most overseas countries, Hewitt said, tenure has little to do with paid vacation time. Instead, it is often the subject of a government mandate.

Many countries mandate a month or more vacation after an employee's first year and some, particularly the Scandinavian countries, are required to provide a cash "vacation bonus" amounting to as much as 10 percent of an employee's annual salary.

Mexico, with six days, offered the least amount of vacation time for an employee with one year of service. Austria, Brazil and Denmark all offered thirty days, although Denmark's allowance is based on a six-day workweek.

and took calls nights and weekends. In 1980, he formed a partnership with two other doctors. From a starting point of about $35,000 his salary steadily grew through the years to around $100,000. He had a home on seven acres and when he walked through town every knew him and said, "Hi."

But after business agreements with his partners and marital difficulties, Asarian went back to school for a master's degree in public health and then returned to being a full-time pediatrician. Rather than join a private practice, he went to work in the Martinez, California, facility of the state's largest health maintenance organization, Kaiser Permanente. Despite fifteen years of practicing medicine, he was given only one year's credit when he joined and started with a $78,000-a-year salary in 1991. In exchange for getting additional compensation in his first year, he would have to forgo an annual raise at the end of it. He was told, however, that over time he would double his salary and that though his vacation time was less than half of what he had in private practice, the benefits were good. He liked the job. He no longer had to contend with insurance paperwork and didn't have to take calls nearly as often as he had in private practice. It was a new age in medicine.

But today, the fifty-one-year-old Asarian said he has gone from being a doctor to being "a high-priced wage slave." The changes began slowly. First, the HMO cut doctors' lunch hours by ten minutes—effectively adding five patient appointments to the weekly load with no additional compensation. Then, because of competitive pressures and costly mistakes by executives who overestimated expansion needs and built facilities that ended up being mothballed, doctors' salaries were frozen for two years. Annual bonuses shrank, and then the HMO stretched the workday by a half hour a day. To offset a wide differential in salaries between long-tenured and newer doctors, doctors with less than seven years at the HMO such as Asarian did get a 10 percent raise in 1997, but all that did was offset the additional hours he was working. His daily patient load grew to about forty a day from about twenty-five when he started. "I have to work five and a half days a week to make what I used to make in five days," he said. While Asarian saw his compensation come under attack, David Lawrence, chairman and CEO of the HMO, was somehow immunized against the forces to which other employees' paychecks succumbed. Lawrence saw his compensation grow to $1.25 million in 1996, a 78 percent increase from the $701,344 he made in 1992, according to data culled by the California Nurses Association from IRS filings by the HMO.

The changes led to employees' altering the HMO's two slogans "Good People, Good Medicine" and "Different from the Ground Up" to simply "Good People Ground Up." Asarian said that along with doctors' extra hours has come less control over their work. Advice nurses who answered patients' questions by phone and who had worked in the department with easy access to the doctors now work in centralized call centers without the interaction they once enjoyed with the doctors. Cost cutting efforts have lead to the use of medical assistants, people with as little as six months of training, instead of more experienced nurses, adding to the doctor's workload. The clerks who handled scheduling for the doctors are no longer within the department either, making it difficult to correct scheduling problems—such as giving too short an appointment for a particular type of ailment—or to prevent them in the future. The end result is that it's not uncommon for Asarian to find that a patient has been given a ten-minute appointment for a twenty-minute problem, adding unpaid overtime to his day and stress to the job. "I feel dehumanized. I'm working an extra half a day a week, which is totally unsustainable," said Asarian. The doctor ultimately decided to leave the HMO and return to private practice. "I learned that lack of control over your life

Crappy Holidays

The corporation I worked for during the last fifteen years has slowly taken away the holidays from their employees. The latest was Easter, but this being just before Thanksgiving prompted me to write.

When they told us we would no longer have Thanksgiving off they said it would only be temporary to see if they would make enough money to keep the doors open.

Well of course they did. That was four years ago. Now, thanks to all the bored people who have to have that little gadget from the local mart on a holiday, many people cannot enjoy their traditional celebrations.

I have known people not to celebrate at all or have to do it on another day other than the actual holiday. Many are mothers and grandmothers, most must work to support their families and have no alternatives.

Please stop and think the next time that you go out for that gadget, of the husbands and children of these people spending the holiday without mom or grandma. Don't go unless it is necessary and maybe they won't lose the only holiday they have left, Christmas! And, if enough of you don't shop maybe, just maybe they will get some of the others back also. They will thank you from the bottom of their hearts.

Pat

makes you sick. I have no control over any part of that job. I can't control my hours, my time off, my appointments, who I work with or my income."

Not getting additional compensation for working overtime is one of the "perks" that comes with being a doctor or other type of employee who is considered exempt from federal overtime laws. But millions of employees have found that while their employers are more than eager to have them work additional hours, they have not always been as willing to pay the time-and-a-half overtime required by law. The U.S. Department of Labor and several class-action lawsuits have addressed the problem in recent years, but it is so widespread that the Employer Policy Foundation, an employer-backed think tank, estimated workers would get $19 billion a year more in pay if employers followed the law. The *Wall Street Journal* called the estimate conservative because it assumes that only 10 percent of the employees eligible for overtime do not receive it. About two-thirds of the workforce is eligible to collect overtime.

Diana Thompson of Puyallup, Washington, was among those workers, though it didn't seem to matter much. Thompson, who spent more than twelve years working in various Albertson's grocery stores in Tacoma, Washington, ran a fish counter that she said often was the highest-producing such counter in the entire company. During her time with the firm, she said, she received several letters of commendation from her division office and supervisor. One reason she was such a good employee is because on average she put in ten hours a week of overtime on the job—some $75,000 to $100,000 worth of work—for which she was never paid. "When I was working the overtime, because I was a company-type person, I didn't think of it. The only way to do the job was to work through lunches, work through breaks and take home work with you. It's something everybody did." One reason people did that, she said, was because managers used intimidation. Managers had quarterly bonuses that were tied to the amount of money they spent on labor. To discourage workers from filing for overtime, she said, managers would tell

Disgruntled Employee Handbook

The Fair Labor Standards Act

The federal Fair Labor Standards Act (FLSA) outlines basic requirements on wages and hours for employees at companies engaged in interstate or foreign commerce. Many states have similar laws that address wage and hours.

Federal law does not require employers to provide much of the basic working conditions employees expect to be part of any job. The law does not require employers to provide vacation, holiday or sick pay; rest periods, holidays off, sick days or vacations; additional pay for working weekends or holidays; fringe benefits or limits on hours worked for anyone more than sixteen.

The law does require an employer to pay a minimum wage and overtime at the rate of at least one and a half times regular pay after forty hours of work in a single workweek.

There is a bizarre list of employees who are exempt from the overtime requirements of the law, ranging from outside buyers of poultry and dairy products to employees of motion picture theaters. Employees not on the exempt list must get overtime unless their employer can show that you are a salaried and not hourly employee and that you do not perform the duties of an executive, administrator, professional or outside salesperson.

If you feel your employer is violating the FLSA, contact your local office of the U.S. Department of Labor's Wage and Hour Division.

Source: The Rights of Employees and Union Members: The Basic ACLU Guide to the Rights of Employees and Union Members

workers that if they couldn't get the job done in the time allotted, there were a hundred people ready to take their position. She also said that any employee who angered a manager risked not getting the hours she wanted or needed to work or the days off she requested.

Thompson lost her job in 1996 after she slipped on a wet floor and shattered her arm at work. Prior to that, she said her typical workweek had grown to sixty hours because she was trying to win a promotion. Despite the extra hours, she still only got paid for forty hours a week at $13.50. She later testified before Congress about the abuses of overtime at the Idaho-based grocery chain, the nation's fourth largest with 85,000 employees. She is also a named plaintiff in a class-action suit against the company—one of seven—that is trying to collect on unpaid overtime for as many as 100,000 past and present employees. "Controlling reported labor hours are Albertson's number one priority. But if you don't complete your assignments, you can be fired for bad job performance. So, you're damned if you do, and damned if you don't," she said. "The inside joke at Albertson's is: 'O.T.' stands for 'Own Time,' because overtime is almost nonexistent." Albertson's has denied the allegations, said it has a written policy that prohibits employees from working unpaid overtime and is fighting the various lawsuits.

One way employees can avoid some of these problems is to be a little more discriminating about who they go to work for. Of course, employees such Sheryl Joseph have found that they can run into additional problems when their employers are a little more discriminating than they should be.

PART 2

Inhuman
Relations

4

Discriminating Employers

"I guess we treat niggers differently down here."

—Comments attributed in a sworn affidavit to Texaco assistant controller James Woolly regarding a black female employee who complained of discrimination after a manager in another office told Woolly it would be illegal to "fire her black ass" as he suggested.
—The New York Times, November 11, 1996

When Sheryl Joseph's birthday came around in 1988, her coworkers celebrated with a cake. Joseph, a secretary with Texaco, Inc., in the oil giant's Harvey, Louisiana, office had just learned that she was pregnant. Excited by the news, she shared it with colleagues. It was a particularly happy birthday, until she saw the cake her boss brought in for her. On it was a caricature of a pregnant black woman with a huge Afro and dark-colored skin. (Joseph had never had an Afro and was light-skinned.) The inscription on the cake read, "Happy Birthday, Sheryl. It must have been all those watermelon seeds." Isn't it nice when the boss remembers your birthday? "When I saw the inscription, I just kind of stared at it and said, 'Oh, thank you,'" Joseph told the *New York Times*. "I didn't feel I could get angry. I had just found out I was pregnant. I needed my job."

Joseph has since left the company, but she was one of 1,400 former and current black employees at Texaco involved in a class-action discrimination suit against the company filed in 1994. In June 1996, the Equal Employment Opportunity Commission found that Texaco had failed to promote blacks in certain employee groups because of their race. At the time, Texaco criticized the ruling and defended its promotion system. But then came the workplace equivalent of the Rodney King tapes. Audiotape recordings secretly made by a former Texaco executive during a meeting appeared to catch high-ranking executives at the company using racial epithets and plotting to destroy evidence relating to the lawsuit. The tapes became public at the end of 1996 when the *New York Times* published a transcript of excerpts of them. Embarrassed by the transcripts and concerned over mounting pressure from a consumer boycott led by civil rights groups, Texaco quickly moved to settle the case.

The company agreed to pay $176.1 million, the largest settlement ever in a discrimination case. Of that, $115 million was to be paid to the plaintiffs, $26.1 million was to go to raises for minority employees over a five-year period and $35 million was to be used to fund a task force that will be responsible for making changes in Texaco's human resource programs. On the eve of the settlement, Texaco CEO Peter Bijur, in an interview with Tom Brokaw on the *NBC Nightly News,* said, "I don't think there is any more discrimination in our company than there is in society in general, but we have some, and it's intolerable, and we're going to eradicate it." It was not clear if Bijur meant to defend the company or attack society.

The former secretary Joseph is more than just part of a high-profile discrimination case. She embodies something relatively new on the discrimination landscape. As a black female without power in the workplace, she represents a monster from the closet for some white males. These men locate the source of their newfound job insecurity in their pigment deficiency and their tendency to urinate standing. As downsizing, stagnant wages and economic insecurity started to spread among white males—"angry white males," as the media would come to call them—it wasn't corporate greed, tax policies, deregulation, weakened labor laws, impotent unions or global-

The Major Federal Antidiscrimination Laws

Title VII of the Civil Rights Act of 1964
Makes it illegal to discriminate in the workplace with respect to race, color, sex, national origin and religion.

The Americans with Disabilities Act
Prohibits employers from discriminating in the workplace against people with physical or mental disabilities. It requires employers to make a "reasonable accommodation" for the needs of disabled employees as long as it does not represent an undue hardship to the employer.

The Age Discrimination in Employment Act
Prohibits discrimination against employees who are forty years old or more.

The Equal Pay Act
Now incorporated into the Fair Labor Standards Act. Prohibits men and women from being compensated differently for doing the same job.

The Civil Rights Act of 1991
Amended Title VII and the Americans with Disabilities Act to extend its coverage to United States citizens working abroad for U.S-owned companies. It also allowed compensatory and punitive damages and jury trials for cases brought under Title VII and the ADA.

ization that was the source of their problems. It was a system of preferences that they believed took from them and gave to minorities and women that was the culprit.

It was a theme that would take center stage in the political arena as the angry white male was christened a new political force credited with reshaping Congress in 1994. Politicians from California Governor Pete Wilson to 1996 Republican presidential candidate Bob Dole seized upon the sentiment and placed affirmative action in the crosshairs. With events such as the Los Angeles police beating of motorist Rodney King (as well as the trials and riots that followed) and the murder trial of O. J. Simpson, racial inequality in America was moving to center stage once again. Only this time, rather than solving any problems, affirmative action was suddenly accused of exacerbating them.

Critics of affirmative action argue that it seeks to cure discrimination through discrimination. They say sexual or racial preferences cause some people to lose out on jobs or promotions that they have earned through their qualifications or performance. In a 1995 *Commentary* cover story, Arch Puddington, a senior scholar at Freedom House, called affirmative action a policy "implemented by stealth and subterfuge and defended by duplicity and legalistic tricks." He stated, "Seldom has a

Ragging on Male Managers

All of the male managers and the one female manager in my office were meeting. She was really pissed about something and let them know it. The big manager told the guys to ignore her because she was on the rag. She then told them that they should check with her doctor because she had had a hysterectomy two years before. Then, amazingly, the meeting was adjourned.

Marge

democratic government's policy so completely contradicted the core values of its citizenry as racial preference does in violating the universally held American ideals of fairness and individual rights, including the right to be free from discrimination."

Affirmative action is part of a long history of trying to address discrimination in the workplace. Antidiscrimination laws touching on the employment arena date back to the Civil Rights Act of 1866, which gave all citizens the right to enter into and enforce contracts the same as white citizens. But the centerpiece of legislation relating to discrimination in the workplace came nearly a hundred years later, contained in the Civil Rights Act of 1964. The sweeping legislation came at a time when television carried vivid images of peaceful civil rights demonstrators in Birmingham, Alabama, being met with fire hoses, dogs and nightsticks. The act outlawed a wide range of discriminatory practices in all areas of life ranging from restaurant service to voting rights. But

Grunty Fun Fact

Women earn 20 to 35 percent less than men, according to a study of eighty-six occupations by the U.S. Bureau of Labor Statistics.

it was Title VII of the act that specifically addressed the employment arena.

Title VII made it illegal to discriminate in the workplace on the basis of race, sex, national origin, color or religion. As important as the legislation was, it didn't do much for a forty-one-year-old, wheelchair-bound homosexual. In part because of political practicality, the scope of the law did not extend to discrimination on the basis of disabilities, age or sexual orientation. In fact, the only reason why sex was included in the statute was because lawmakers opposing the original bill amended it to include sex in the hope that it would create enough opposition to kill it. The U.S. Equal Employment Opportunity Commission has the responsibility to oversee and enforce the law. Nowhere in Title VII, though, is there a prescription for affirmative action. In fact, the law is fairly explicit in saying it is not intended to require that an employer give preferential treatment to anyone or any group of people.

Soon after the passage of Title VII, President Lyndon Johnson issued executive order 11246. The order prohibits federal contractors and subcontractors from discriminating against any employee or job applicant on the basis of race, color, religion, sex or national origin and requires them to take—here's the magic term—"affirmative action" to insure that they don't. The order required contractors with more than fifty employees and a contract of $50,000 or more to write affirmative action plans that included such things as a breakdown of the company's workforce by sex and race, a similar breakdown of the overall labor force, an analysis of whether the company had disproportionately few women or minorities in any job areas and the creation of a plan and time line to remedy any deficiencies.

It wasn't the first time that an executive order was used to address some of the discrimination that was prevalent in the workplace.

Girls'-Clubbed

I belong to the class that's okay to hate—white male with no military experience or disabilities.

I took a job with a temporary agency as a Level 3 accountant. The title merely meant I had more education and experience as an accountant and financial analyst than a bookkeeper or staff accountant.

The agency sent me out on a long-term assignment with a large multinational company that had just purchased a smaller company and needed help getting the books in order so they could be absorbed.

They thought a temp could no longer perform a temporary position. So, they hired a full-time employee to handle the responsibilities that I was already performing. I worked closely with the area manager to develop the position and create the system of checks and balances that were in place. He approached me, said they were going to requisition the position formally and suggested that I apply for it.

There were three candidates including myself. One was a younger gentleman who did not have the necessary education. The other was a woman, fresh out of college with no real world experience. She did not have an accounting or finance degree, as I did, but more of a general business degree that had some bookkeeping focus.

Though the manager thought I was a sure fit, the department head selected the woman. He had thoughts of increasing his own bonus by further diversifying the department.

Imagine that in a world supposedly dominated by my class, a woman with no hard experience and a fluff education was selected over the person who developed and created the position. Even when she was brought in, they expected me to train her.

I had no choice but to jump ship into a new field: computer consulting. I am happier and doing fine, but am now starting to find myself in another girls' club that I may not fit into.

P.P.

Franklin Roosevelt, under the threat of a march on Washington from black demonstrators, issued executive order 8802 in 1941. The order prohibited defense contractors from discriminating in employment. Later, under the Nixon administration, affirmative action expanded further, particularly into the building trades. But it wasn't long after its introduction that affirmative action was facing challenges in the courts and that the courts began to spell out when affirmative action was discrimination and when it was, as in the case of Kaiser Aluminum & Chemical Corp., an appropriate way of eliminating racial imbalances in jobs that had been historically segregated.

Kaiser had set up an affirmative action program through an agreement with the United Steel Workers of America in an effort to raise the number of blacks in craft positions to a percentage that was equal to the percentage of blacks in the local labor force. Because of historical exclusions from craft unions, few blacks had the requisite skills to be hired directly into these positions. Prior to 1974, only 5 out of the 273 skilled workers at the Kaiser plant were black. That was less then 2 percent, at a time when blacks accounted for nearly 40 percent of the local workforce. To remedy that, Kaiser created a training program to take unskilled workers and prepare them for craft

Wrong Way on a One-Way Street

I work at a major educational institution. The university underwent reorganization several years ago. Job openings in a number of departments, normally filled by males—carpentry, plumbing, electrical—were reserved specifically for women. Men were told not to apply. Our union (or lack of it) was told it was a concerted effort to promote equality in the workplace. No problem. If a woman did not possess the needed skills, she would be given time to take courses to become qualified for the position. Fine.

When several males asked that this become a two-way street—that men be offered typing courses, WordPerfect and other skills training needed for work in an office—the laughter was heard for days. There are just as many men interested in working in an office as women interested in working with tools, the university was told.

"A man can apply for any office (clerical) position, providing he has the skills needed for the job," was the answer from the administration. There would be no courses offered to men "for the purpose of becoming qualified for a clerical position."

It just goes to prove that equality is and always will be a one-way street.

S.T.

positions. Though admission to the training programs was based on seniority, the agreement with the union called for at least half the positions to be filled by blacks. The requirement was set to expire when the racial makeup of the skilled positions mirrored the racial makeup of the local labor force.

Frank Weber didn't think it was fair when he got shut out of the program. Weber, a white production worker at the Kaiser Aluminum plant in Gramercy, Louisiana, had greater seniority than the most junior black worker admitted into the program. Weber filed a class-action suit and charged that the program discriminated against him and others on the basis of their race, in violation of Title VII. Both the circuit court and appellate court ruled in Weber's favor, saying that any employment preference on the basis of race violated Title VII, but the Supreme Court in *United Steel Workers* v. *Weber* reversed the decision in 1979.

The Court approached the case from a narrow perspective, saying that the only question to consider was whether Title VII prohibits a private employer and union from agreeing on a voluntary affirmative action plan. The Court had already ruled that Title VII protects whites as well as blacks in a 1976 case (*McDonald* v. *Santa Fe Trail Trans Co.*), which did not involve affirmative action. The Court, looking at the legislative history surrounding Title VII, said it was never intended to prohibit such private, voluntary action from employers. Instead, it was designed to address the "steadily worsening" position of black workers in the economy. The Court quoted Senator Hubert Humphrey's remarks in support of the legislation when he said, "What good does it do a Negro to be able to eat in a fine restaurant if he cannot afford to pay the bill? What good does it do him to be accepted in a hotel that is too expensive for his modest income? How can a Negro child be motivated to take full advantage of integrated educational facilities if he has no hope of getting a job where he can use that education?" In ruling in favor of the plan, the Court said it mirrored the purpose of the law because it sought to break down old patterns of segregation and open new employment opportunities for blacks in areas that had been traditionally closed off to them. The Court said the program fell within the "area of discretion" left by Title VII for private employers to eliminate racial imbalances in job areas that had been traditionally segregated.

In delivering the opinion the Court sought to spell out some groundwork for determining whether an affirmative action plan was permissible or not. In the case of the Kaiser plan, the Court noted that it not only sought to address long-standing segregation, but that it did not require white workers to be fired and replaced by blacks, it did not create an absolute bar to advancement for white employees and it was a temporary program put in place until balance was achieved. Though that standard largely continues to be used by the Court today, it has been narrowed some, in that the measure of imbalance is no longer the employer's workforce compared with the labor force as a whole, but those within the workforce who are qualified for the po-

Pay Daze

Last week, I was looking on our shared computer drive for our price lists and came across a file marked "workcomp." I clicked on it and it was everyone's salary in the whole company. The file had been in public access for over three months!

I ran an analysis of the managers (of which I am one) and found out that there are 123 male managers, 20 female managers. The male managers make an average salary of $82,000 and the female managers make an average salary of $65,000. There were several men making six figures, but not one single female. I am one of the lucky females, the third-highest paid.

However, I am still furious over the blatant discrimination. There are several women in the same positions who are making much less.

It is astounding that this information was made public. I don't know how many other people have seen this file. It was a fluke for me, but if I were surfing, it would have been easy to find. The moron who put it on there filed under the Excel application, which is stupid to begin with.

Anonymous

sitions in question. In the 1995 case of *Adarand Constructors* v. *Pena,* a case involving a company that lost out on a subcontract to a minority-owned competitor even though it had entered a lower bid for the job, the Court emphasized the need for affirmative action programs to meet this strict criterion in order to be valid. In a speech as bold as the yellow line that runs down the middle of a road, President Clinton said he was directing federal agencies to comply with the Adarand decision. Though the case was about federal contracting rather than employment, it echoed the Kaiser criteria. Clinton said affirmative action programs must have "no quotas in theory or practice; no illegal discrimination; no preferences for people who are not qualified for any job or opportunity; and as soon as a program has succeeded, it must be retired."

Despite the perception among some that affirmative action has turned discrimination on its head, for the most part discrimination still exists in its traditional form, as the Federal Glass Ceiling Commission found when it issued its report in 1995. (The "glass ceiling" refers to the invisible barriers in the workplace that prevent women and minorities from rising to top positions.) The commission, a

Was That Dr. Kevorkian?

One of our department managers loved to keep track of the female employees' menstrual cycles. He kept a chart, then disciplined them if they called in sick claiming they were disabled by cramps when his chart showed they shouldn't be having their period.

One day he left work mid-shift to go to his doctor because he was having chest pains. His doctor said, "Omigod! We've got to get you right to the hospital, but first I've got to stop by a friend's apartment."

The friend was his girlfriend, one of our company's employees (the doctor was married). Their plans couldn't wait so the doctor ripped off a little nooky. When the doctor returned to his convertible, there was his patient, dead as a doornail. When I heard of the manager's death I thought THERE IS A GOD AFTER ALL!

Oldduck

twenty-one-member bipartisan body, was created through the Civil Rights Act of 1991 under the Bush administration. What the commission found in its study was that what is different in today's workplace is not that discrimination hurts white males, just that these males fear it does. In summarizing the research papers, findings of focus groups and public testimony underlying the study, the commission said these new worries among white males are actually helping to perpetuate the glass ceiling. "The glass ceiling exists because of the perception of many white males that as a group they are losing—losing the corporate game, losing control and losing opportunity," the report said. "Many middle- and upper-level white male managers view the inclusion of minorities and women in management as a direct threat to their own chances for advancement. They fear that they are losing competitive advantage. White male middle-level corporate managers, who were interviewed in independent studies, frequently alluded to loss of opportunity."

There is no doubt that the dominance of the white male in the workplace is on the wane. White men are expected to represent 47.5 percent of the U.S. civilian labor force by the year 2000, according to the Bureau of Labor Statistics. This reflects a slow and steady decline from 55.6 percent in 1970. But despite these males' fears of losing their position at the top of the workplace food chain, the reality is quite different. While the report did find that women and minorities have advanced in the workplace, it concluded that the progress has been "discouragingly slow." It noted, "Despite the recognition of corporate leadership that inclusion is a bottom-line issue, a glass ceiling is still firmly in place and barriers to the advancement of minorities and women continue to exist on three levels: societal, internal and governmental."

So while women and minorities will account for half the workforce in the year 2000, the executive suite remains overwhelmingly occupied by white males. According to the study, 97 percent of senior managers at Fortune 1000 industrial companies and Fortune 500 companies are white. Of those managers, about 95 percent are male.

White Men Need Not Apply

I cannot believe people cannot see that affirmative action promotes the very thing that it was created to eliminate.

Can "women and minorities are especially encouraged to apply" mean anything other than "whites males need not apply"? I have been under-employed for the past few years after being displaced in the construction industry for 17 years. I returned to school, got a BS in education and an MBA, graduated with a 3.9 GPA, but can't even get an interview. I do, however, get a lot of affirmative action information forms to fill out.

A friend of mine and I applied for an adjunct professor position in business administration at a small community college in Maryland. Both of us are white males. Both of us have business experience and MBAs. When neither of us were offered interviews, my friend called the school's personnel department to ask why.

He was told that the candidate selected had better qualifications than he did. He informed the personnel director that he knew the woman that was offered the position and that he knew that she was still working on her MBA at the same university we attended. She was behind us in school and that she had little or no real business experience. The personnel director hung up on him.

I worked as a graduate assistant while completing my MBA. As part of my duties I was asked to compile the statistics for several applicants for a history professor slot that opened up. My supervising professor was on the selection committee. The university president's office informed the committee that they were to hire a woman or a black regardless of the qualifications of the white males that applied because they needed to improve the "diversity" of their faculty.

I saw the memo. I saw the resumes of highly qualified males tossed out. They could hire an inexperienced woman who was ABD, had not even finished her degree and still hasn't as far as I know.

Who suffered here? Hundreds of students and parents that are paying for the education. My wife works as a pharmacist for one of the largest retail pharmacy chains in the U.S. Recently she tried to hire a male pharmacy technician who was more than qualified for the position. Her boss sent her a memo.

It said that NO men were to be hired as pharmacy technicians or cashiers because of the need to meet affirmative actions and quotas.

Richard S.

In Fortune 2000 companies, only 5 percent of the senior managers are women, and of those managers virtually all are white. Then–U.S. Labor Secretary Robert Reich summed it up by saying the report shows that the world at the top of the corporate hierarchy does not yet look anything like America. "It is interesting that few white men perceive the historical denial of opportunity suffered by minorities and women as 'loss,' " he said. "The loss they see is that which they fear will happen to them."

At the same time that women and minorities continue to find themselves pressing up against the glass ceiling, there are indications that, despite all the controversy, reverse discrimination has not become a sizable problem in the workplace. Alfred Blumrosen, a Rutgers University professor of law and former official with the Equal Employment Opportunity Commission who helped develop commission guidelines on affirmative action, analyzed court opinions in discrimination cases between 1990 and 1994. He found that reverse discrimination accounted for 1.7 percent of all those cases. Of more than three thousand opinions issued, less than a hundred involved cases of reverse discrimination. In reviewing the opinions, Blumrosen found that a high percentage of the reverse discrimination cases were without merit. Several job candidates had lost out to females or minorities who were more qualified than they, and had then filed suits. In six cases where reverse discrimination was established, Blumrosen said the court ordered appropriate relief. A total of twelve cases involved affirmative action programs, most of which had been established by consent decrees. In half those cases the courts upheld or modified the programs and in half the courts either invalidated or reexamined them. "This research suggests that the problem of 'reverse discrimination' is not widespread; and that where it exists, the courts have given relief," Blumrosen wrote. "The paucity of reported cases casts doubt on the dimension of the 'reverse discrimination' problem."

Blumrosen notes that none of the cases in the study involved Johnson's executive order 11246, which established affirmative action programs among federal contractors. He said there is an absence of such litigation because programs created under those federal guidelines do not provide a basis for a reverse discrimination claim. Not surprisingly, Blumrosen's report didn't seem to do much to quiet the clamoring of critics that see such programs as discriminatory against whites and males. They say that because those programs don't trigger court cases, the analysis grossly understates the true nature of the problem of reverse discrimination.

Though affirmative action has focused on the underrepresentation of women and minorities in the workplace, discrimination takes on many forms. It is not always about judging people by the color of their skin, but sometimes by the fat content of their heart. That's what John Rossi found out when he lost his job at Kragen Auto Parts. Rossi, tipping the scales at more than four hundred pounds at the time he lost his job, charged he had been fired because of his

Free from the Drug Chain Gang

I was a pharmacist for a large, family-owned chain of drugstores. A major drugstore chain gobbled up the chain, and we were promised a lot of things before the takeover.

Twenty-eight-hour-a-week job-sharers were promised vacation and health benefits. None were given. Brand new pharmacist graduates were paid several thousand dollars more than long-time pharmacists. Raises to equalize salaries were hinted at.

We were paid by the hour, but when they called a 10 P.M. mandatory meeting, suddenly we were "salaried," and free pizza became our pay. When store hours were shortened, so were our paychecks. This chain chose the best of two worlds—one foot in each class of employment. Overtime pay—forget it! The district supervisor warned, "Don't rock the boat!" They would rather have a fast turnover of employees so benefits would not build up.

So, I gave my one-week's notice and enjoyed a free Christmas like a normal human being. (According to the employee handbook, only one week was required, not two weeks.)

And who was hired to replace me, but a younger male pharmacist who was paid 30 percent more than I received for the same position.

Name withheld

weight. At the age of thirty-six, Rossi won a $1 million jury award—enough to buy one fuckload of Twinkies. Unfortunately for the good folks at Hostess, though, Rossi told reporters he planned to use the money to get the medical help he needed. It was believed to be a record award for a case involving discharge from employment due to obesity.

Rossi had worked ten years for Northern Automotive Corp., which operates hundreds of Kragen stores. At the time he was fired he was managing a store in Berkeley, California. Rossi sought help from his employer for his morbid obesity. Attorneys for Rossi said that after denying him help, the company complained about his job performance. Critical to the case was testimony from a doctor stating that obesity is 20 percent environmental and 80 percent genetic, thereby qualifying it as a disability. Though the case was brought under California's Fair Employment Act, it mirrors the protections of the federal Americans with Disabilities Act.

The Americans with Disabilities Act is considered by many to be the most significant piece of civil rights legislation passed since the Civil Rights Act of 1964. Passed in 1990, the law was an effort to protect one of the widely discriminated groups that Title VII had failed to include. A total of 49 million Americans have disabilities,

Getting His Irish Up

Michael J. Daly, a former real estate agent who speaks with an Irish brogue, has sued his former employer, charging he was fired because of his accent, the *Wall Street Journal* reported.

The lawsuit, filed in U.S. District Court in Orlando, Florida, charges that Park Square Enterprises Inc. fired Daly as a sales associate after a consultant's report said his "communication skills are hampered by his Irish background."

Daly told the *Journal* that he thought the signs that read "Irish need not apply" had been long taken down.

I wonder if his boss is familiar with the Gaelic expression "Kismearse yafahkin coont."

6/24/97

according to the 1990 U.S. Census. The Census Bureau found that more than 60 percent of working-age Americans with disabilities, and 76 percent with severe disabilities, do not work, and that those who do on average earn 35 percent less than workers without disabilities. A 1994 Harris Poll found that 79 percent of people with disabilities wanted to work but were not working. The Rehabilitation Act of 1973 prohibited the federal government or federal contractors from discriminating against the disabled; the Americans with Disabilities Act made it illegal for any employer with a workplace of fifteen people or more to discriminate against someone with a disability. Under the ADA, a disability is considered to be a significant impairment that limits or restricts one or more major life activities, such as hearing, seeing or walking. It applies to both mental and physical disabilities. That doesn't mean that airlines now had to hire a blind applicant who wanted to be a pilot, but rather that employers couldn't discriminate against someone who could perform the essential functions of a job. It also required that employers make a "reasonable accommodation" to someone with a disability, as long as it

Well, at Least He's Not Gay

A week before his thirty-fourth wedding anniversary, Georgia's former Attorney General Michael Bowers said he had had a decade-long affair with a former waitress at a Playboy club, the *Wall Street Journal* reported.

The announcement came shortly after a federal appellate court upheld the right of Bowers to withdraw a job offer to Robin Joy Shahar, a female attorney who planned on marrying another woman.

Bowers, who successfully defended Georgia's law that makes sodomy a crime, argued that by allowing Shahar to be a part of his staff, he would send confusing signals to the public about his stand on homosexuality and same-sex marriages. The strength of his anti-gay stance helped propel him to become the leading contender for the Republican nomination in Georgia's 1998 gubernatorial race.

As the Journal *aptly pointed out, like sodomy, adultery is a crime in Georgia.*

6/20/97

does not represent an undue hardship to the employer's business. That can mean modifying equipment, restructuring a job or allowing someone to have a flexible work schedule. An employer, though, is not required to lower production or quality standards to make an accommodation.

While all of this may seem straightforward enough, it does leave a lot of gray areas between an employer's and an employee's reading of the law. For instance, the Equal Employment Opportunity Commission brought suit against United Parcel Service in March 1997 under the Americans with Disabilities Act, charging that the delivery service illegally discriminated against employees with vision in just one eye by prohibiting them from driving. The Atlanta-based company said in a statement that the suit was without merit and that UPS had complied with the law, calling it a safety and not a disability issue. The case is currently being litigated.

Unlike disabilities, which affect only a portion of the workers, everyone can look forward to getting old—providing that they live so long. The Age Discrimination in Employment Act, passed in 1967, prohibits employers with more than twenty employees from discriminating against people who are forty or older because of their age. Tom Osborne, an attorney in the American Association of Retired Persons Litigation Group, said that when the law was enacted the focus was on age discrimination in hiring. But today, he noted, a large number of cases being filed arise as a result of terminations. Older employees can be attractive targets of downsizing because of their higher salaries and benefits costs. "That has been exacerbated by downsizing," Osborne said.

Such cases have become a bit harder to win because of a 1993 Supreme Court decision that involved Walter Biggins, a chemical engineer for the Holyoke, Massachusetts–based Hazen Paper Co. Biggins was fired just two months before his sixty-second birthday—months before he would be vested in the company's pension plan. The company had said he was fired for business associations with competitors and for refusing to sign a confidentiality agree-

Filing a Charge

If you believe you have been discriminated against by an employer, labor union or employment agency when applying for a job or while on the job because of your race, color, sex, religion, national origin, age or disability, or believe that you have been discriminated against because of opposing a prohibited practice or participating in an equal employment opportunity matter, you may file a charge of discrimination with the U.S. Equal Employment Opportunity Commission (EEOC).

Charges may be filed in person, by mail or by telephone by contacting the nearest EEOC office. If there is not an EEOC office in the immediate area, call toll free 800-669-4000 or 800-669-6820 (TDD) for more information. To avoid delay, call or write beforehand if you need special assistance, such as an interpreter, to file a charge.

There are strict time frames in which charges of employment discrimination must be filed. To preserve the ability of EEOC to act on your behalf and to protect your right to file a private lawsuit, should you ultimately need to, adhere to the following guidelines when filing a charge.

Title VII of the Civil Rights Act—Charges must be filed with EEOC within 180 days of the alleged discriminatory act. However, in states or localities where there is an antidiscrimination law and an agency authorized to grant or seek relief, a charge must be presented to that state or local agency. Furthermore, in such jurisdictions, you may file charges with EEOC within three hundred days of the discriminatory act or thirty days after receiving notice that the state or local agency has terminated its processing of the charge, whichever is earlier. It is best to contact EEOC promptly when discrimination is suspected. If charges or complaints are filed beyond these time frames, you may not be able to obtain any remedy.

The time requirements are the same for the Americans with Disabilities Act and the Age Discrimination in Employment Act.

Equal Pay Act (EPA)—Individuals are not required to file an EPA charge with EEOC before filing a private lawsuit. However, charges may be filed with EEOC, and some cases of wage discrimination may also be violations of Title VII. If an EPA charge is filed with EEOC, the procedure for filing is the same as for charges brought under Title VII. However, the time limits for filing in court are different under the EPA; thus, it is advisable to file a charge as soon as you become aware the EPA may have been violated.

Source: Equal Employment Opportunity Commission

ment. Because the jury in the lower court found the company's violation of the Age Discrimination in Employment Act was willful, it awarded him back pay of $560,000 and damages equal to that amount. The judge, though, set aside the jury's determination that the discrimination had been willful because he thought the evidence was not significant enough. An appeals court reversed the judge and the Supreme Court reaffirmed that decision. There was bad news for employees, though, in the decision, which held that just because an employee is fired as he is about to become vested in a pension program doesn't mean he is being discriminated against because of his age. The court said plaintiffs must show that the employer relied on the employee's age and not some corollary in making the decision to terminate. "We see a number of cases where people get fired and made to leave. It's just harder to prove now," said Osborne. "You can't rely on that proxy theory. The courts are fairly skeptical."

Paul Tobias, an attorney and chairman of the National Employee Rights Institute, a nonprofit educational and advocacy group, said the antidiscrimination laws have done a lot to improve conditions in the workplace but that discrimination continues to be a problem. In part, he said, this is because of the difficulty of enforcement, given the excessive workload the Equal Employment Opportunity Commission must try to manage. The commission, charged with enforcing the nation's antidiscrimination laws, has seen a dramatic rise in its workload thanks to new legislation meant to protect a greater number of workers. Both the Americans with Disabilities Act in 1990 and the Civil Rights Act of 1991, which made it more attractive to sue employers, fueled this rise. The number of private sector charges filed in fiscal 1994 reached nearly 92,000, up from about 64,000 in fiscal 1991. That helped to push the pending inventory of cases to about 97,000 in fiscal 1994, from just less than 46,000 three years earlier. During that same time the average caseload per investigator rose to 122 cases, up from 59 in fiscal 1991. Without the budget or staff necessary to handle the increased number of charges brought under the new statutes, the EEOC has struggled to meet its mandate.

"We've been working with one hand tied behind our back," said David Grinberg, a spokesman for the commission. "It's changed the way we process discrimination cases. It used to be a one-size-fits-all process. Now we have a priority system."

In 1995, the commission developed a national enforcement plan, an acknowledgment that its "effectiveness as a law enforcement agency had been reduced by the overwhelming increase in its inventory of individual charges of discrimination, by the lack of financial resources needed to address the increased workload and by a failure to strategically utilize its resources to pursue its mission through vigorous investigation, conciliation and litigation," the commission said. The task force working to outline a national enforcement plan concluded that the agency was unable to use its limited resources to pursue its mission of eradicating workplace discrimination through its existing policy of "full investigation and enforcement." Instead, it called for the creation of enforcement priorities.

The foundation of the plan laid out by the task force calls for directing resources at cases that could have significant impact beyond the parties directly involved, cases having the potential of promoting the development of laws supporting the antidiscrimination goals of the statutes enforced by the commission and cases involving the integrity or effectiveness of the commission's enforcement process. The end result is that today, while the Equal Employment Opportunity Commission is suing fewer employers, it is winning more in settlements for victims. The EEOC filed 161 lawsuits in fiscal 1996, down from 322 the previous year. Nevertheless, it won $49.3 million in damages for discrimination victims through litigation, compared with $24.6 million in fiscal 1995.

The commission's lack of resources has made the plaintiffs bar strictly select who gets to seek legal remedies and who doesn't. "Cases are tough. It's hard to get a lawyer to take a case. Lawsuits are expensive," said Tobias of the National Employee Rights Institute, who cautioned that employees looking to sue generally need to have dramatic evidence of a violation of the law to persuade a lawyer to take the case. "Once you get into a pissing match with corporate America, they buckle down and hire their guns. Some big companies take high-level positions to never settle a case. What's money to them? They'll spend a couple of hundred thousand dollars to fight a case." Because of that, employees need more than just a sense that they have been the victims of injustice. They need witnesses, smoking guns or paperwork. "In the eyes of God," said Tobias, "the company's done terrible things," said Tobias, "but we're not in church and the law is administered by Reagan-Bush conservatives and they've got cold hearts."

The fastest-growing type of discrimination case these days is one many people don't even think of as a form of discrimination. As Pamela Martens found out, though, it's that and a whole lot more.

5

The Employee Relations Department

"Clinton asked Jones: 'Are you married?' She responded that she had a regular boyfriend. Clinton then approached the sofa and as he sat down he lowered his trousers and underwear exposing his erect penis and asked Jones to 'kiss it.'"

—FROM COMPLAINT OF PAULA CORBIN JONES,
Plaintiff, v. William Jefferson Clinton, *filed May 6, 1994 Civil Action No. LR-C-94-290
United States District Court for the Eastern District of Arkansas, Western Division*

PAMELA K. MARTENS entered the broker training program at Smith Barney Inc. in 1985 through its Garden City, New York, office. She worked there for ten years until she was terminated. Despite her book of a thousand clients with assets of $187 million, Martens's efforts to move to a new firm were made difficult because Smith Barney, according to a lawsuit, bad-mouthed her to prospective employers and also placed a permanent mark on her otherwise spotless record with the National Association of Securities Dealers. On the form that is filed with the regulatory agency when a broker's tenure is ended with a firm, Smith Barney said she was terminated for "incompatibility with local management." The firm, the suit said, gave male brokers it terminated the option of resigning with a clean record, but Martens was only allowed to resign with a clean record if she agreed not to sue the company for retaliation. It was Smith Barney's final flip of the bird to Martens, whose lawsuit notes that after years of harassment and discrimination the company even discriminated against her in the way it fired her.

Martens was one of three women in the Garden City office who filed a sexual harassment and discrimination suit against Smith Barney in 1996. A spokeswoman for the firm at the time dismissed the allegations as "totally absurd and without merit," telling the *Wall Street Journal,* "The suit is actually about one former broker and two of her associates who were unhappy with one branch out of about four hundred seventy branches." Unfortunately for the firm, other women at Smith Barney didn't agree. Twenty-two others joined the suit from Smith Barney offices around the country and expanded it into a class action that some came to see as a symbol of the pervasive harassment and discrimination against women on Wall Street. In 1998, the firm settled the suit by agreeing to spend $15 million to recruit women and agreeing to offer settlements to class members, who could individually go before a panel of mediators.

Martens's lawsuit paints a graphic picture of life in the Garden City office where she worked. According to the suit, the office was home to the now infamous "Boom Boom Room," a fraternity-style lounge in the basement of the office featuring a toilet hanging from the ceiling and an oversized garbage can from which branch manager Nicholas Cuneo served Bloody Marys to male brokers whom he summoned over the PA system. The brokers joked that female employees—"slits and tits," as they were affectionately known at the office—would be "dealt with" in the Boom Boom Room when they did not behave and that sexual harassment charges would be deliberated there as well.

Anne Clark Ronce, an executive recruiter in San Francisco who often serves as an expert witness on sexual harassment cases, described the state of sexual harassment in the workplace today as "brutal." She noted, "Part of why it is brutal is that we still are not really seeing the real spectrum of what goes on. What frustrates me is what makes it into the media is the extremes at each end of the curve, so normal people throw their hands up in the air and say that's ridiculous." At one end, she said, an employee files a lawsuit claiming a hostile work environment because she watched a man hug a female colleague who he'd learned had suffered a death in her family. At the other end, she said, a postal worker who has repeatedly turned down her boss for dates finds a blue Play-Doh dildo left for her on her chair. "What sexual harassment is really about is a relentless, debilitating lack of respect that wears people down and tells them on a daily basis they are second-class citizens," said Ronce. "It's not about the battle of sexes and sex and flirtation in the workplace. It's about human dignity and respect."

That certainly seems clear in the Smith Barney case. From the start, Martens got a taste of what would be in store for her during her tenure. When she interviewed for a position in the broker training program, her suit said, Cuneo tried to talk her out of it. He told her that she would not receive the same stipend as male trainees and that although she could try to sue him, many others had tried and failed. Cuneo, Martens said, told other women they would not earn as much as their male counterparts because they were not heads of households. Martens nevertheless took the job because she felt that once she proved herself Cuneo would change his tune. Apparently he was tone-deaf.

At an all-female sales assistants' meeting, the suit continued, Cuneo told the women they would be required to work at his charity golf tournament and dress in short skirts to serve coffee to male brokers. He told the women that if they refused, they would be denied raises, bonuses or time off without pay. The complaint described this last demand as quid pro quo sexual harassment, a type of sexual harassment where job status or monetary rewards are tied to the harasser's demands. The Smith Barney lawsuit, though, mostly describes the other type of sexual harassment that creates what in legal terms is known as a "hostile work environment."

Quid pro quo sexual harassment—sleep with me and the promo-

Grunty's Tips on Sexual Harassment

Oftentimes it seems difficult for people in today's workplace to know where the line is drawn between reasonable behavior and sexual harassment. Sometimes the mere choice of a word or phrasing of a simple request can be taken the wrong way. This has had a chilling effect on people, who are afraid to say the most innocent things for fear of being misunderstood.

To help you, Grunty offers some examples below of things you can say in today's office and things that could get you in trouble.

It is okay to call colleagues by their first name, such as "Pete, William and Richard."
You can get in trouble if you say "Peter, Willie or Dick."

It is okay to say, "Did you see the new proposal those boobs in marketing came up with?"
You can get in trouble if you say, "Did you see those new boobs in marketing?"

It is okay to say, "I'll put it in your mailbox."
You can get in trouble if you say, "I'll shove it in your box."

It is okay to say, "Spread those papers on my desk."
You can get in trouble if you say, "Spread 'em on my desk."

It is okay to say, "Can you lick this envelope?"
You can get in trouble if you say, "Can you lick this?"

It is okay to say "staple," "clip" or "tack."
You can get in trouble if you say "nail," "screw" or "mount."

It is okay to say, "You've got the best department head."
You can get in trouble if you say, "You've got the best head in your department."

It is okay to say, "I'll skip lunch and grab a snack."
You can get in trouble if you say, "I'm just going to nibble."

It is okay to say, "Nice chair."
You can get in trouble if you say, "Nice seat."

It is okay to say, "Right now, I've got to clean out my in box and my out box."
You can get in trouble if you say, "Time for a bit of the old in and out."

tion is yours, don't and you're fired—had long been the only type of harassment recognized by the courts. But that changed dramatically after the Supreme Court tackled its first sexual harassment case in 1986 when Mechelle Vinson, an assistant bank manager with Meritor Savings Bank, sued her employer, charging that her boss's persistent sexual harassment had created a hostile work environment. Meritor branch manager Sidney Taylor hired Vinson as a teller trainee in 1974 and during her four years at the bank she had moved up the ranks—on merit—to become assistant branch manager. She took an indefinite sick leave in September 1978 and was fired two months later for taking excessive leave. During her time at the bank, Vinson testified, she was constantly subjected to Taylor's harassment.

When she began working there, Vinson said, Taylor treated her in a fatherly manner, but that soon changed. He invited her to dinner and during the meal suggested that the two go to a motel and have sex. At first she refused, but she said she became concerned her job was on the line and consented. After that, Taylor made repeated sexual demands, usually at the branch, both during and after hours, giving what one sexual harassment expert described as new meaning to the term "safe sex."

Vinson estimated he, shall we say, *visited her vault to make a deposit* forty to fifty times. In addition, she said, Taylor's charming ways included fondling her in front of other employees, following her into the bathroom when he knew she'd be in there alone, exposing himself and even forcibly raping her on several occasions. The sexual relationship ended in 1977 when she began dating a steady boyfriend. Though the bank had a complaint procedure, Vinson said she never used it because it required that she make her complaint to her supervisor, which in this case was the harasser.

Taylor denied having any sort of a sexual relationship with Vinson, and like many sexual harassment cases it went from being a story of kiss-and-teller to he-said-she-said. The trial court didn't care whether the allegations were true, ruling that if a sexual relationship

Sexual Harassment: The Basics

What Is Sexual Harassment

Sexual harassment is a form of discrimination that violates Title VII of the Civil Rights Act of 1964.

The U.S. Equal Employment Opportunity Commission defines sexual harassment as unwelcome sexual advances. That can include requests for sexual favors and other verbal or physical conduct of a sexual nature when submission to or rejection of this conduct explicitly or implicitly affects an individual's employment, unreasonably interferes with an individual's work performance or creates an intimidating, hostile or offensive work environment.

The victim or harasser can be male or female and the two can be of the same sex. The harasser can be a supervisor, coworker, agent of the employer or nonemployee, such as a client. The victim does not have to be the person harassed, but could be anyone affected by the offensive conduct.

Sexual harassment can occur without any economic injury to the victim.

The harasser's conduct must be unwelcome.

What to Do If You Are Sexually Harassed

It is best to firmly communicate to the harasser that the conduct is unwelcome. The EEOC also advises keeping a written record of what happened, including the details of where it occurred, when, whether others were present and how you responded.

Because retaliation is common and it is easier to dismiss the complaints of one person than those of a group of people, it is a good idea to talk to other employees if you think they might have been victims of unwelcome conduct from the same person.

You should also report the harassment to your supervisor. If your supervisor is the harasser, complain to his or her boss.

If there is a formal complaint process at your workplace, use it. If you are a member of a union, file a complaint there. If those avenues don't exist, complain to your human resources department.

If the above fails to stop the harassment, you may want to consult an attorney or file charges with the U.S. Equal Employment Opportunity Commission. To file charges of sexual harassment with the EEOC, contact a field office near you. You can find the nearest field office by looking in your local phone book. Information about sexual harassment can be obtained from the EEOC by calling 800-669-EEOC.

Source: U.S. Equal Employment Opportunity Commission, Women's Legal Defense Fund

existed, Vinson participated in it voluntarily and it had nothing to do with her continued employment or with the advancement of her career. In other words, it was not a case of quid pro quo sexual harassment. The court of appeals disagreed, and so did the Supreme Court.

In the unanimous opinion of the Supreme Court, written by Chief Justice William Rehnquist, the Court dramatically reshaped the sexual harassment arena by dismissing the notion that plaintiffs had to demonstrate they'd suffered an economic loss. The Court said that Title VII of the Civil Rights Act is concerned with "the entire spectrum of the disparate treatment of men and women in employment."

Rehnquist noted that other courts have held the principle of a "hostile environment" in race-based discrimination cases and that sexual harassment should be no different. In that regard, he quoted from a 1982 decision handed down by the Eleventh Circuit Court of Appeals in *Henson* v. *Dundee*: "Sexual harassment which creates a hostile or offensive environment for members of one sex is every bit the arbitrary barrier to sexual equality at the workplace that racial harassment is to racial equality. Surely, a requirement that a man or woman run a gauntlet of sexual abuse in return for the privilege of being allowed to work and make a living can be as demeaning and disconcerting as the harshest of racial epithets."

The Supreme Court faulted the trial court not only for its presumption that sexual harassment could not exist in the absence of economic harm to the plaintiff, but also for its supposition that if sex did occur between Vinson and Taylor, it was voluntary. "The gravamen of any sexual harassment claim," wrote Rehnquist, "is that the alleged sexual advances were unwelcome." The case was sent back for further proceedings and was settled out of court for an unspecified amount.

The Supreme Court would revisit the issue of sexual harassment in 1993 in the case of *Harris* v. *Forklift Systems, Inc.* Teresa Harris, the plaintiff in the case, had worked as a manager at an equipment rental company. She testified that her boss, Charles Hardy, had created a hostile work environment through persistent sexual harassment. In addition to unwanted sexual innuendos and insults, Hardy would say things such as "We need a man as the rental manager" or "You're a woman—what do you know?" and called Harris a "dumb-ass woman." Once, in front of other employees, he suggested that he and Harris go to the Holiday Inn to negotiate her raise. Harris wasn't the only target of Hardy's rapier wit. He occasionally asked Harris and other women to fish coins from his pants pockets or threw objects on the floor so he could watch them bend over and pick them up.

In mid-August 1987, two years after she joined the company, Harris complained to Hardy about his behavior. He was surprised she was offended and apologized, saying he was joking and that he would stop. But the following month, he started again. While she was working with a customer on a deal, Harris, in front of other employees, asked her, "What did you do, promise the guy some [sex] Saturday night?"

The United States District Court for the Middle District of Tennessee, adopting the report and recommendation of a magistrate, said that while Hardy's conduct may have been offensive to some people, it wasn't offensive enough to reasonably expect it to seriously affect Harris's psychological well-being. But in the unanimous Supreme Court decision written by Justice Sandra Day O'Connor, the Court ruled that for a hostile work environment created by sexual harassment to exist, it does not have to seriously affect an employee's psychological well-being or lead the plaintiff to suffer injury.

"A discriminatory work environment," wrote O'Connor, "even one that does not seriously affect an employee's psychological well-being, can and often will detract from employees' job performance, discourage employees from remaining on the job or keep them from advancing in their careers."

While psychological harm is one factor that should be considered in determining whether a work environment is hostile, O'Connor said it was only one. Other considerations should include how often the conduct occurred, how severe it was, whether it was physically threatening or a mere offensive remark and whether it reasonably interferes with employees' ability to do their jobs. While relevant, psychological damage is just one factor to consider, and the court said "no single factor is required." Harris was later awarded $150,000 in lost wages, bonuses and interest.

Though the decision once again broadened the concept of sexual harassment, it had been a Supreme Court decision of another kind that turned sexual harassment into a hot topic of discussion within the nation's workplaces just a few years before that. The decision was the one George Bush made when he chose Clarence Thomas as his appointment to the Supreme Court. During the televised and widely watched 1991 confirmation hearings, Thomas faced allegations that while he headed the Equal Employment Opportunity Commission—ironically, making him the chief of the sexual harassment police—he was guilty of sexually harassing former EEOC employee Anita Hill. While the hearings fueled many jokes in offices about the cinematic prowess of Long Dong Silver, reportedly one of Thomas's favorite actors, and speculation on the size of his nominee's *gavel,* which he reportedly boasted was larger than normal, and made it all the rage to stand up at the office and yell, as Thomas allegedly did, "Hey, who put this pubic hair on my can of Coke?" it also got people talking about sexual ha-

Harassment Grab Bag

A divided Eighth Circuit Court of Appeals ruled that Phil Quick, who charged he was sexually harassed by male coworkers at the Iowa factory where he worked as a welder, had a right to bring his case to trial.

Quick complained he was taunted for being a homosexual, which he is not, and was the victim of "bagging," a practice in which males grab each other's crotches.

Officials of Donaldson Co., Inc., where Quick worked, were quoted in the *Omaha World-Herald* as saying it was a matter of horseplay and not harassment and that "bagging" was once widespread.

The good news is that the Donaldson Co. men's choir never has trouble hitting the high notes.

rassment. The high-profile Thomas hearings threw national attention on the issue and brought it out of the closet, where many women—and some men—had suffered in silence for years.

Though some people say the Thomas hearings created a chilling effect on the workplace, leaving people afraid to joke and deal warmly with colleagues, Helen Norton, director of equal opportunity programs for the Women's Legal Defense Fund in Washington, D.C., said there's no reason for confusion. "This isn't a gray area. I think responsible adults in the workplace know how to act," she said. "You know if you are thoughtful and aware that you don't act in a way that would offend you or your daughter or mother or sister."

Even some male corporate executives who may not fully understand why women get upset by certain behavior are learning to take sexual harassment seriously because of high-profile cases with large settlements. Those who don't simply run the risk of being sued. "I'd say seventy to eighty percent of those who get sued don't get it, especially if they admit to the conduct," said Pat Gillette, head of the employment law practices group at the San Francisco law firm of Heller, Ehrman, White & McAuliffe and a specialist in defending corporations against charges of sexual harassment "They ask, 'Why should she be upset by that?' What I generally tell my clients is I don't care if they buy into it, cut it out or they are going to pay big dollars."

Part of the problem is that too often corporations try to insulate themselves against liability—

No Support Without a Bra

"I walked past my supervisor's door, there are five women in there, and after four years of being with this company, I ask, 'How do I get to be in this group?' There's a giggle, and as I walk away, the reply is 'Either you have a sex change, or you buy a push-up bra.'"

Tracy Tinkham, one of eight men who filed a 1994 sexual harassment and discrimination suit against the Jenny Craig diet firm, in an interview with NBC's Dateline.

seeking insurance policies or requiring employees to sign agreements to submit such claims to arbitration rather than the legal system—instead of addressing the causes of the problem. "If folks are
only concerned about their liability, they are missing some of the bigger picture," said Norton of the Women's Legal Defense Fund. "How
do you treat your workers so they want to work well, so they want to
be productive and want to stay working for you?"

Though more victims of sexual harassment are coming forward
today—there were more than 15,300 sexual harassment charges filed
with the EEOC in 1996, compared with a little more than 6,100 cases
in 1990—various surveys of industry groups and of leading corporations consistently find that only a small percentage of those who say
they are harassed actually speak up to complain. A 1992 survey by
Working Woman magazine based on a representative sample of 9,700
readers found that more than 60 percent of the respondents had been
harassed, but that only one in four women reported the harassment.
A separate study done a year earlier by Klein Associates found that
less than 10 percent of people who are sexually harassed report it because of fear of retaliation and loss of privacy.

Defense attorneys say retaliation can sometimes create more
trouble for a sexual harasser than the harassment itself. Often, retaliation is what sets an employee otherwise willing to put up with
harassment in pursuit of legal remedies. "Retaliation claims can be
the most dangerous claims you try," said Heller, Ehrman's Gillette.
"Retaliation smacks of punitive damages. It's one thing to say, 'I
didn't know it was offensive.' If you can show someone retaliated
for doing something they are legally entitled to do, juries can really
get mad."

The sexual harassment expert Ronce said that in the cases she
has been involved with, company's are not made to pay severely
for their retaliatory acts. Even when juries seek to punish them
harshly, judges have come back and reduced the penalties levied.
Without fear of consequences, she said, retaliation remains the
norm. "I have never seen a case where there wasn't retaliation,"

said Ronce. "The complainant may prevail in the end, but not without retaliation."

Retaliation comes in many forms, including ostracism, reduced access, termination, public maligning, wiretapping and transfers from nice offices in the executive suite to a basement office by the Coke machine. Ronce told the story of a female utility worker who was demoted and given impossible work schedules. She was required to report to work at 5 A.M., but also required to attend meetings at 5 P.M. In addition, her employer tapped her phone. When she approached the company about this, officials accused her of being paranoid. In other cases women who complained of sexual harassment faced death threats to themselves and their families. One woman was thrown up against a locker by a supervisor who held her in place and told her, "I know your child walks home from school alone every day."

Laurie Nardinelli knows about retaliation. Nardinelli was one of the lead plaintiffs in a sexual harassment and class-action discrimination suit filed against Chevron Corporation. Chevron said its own internal investigation of the allegations never found any culprits and the company did not admit guilt, but it paid $2.2 million to Nardinelli and three other women to settle charges of harassment and later reached a settlement on a related class-action sexual discrimination case for a minimum of $8 million. Attorneys for the plaintiffs said the second settlement could grow into tens of millions of dollars depending on how many of the individuals covered by the suit choose to arbitrate their settlement.

Nardinelli, a communications analyst with the Chevron Information Technology Co., started working at Chevron in 1987. Beginning in March 1990, according to the suit, Nardinelli began receiving violent pornographic material through interoffice mail. One time her mail featured a series of three pictures showing a woman being gang-raped and dismembered. Another photograph featured a woman being tortured and had a caption typed below it reading, "Taming of the Arrogant Little Techno-Bitch."

The manager who Nardinelli believed was responsible for the mail repeatedly made comments and asked questions of a sexual nature. She also had to deal with sexual talk and obscene images throughout the office, including on the computers she was required to check as part of her job. On computer screens, she would find graphics of a man masturbating, and under the image the words: "We love our hardworking CITC [Chevron Information Technology Co.] cuties." Chevron contended that it conducted a thorough and good-faith investigation into Nardinelli's reports of harassment, but according to court filings from Nardinelli's attorneys the company spent more time investigating Nardinelli and trying to prove she was fabricating the events and sending the pornography to herself than in trying to find out who was really behind everything.

Filings with the court say the company broke into Nardinelli's personal electronic mail library and reviewed several years of her personal E-mail, secretly monitored her phone calls, set up a surveillance camera outside her office with a motion detector, conducted a secret review of her and her husband's credit card records and the credit card records of two nonemployees the company believed were living with her, contacted her private psychotherapist without her consent or knowledge and hired a private investigator to check her and her husband's DMV records. The company did not take similar steps to investigate the manager she told it she suspected was sending the photographs.

In response to the company's motion for summary judgment, Nardinelli's attorneys wrote, "Defendants were hardly acting as the benevolent, caring employer struggling to assist their victimized employee in any way they could, as their motion suggests. On the contrary, the evidence reveals a cold, calculated and downright nasty campaign by defendants to attempt to discredit Ms. Nardinelli in any way they could, and to blame her for the horrible and terrifying incidents to which she had been subjected—just as rape victims are, all too often, blamed for the violence and degradation perpetrated against them." At one point, when Nardinelli had complained to corporate security about receiving the sadistic pornography, their response, filings from her attorneys say, was to cross-examine her. Rather than expressing concern, security wanted to know "what she had done that could have caused any of her male coworkers to believe she was interested in, or attracted to, them."

Court filings from Nardinelli's attorneys said that as part of the investigation the company called in two psychologists to determine whether the accused manager was a violence risk. They interviewed the other women as well. Nardinelli was put through two interviews totaling more than six hours, which included prying questions about her private life. The accused manager was interviewed for two hours and was not asked about his personal life or pornography. After the interviews were completed, Chevron Information Technology president William Houghton met with the woman. They were concerned that now that the manager knew the names of his accusers, he might act violently toward them. But rather than address or acknowledge their fears, the filing said, Houghton expressed sympathy for the manager and told the women he had "nightmares of being in the same situation" where someone accused him of "these kinds of things." He told the women he could not put himself in their shoes and understand their fears, and got angry when they asked questions. "You don't seem to appreciate that we've taken a 1B manager with thirty-five years' experience and put him through a horrible morning."

Needless to say, management often has a perspective that is different from that of the employees who are victims of sexual harassment. While only 21 percent of the 1992 *Working Woman* survey respondents said complaints of sexual harassment were dealt with justly, more than 60 percent said the charges were ignored or the harasser had been given a slap on the hand. In 55 percent of the cases, nothing happened to the harasser. By contrast, more than 80 percent of the executives surveyed by the magazine said the harasser was justly dealt with. "In every workplace we've surveyed, we find that a majority of employees don't have faith in corporate channels for

Fish Stinks from the Head Down

The problem with all of this is there's the big guy, you and your staff. The big guy is fucking someone on your staff. Where it comes into play is where some other woman above the woman the boss is fucking isn't getting the promotion, raise, bonus and recognition. It's a mess. It's not just a morale mess, it's a legal mess. It's awful for morale.

Shortly after I joined a major investment banking firm as a department manager I hired a woman at the boss's suggestion for a newly created, low-level position. If he wants to give me extra staff, I'm not going to complain. She was not particularly bright—she couldn't spell "YMCA"—but I didn't think much about it. Soon, her dresses got a little tighter and her heels a little spikier. All of a sudden the boss is relying on her more than the woman over her.

She was married and the boss was married, but they became involved. It seemed everyone picked up on it before me. One day the big guy comes to me and said he needs an assistant and he wants her. She's presentable. I don't give a shit who gets his dry cleaning. She's not a sophisticated person. Not exactly the person you'd take to a meeting in Washington. She gets a $15,000 raise to $55,000 and a $30,000 bonus, three times what she was supposed to get. There were other people there who were doing more and better. They are not on welfare, but they are relatively disadvantaged. There was a general bitching in the air. But if they went into another industry, they could expect to make three quarters of what they were making.

It was a horrendous morale problem. It's very clear why the one was rewarded and the others were not. I asked the one woman who was relatively victimized if she wanted me to have a discussion with the boss—veiled or otherwise. She asked me not to do it and I can't say I wasn't glad. It was humiliating for her, but she was trapped having recently bought a house. She was making something like a $100,000 a year. She didn't get the promotion, didn't get the bonus, didn't get the raise.

It could just go away because the victim is making a lot of money. Money is the salve of all wounds. Victims of office politics don't get promotions, don't get whatever, but if they are well paid, they just sort of go on and collect the bucks. They are not always proud people to begin with. There are a hell of a lot of people who are in it only for the money. The money is what really, really counts.

Interview with Wall Street Executive

complaint," Freada Klein, a consultant who runs sexual harassment training sessions for corporations, told *Working Woman*.

If a thirst for justice doesn't move some to speak up when they are victimized, the promise of a fat payday might help—even when sexual harassment might not really have occurred, according to some plaintiffs' attorneys. They thank Rena Weeks, a legal secretary who successfully brought suit against the world's largest law firm, Baker McKenzie, for what they dub the "new California lottery." Attorneys say the Baker McKenzie case was unremarkable from a legal perspective, but it showed how a little arrogance can go a long way in getting a jury to want to punish a defendant, especially when that defendant is a big law firm.

Rena Weeks had been with the firm for about three months and had spent about a month of that time working for attorney Martin Greenstein. During her brief stint with Greenstein, she charged, he dropped M&M candies into her breast pocket, grabbed her breast, pulled her arm back to see which breast was bigger and made comments of a sexual nature. Weeks was moved by the firm when she complained, but according to the testimony of other women from Baker McKenzie, Greenstein had a history of harassment and the firm had failed to take steps to discipline him adequately before the Weeks incident. The jury was angry enough to deliver a $7.1 million award, $6.9 million of which was to be paid by the firm. A judge later cut the award in half. "It was a law firm and juries don't particularly like law firms. In my mind it was a case of a terribly wrong jury verdict," said Jeff Tanenbaum, a partner with the Littler, Mendelson, Fastiff, Tichy & Mathiason, which specializes in employment law from the defense side. "We saw a tremendous increase in the number of cases that were filed after the Weeks verdict was announced. People saw the money."

Rena Weeks may have provided inspiration to sexual harassment victims, but defense attorneys see Adelyn Lee as an example of the type of plaintiffs she inspired. "Her case really typifies what's gone on," said defense attorney Gillette, who represented software tycoon

Larry Ellison in a civil case brought by Lee. "It's such an easy allegation to make—why not roll the dice and make it." Ellison, founder and CEO of the nation's second-largest software company, Oracle Corp., had an affair with Lee, who was an executive assistant to the head of sales at the company. According to the lawsuit she filed, she showed up at Ellison's home for a date one day and told him she wanted to break off the relationship. He threw her down on the bed and forced her to have sex. The suit said he told her if she ever left him, she would leave Oracle as well. Five days later she was fired. The company contended she was fired because of poor performance. The suit was settled out of court for $100,000 in exchange for Lee's retracting her allegations. But that didn't end the story.

One strong piece of evidence Lee had in her favor was a smoking gun in the form of E-mail from Lee's boss to Ellison saying he had done what Ellison had told him to do and fired Lee. Lee was later charged with forging the E-mail, and was found guilty. During the forgery trial former Oracle employee Andrea Zeman, who had also dated Ellison, testified that Lee had called her and suggested the two could get $1 million from Ellison if they threatened to go public about his affairs with employees.

While defense attorneys love the Lee case because it shows how the charge of sexual harassment can be abused by an employee, what it really shows is some of the potential dangers of dating an employee. With more women in the workforce than ever before, the office has replaced singles bars as the place to meet in the 1990s. But while labor and love might be an increasingly common combination that unites the star-crossed in blissful romance, it's a volatile combination that can wreak havoc on coworkers' morale, destroy careers and entangle employers in costly litigation.

Oracle didn't have any policies prohibiting office romances then, and it still doesn't. In fact, while such policies do exist, most corporations have steered clear of them. A 1994 survey of nearly five hundred companies by the American Management Association for *Money* magazine found that only 6 percent of them had a written policy on employee dating and that only two of those companies barred all employee dating. There's a good reason for that. Such policies are difficult to write and enforce, as they must strike a delicate balance between an employer's right to maintain a well-functioning workplace and an employee's right to privacy. "There's no clear legal doctrine," said John True, a partner with the San Francisco law firm Rudy, Axelrod, Zieff & True. "There are only competing interests."

Office romances certainly can undermine employee morale if coworkers feel a colleague is getting special treatment for merely sleeping with his or her supervisor. At the same time, employers may wish to protect themselves against the problems that can arise when an office romance turns sour and an employee charges they were sexually harassed, being punished in the workplace for breaking off a relationship or shunning the advances of a higher-up. In some instances, employers have not only concerned themselves with romantic relationships employees may have with a coworkers, but with outsiders as well. Some policies employers have put into place have sought to prohibit employees from engaging in relationships with workers at competing companies. In other instances, conflict-of-interest policies have been broadly interpreted to prohibit relationships with nonemployees. In one instance, a California deputy attorney general wrote a strongly worded opinion that the state's Public Utilities Commission's conflict-of-interest policy prohibits any worker at the regulatory agency from marrying any worker at any of the utilities it regulates.

There have been so-called nonfraternization policies that courts have upheld, notably the one instituted by United Parcel Service, which prohibited managers from socializing with rank and file. More often, say attorneys, the language has no meaning and renders the policies unenforceable. For instance, what is meant when an employer prohibits certain relationships? Does it mean when two people have gone out on a date? Think they are attracted to each other? Had sex?

If a company does seek to institute such a policy, it does not prevent relationships from arising. "It doesn't matter what rule you put in place. You cannot legislate love. You can't tell people who they should fall in love with," said Cliff Palefsky, a partner with the San Francisco law firm McGuinn, Hillsman & Palefsky, which represents plaintiffs in employment-related cases. "History has shown us if people violate their marriage vows, they are going to violate your policy. It basically causes people to sneak around, hide and lie, rather than deal with it and their coworkers honestly." Palefsky said employers

Love Stinks in the Workplace

I'm a page layout tech (read: peon) at a subsidiary of a large publishing company that produces computer books.

Turnover is high and our production department is continually filled with young, single, recent college graduates. And everyone is dating EVERYONE. There is a company policy of not hiring spouses of employees, but there isn't one about not dating someone you meet in the workplace.

You can imagine the complications of office politics. It gets really interesting when management gets involved; two of the managers met and married each other, and collectively have control over half the policy-making power in the department. It's impossible to get promoted without being in their good graces. (And, big surprise, I'm not.)

To make matters more interesting, my boss began dating an employee from another team soon after his divorce was final. They both started coming in late, leaving early and taking two-hour "quickie" lunches. During the workday, people would go to her work area first if they were looking for him because he spent most of the day sitting on her desk talking to her. If you weren't careful, you'd stumble upon them kissing in the breakroom or the copy area.

I made the stupid mistake of falling in love with my friend/coworker, and the even stupider mistake of telling her so. She did not return my affections, but did me the generous favor of sending my love letter through the E-mail to several of my coworkers. (This damned E-mail is just too easy to use.)

Of course, she's no longer my friend. We don't speak to each other and my coworkers no longer have respect for me. I had to make a formal complaint of discrimination against one of them, which she got reprimanded for.

The lesson: office romance = bad idea.

Name withheld

who become aware of a relationship have some obligation to make sure it is consensual. But once they determine that, he said, they should stay the hell away.

When two lovers try to hide their relationship in the workplace, it can cause enormous tension. They can become the subject of unwelcome gossip, and once a relationship hits the skids, going to a once enjoyable job might become a dreaded and uncomfortable task. Nevertheless, those thinking about starting up an office romance need to go into it with their eyes open because eventually they may have to decide whether they value their lover more than their job. Even if an employer never says anything about the relationship, it can undermine an employee's opportunities for advancement. When Ken, a young California attorney, had a yearlong fling with a legal assistant in his office, he didn't think much about the effects it would have on his career. But after the affair ended, he discovered his dalliance hadn't done much to move him through the ranks. "I found out years later that the partners definitely looked down upon it. It was looked at as most inappropriate," he said. "They said, 'Is this guy an idiot? Doesn't he have any sense?'" In a case of do-as-I-say, not-as-I-do, sometime after that the partner who was most critical of the affair ended up having one of his own with his secretary, who was married. Both attorneys have since left the firm.

Ethan Winning, a Walnut Creek, California–based employee relations consultant and author of *Labor Pains: Employer and Employee Rights in the Workplace,* said that while most employers want to avoid dealing with the issue of office romances, not dealing with it can be problematic. He tells the story of a vice president of a San Francisco Bay Area company who began a relationship with a low-level supervisor. Other employees weren't happy about the relationship because they felt she received special treatment. The two soon were living together and the relationship ran into problems. They started fighting at work and five months after it started, she threw his belongings all over their front lawn. Since he had the power to do so, he terminated her. She claimed it was a wrongful termination and alleged he had raped her on company premises. The company fired him and settled with her.

Winning said that while he doesn't think it's practical to institute policies that prohibit relationships, he has helped create policies that dictate there can be no direct reporting lines for people romantically involved. If such policies are developed, they are going to be in an administrative handbook rather than an employee manual. "The best thing to do is communicate," he said. "Go to the two people involved and say, 'It's you're business that you are dating, but when your dating begins to interfere with this business, one of you will have to go, and it's going to be the lesser-valued employee.' " Winning says if there are no openings available in another department to transfer one of them and the relationship is a problem, he usually advises to buy out the less-valued employee as the best way to avoid ugly and costly court cases. "It may cost you a heck of a lot more to defend yourself than just paying off one of the employees," he said. "I'm a practical consultant. It's cheaper than fighting a discrimination or wrongful discharge suit."

That's something with which the folks at IBM might agree. The computer giant was sued for wrongful termination after it gave Virginia Rulon-Miller an ultimatum: End a romantic relationship with a former colleague who now worked for an IBM competitor or be demoted from the ranks of management. Rulon-Miller had risen from the position of receptionist to become a highly regarded marketing manager. Though the company gave her the ultimatum, she had never been accused of sharing competitive information with her lover. She was awarded $300,000 in the case.

Of course, all of that could have been avoided if the company had just followed its own policies, spelled out in a memo from CEO Tom Watson in 1968 in which he told managers that the only time they should be concerned with an employee's off-the-job behavior is when it "reduces his ability to perform regular job assignments, interferes with the job performance of other employees or if his outside behavior affects the reputation of the company in a major way." Watson said when on-the-job performance is acceptable, he could think of few situations where outside activities could result in discipline or dismissal. "IBM's first basic belief is respect for the individual, and the essence of this belief is a strict regard for his right to personal privacy. This idea should never be compromised easily or quickly."

Unfortunately, today employers will invade their employees' privacy, as workers at Kmart will tell you, faster than you can say "blue-light special."

6

The Research Department

> "Would you buy a new vehicle or piece of equipment without checking it out first? Then why hire people on face value when you can find out about their past for less than the cost of a day or two on the payroll?"
>
> —On-line brochure for 21st Century Pre-Employment Screening

ALBERT POSEGO SEEMED like any other worker at Kmart Corp.'s Manteno, Illinois, warehouse. He did the work like everyone else, invited coworkers to go out for beers at the end of the day and even gave up a day off to help a coworker who needed some extra muscle when he was moving his family into a new home. But Posego was not a normal Kmart employee. He really worked for Confidential Investigative Consultants, Inc., a Chicago firm retained by the retailer to gather information about its workers. Posego was one of three people Kmart put into place to spy on workers during a six-month period at the distribution center.

The three undercover agents, according to comments by Kmart in press accounts, were retained to break a theft ring at the warehouse. But according to the attorney representing workers suing Kmart over invasion of privacy and other alleged wrongdoings, 190 pages of reports show the investigators routinely revealed information about the personal lives of the workers, including their family problems, dating habits, future work plans, any disenchantment with the company they expressed, attitudes they held about unions, how they spent their time away from work and where they shopped. "It's kind of unique—the old-fashionedness of using actual spies, or what they call 'investigators,'" said Phillip Snelling, an attorney with the Chicago law firm of Johnson, Jones, Snelling, Gilbert & Davis, who is representing the Kmart workers. "There have been cases relating to electronic surveillance, but I haven't come across something as pervasive as this. You do have those traditionalists."

While Kmart took a decidedly low-tech approach to employee surveillance, many employers today are using ubiquitous technology to peer into their employees' lives, thoughts and bodies. They have moved well beyond the simple approach of name, rank and Social Security number to gather enormous details about their employees' conduct on and off the job. Cellular phones, voice mail, E-mail and computers all serve as portals for employers to listen in on and read over the shoulders of their workforce. Psychological and honesty tests let prospective employers weed out people they may deem undesirable because they have the wrong thoughts. And, for a modest fee, an employer can contact one of several companies that tap into or maintain databases of employees to find out if a job applicant has ever sued a past employer, filed a workers' compensation complaint, or been convicted of a crime.

Big Brother is here, but Orwell got it wrong. It's not the government that has stripped us of our privacy, but our employers. No longer content with merely the blood, sweat and tears of their workers, employers increasingly want their urine and DNA too. They want to know the most intimate details of their employees' lives. They want to know not only what they are doing at work every minute of the day, but what they do after hours. Employers these days will get rid of employees not only because they don't approve of their sex partners, but because they don't like the fact that they smoke afterward. They justify their intrusions under several banners: They need to operate a workplace that is safe. They need to guard against theft and sabotage. They need to insure productivity. Whatever the justification, it all comes down to money. At least those employees stripped of their privacy can take solace in the fact that they work for a more fiscally sound company than they might otherwise.

"The daily abuse of civil liberties in the workplace is a national disgrace," said Lewis Maltby, director of the American Civil Liberties Union's Workplace Rights Project. "Despite a dramatic increase in workplace surveillance, most Americans aren't even aware that they are being monitored, let alone that there are virtually no laws in place to protect them." Though the Fourth Amendment to the Constitution protects people against unreasonable search and seizure, it only protects public employees in the workplace. The founding fathers knew how oppressive kings and queens were, but never imagined what kind of royal assholes employers could be. In the absence of such protections and with most employers having the power to terminate workers without cause, employees often find they must submit to the unreasonable intrusions of their employers or lose their jobs.

That's what workers at an Anheuser-Busch brewery in Van Nuys, California, found out in August 1995 when they discovered that security guards had locked entrances and exits to the parking lot and locked the turnstiles that connected the parking lot to the plant

Bowl Games

Two secretaries for G.T. Machine & Tool Co. of Long Island City, New York, charged in a lawsuit that their boss secretly videotaped them going to the toilet, *Newsday* reported.

The camera is believed to have been hidden in a ventilation grate "precisely at crotch level and aimed dead-on at the toilet seat," the report said.

"Harry would tell us [to] feel free to use his bathroom," one of the plaintiffs said of her boss. "It was like he was being nice to us. It was like he was being concerned."

You'd think they'd have been a little suspicious about the 500-watt bulb shining up from the floor.

7/28/97

Big Blue Line: The Watson Memo

When IBM discharged model employee Virginia Rulon-Miller for having an affair with a former IBM employee who went to work for a competitor, she complained IBM was sticking its nose in places it didn't belong. Rulon-Miller prevailed in her court case, in part because of this 1968 memo from then IBM CEO Thomas Watson, Jr. The jury found IBM failed to follow its own policies and awarded $300,000 to Rulon-Miller.

To: All IBM Managers:

The line that separates an individual's on-the-job business life from his other life as a private citizen is at times well-defined and at other times indistinct. But the line does exist, and you and I, as managers in IBM, must be able to recognize that line.

I have seen instances where managers took disciplinary measures against employees for actions or conduct that are not rightfully the company's concern. These managers usually justified their decisions by citing their personal code of ethics and morals or by quoting some fragment of company policy that seemed to support their position. Both arguments proved unjust on close examination. What we need, in every case, is balanced judgment that weighs the needs of the business and the rights of the individual.

Our primary objective as IBM managers is to further the business of this company by leading our people properly and measuring quantity and quality of work and effectiveness on the job against clearly set standards of responsibility and compensation. This is performance—and performance is, in the final analysis, the one thing that the company can insist on from everyone. We have a concern with an employee's off-the-job behavior only when it reduces his ability to perform regular job assignments, interferes with the job performance of other employees or if his outside behavior affects the reputation of the company in a major way. When on-the-job performance is acceptable, I can think of few situations in which outside activities could result in disciplinary action or dismissal.

When such situations do come to your attention, you should seek the advice and counsel of the next appropriate level of management and the personnel department in determining what action—if any—is called for. Action should be taken only when a legitimate interest of the company is injured or jeopardized. Furthermore the damage must be clear beyond reasonable doubt and not based on hasty decisions about what one person might think is good for the company.

IBM's first basic belief is respect for the individual, and the essence of this belief is a strict regard for his right to personal privacy. This idea should never be compromised easily or quickly.

Thomas Watson, Jr.
4/4/68

for a drug search. The gates, which were locked at 4:30 P.M., remained locked until after 7 P.M. The exercise was repeated for the graveyard shift at 11 P.M. Security guards told employees who tried to leave the plant that they were not allowed to go. According to a lawsuit filed over the matter, one employee called the police and was told that it was unlawful for the company to hold the workers. When that employee complained that what the company was doing was illegal, he was told that the search was authorized by corporate headquarters and that CEO August Busch "indicated" that it had better be conducted by the end of the following week or "fucking heads would roll."

Those conducting the random search told employees they could either agree to cooperate and allow their cars and themselves to be searched for drugs, or face suspension. Anheuser-Busch told the *Los Angeles Times* the search was conducted because of safety concerns. "These are people driving forklifts and operating high-speed machinery," a brewery spokesman told the newspaper. It's nice to know the makers of Budweiser wouldn't want people to ingest substances that could impair them. Despite the altruistic motivation of the company, twenty-one ungrateful employees filed suit, charging, among other things, that the company invaded their privacy, made false arrests and wrongfully terminated workers. They also said that contrary to the company's pronouncements about safety, it had targeted employees who'd complained of unsafe working conditions at the plant. Before drug-sniffing pooches began their attempt to identify any cars that smelled suspicious, five workers had been made to report to a room and empty their pockets, take off their shoes and socks and let their wallets be searched, the suit said. All of them came up clean.

The company suspended workers who refused to consent to the search and later fired them. The drug-sniffing dogs searched three hundred cars and turned up marijuana in three vehicles, as well as dog biscuits in some others—an indication that one thing employees can do is band together and keep a box of Milk-Bones in each of their cars to foil such attempts by employers. Before the search, the plant had put up notices that "persons and vehicles on the property are subject to search." Though the case is still pending, such notices go a long way in stripping away whatever claim to privacy employees might have. In the absence of clearly delineated lines where employers can and can't go, courts have generally taken the position that a right of privacy within the workplace can only be exerted where there is an expectation of privacy. For instance, placing secret video monitors in the lobby of an office probably wouldn't be seen as an invasion of privacy because of the public nature of lobbies, but installing them in a bathroom probably would. "The single most important point for employers regarding privacy in the electronic workplace is the need to be open and clear about the company's intentions, thereby reducing employees' expectations of privacy in the workplace," the 1996 *National Employer*, a legal workplace

Is Your Life an Open File?

While the information employers collect about their employees is often disturbing, what they do with the information they have can be just as troubling.

Oftentimes, in the absence of formal policies on disclosure, it is up to a person in charge of an employee file—whether it is an executive or a record clerk—to release information, according to David Linowes, a professor of political economy and public policy at the University of Illinois at Urbana-Champaign, who conducted a survey of Fortune 500 companies and their disclosures of employee information. A total of eighty-four companies with 3.2 million employees participated.

Linowes found that 38 percent of the companies do not tell their employees about the types of information stored on them and 44 percent do not tell them how personnel records are used.

The survey found 70 percent of the companies surveyed disclose personal information to nongovernment credit grantors, 47 percent gave information to landlords and 19 percent gave information to charitable organizations.

"If this kind of liberal cooperation with credit grantors is to prevail, the subject individual at least should be informed," said Linowes. "More than one-half are not."

guide produced by the law firm Littler, Mendelson, Fastiff, Tichy & Mathiason, tells employers. "Examples abound where employers have successfully defended against privacy claims by following this simple advice."

Though courts have held this view about privacy, employee advocates say it's based on faulty reasoning. "That is an inherent doctrinal flaw in the way courts analyze privacy. To me it's not a valid interpretation of the right of privacy to say you only get enough privacy in the workplace as your employer wants to give you," said Craig Cornish, a plaintiffs' attorney with Cornish & Dell'Olio in Colorado Springs, Colorado, and a leading expert in workplace privacy rights. "What should be the rule in privacy cases is that courts should balance the need of the employer to conduct electronic surveillance in specific situations against the importance of allowing the employee a certain modicum of privacy in certain segments of the workplace."

Part of the reason privacy is such a murky area in the workplace is because there is no single federal law that addresses the privacy rights of employees at work. Some of the best protections of workplace privacy come from seemingly unlikely places, such as the Americans with Disabilities Act. The ADA has gone a long way in stopping employers from making inquiries about a job applicant's health and medical history or requiring a physical examination prior to making a conditional job offer. It also limits the ability of employers to subject an existing employee to a physical examination and restricts how the information from the exam is used. The Fair Credit Reporting Act, designed to protect consumers, extends to employers in their use of credit checks on job applicants and employees and serves as another safeguard of a limited nature. Other laws touching on privacy in the workplace include the Employee Polygraph Protection Act, which restricts the use of lie detector tests except in very limited circumstances, and the Federal Omnibus Control and Safe Streets Act, which has been seen as prohibiting employers from listening in to the personal phone calls of their employees.

Signs Your Employer May Be Monitoring You

Millions of employees are monitored secretly by their employers every day. Just because your boss might not tell you that he is videotaping you, reading your E-mail or listening in on your phone calls doesn't mean he isn't. Below are some tips from Grunty that might help you detect if you are being monitored.

You notice when you walk by the oil painting of the founder that the eyes move with you.

There are no urinals in the bathroom, only Dixie cups.

When you go to get first aid for a cut, instead of using a disposable towel, your boss wipes the cut with a glass slide.

Your employer tells you the parabolic microphone outside his office is there "just for decoration."

You notice a small surgical scar behind your ear, but can't recall ever having had surgery.

For the most part, though, privacy protections vary from state to state, court to court and employer to employer. But even in states that provide a constitutional right to privacy, such as California, employees often find themselves fighting a losing battle. Article 1, Section 1 of the California Constitution was amended by voters in 1972 to list privacy as an inalienable right. But in two California Supreme Court cases that centered on drug testing, the court found that other considerations outweighed privacy concerns.

In 1994, the California Supreme Court took up the case of Jennifer Hill, an athlete at Stanford University who challenged the National Collegiate Athletic Association's drug testing program as a violation of the state's constitutionally protected right to privacy. Though the case is not about an employer and employee, it did look at the question of how private institutions fall under California's constitutional mandate and established tests for future cases in which privacy issues are considered. In his majority opinion upholding the NCAA program, Chief Justice Malcolm Lucas laid out the "correct legal standard to be applied" in assessing claims of invasion of privacy. The three-part test asks whether confidential or sensitive information has been made public or wrongly used, if there has been a reasonable expectation of privacy, and whether or not the invasion of privacy was significant enough to "constitute an egregious breach of the social norms underlying the privacy right." If this is established, the defendant must show that the invasion of privacy was justified by a competing interest that is legally authorized or has some broader social benefit more important than the privacy claim. In the case of the NCAA test, the court felt that athletes had a diminished expectation of privacy and that the NCAA's competing interest in enforcing a ban on steroids and other illegal substances to insure fair competition justified its actions.

Though Lucas in his opinion was careful to warn against anyone reading into the decision a blanket approval of drug testing in the workplace, the test laid out in *Hill* v. *NCAA* established a road map for handling privacy issues in private employment settings in California. It should be disturbing to employees to see how little it takes for a court to see an interest greater than a constitutionally protected right. California's Justice Stanley Mosk, in a strongly worded dissenting opinion, called the justification for the NCAA's testing of athletes an invasion of their privacy and an "affront to their dignity" that was "unacceptable." He wrote, "Today, the majority take away from Stanford student athletes—and all other Californians—the right of privacy guaranteed by the California Constitution. At the same time, they grant to the NCAA—and any other intruding party—a 'right of publicity' based on nothing more than their own views of 'good' and 'bad' policy."

The California Supreme Court took on drug testing once again, this time involving the workplace, in a 1997 ruling on *Loder* v. *City of Glendale*. In this case, a taxpayer brought suit against Glendale's policy of requiring all applicants to whom they had made a job offer and all existing employees given a promotion to submit to a drug test. Though the court found that the policy of testing existing employees violated their Fourth Amendment rights, it said it saw no state or federal constitutional problems in the city's policy of testing those given a job offer. The decision stunned civil libertarians, particularly in the face of a U.S. Supreme Court decision that recognized the Fourth Amendment rights of public employees and the Court's interpretation that drug testing constitutes a search.

In 1989 the U.S. Supreme Court ruled in two landmark drug testing cases on the same day. In balancing the privacy rights of employees against the government's interest, the court in *National Treasury Employees Union* v. *Von Raab* ruled that employers were justified in performing drug tests on employees in safety-sensitive positions. In *Skinner* v. *Railway Labor Executives,* the Court ruled that Fourth Amendment privacy protections could extend into the private workplace if the industry in question was subject to heavy government regulation. Nevertheless, the Court found in Skinner that the public safety issue trumped the employee's right to privacy.

Like it or not, the piss test has taken its place along with the telephone, computer and filing cabinet as standard operating equipment in today's workplace. The share of major U.S. firms that tests for drugs rose to 81 percent in January 1996 from 78 percent in January 1995, according to a survey by the American Management Association. It was the highest level since the group began its surveys in 1987 and was nearly four times the 21.5 percent rate of that year. The rise in drug testing is attributed to new government mandates for testing in certain industries, the effect of court decisions, requirements imposed by corporate customers and incentives from insurance companies to reduce potential liabilities. As employers test a greater number of employees and no longer test only when they are suspicious of drug use, but routinely as a part of preemployment screening and in random programs, the rate of employees testing positive fell to 1.9 percent in 1995 from 8.1 percent in 1989.

In the private sector, where the Fourth Amendment does not extend its reach, lawsuits brought under state constitutions and statutes have produced mixed results, an American Civil Liberties Union report on drug testing said. "For the most part," the report said, "unless

Ask Grunty: You're'n Trouble

Dear Grunty,

My company has a random drug testing policy. I have a real problem with this because it invades my privacy. What I do at home is my business. Next, they will want to know what color my underwear is. What can I do to stop the invasion of MY privacy?

Pissed

Dear Pissed:

The founding fathers were too busy growing hemp to worry about corporations conducting drug tests on their employees.

The federal Constitution provides no protection against searches by private individuals or companies. It only restricts the government. Some states have privacy protections in their constitutions. But in general, there is little protection against drug tests in the workplace, especially where the work can be considered safety-sensitive in some way, such as flying airplanes or carrying a gun.

There are several things that people say can beat a drug test, but many of them are detectable. Substituting someone else's urine seems to work as long as you can keep it warm and aren't being monitored. They do check the temperature.

Grunty does not have any firsthand knowledge of tricks for beating drug tests, although Abbie Hoffman did write a book on the subject and you might call the folks at *High Times* magazine, which has published several articles on the subject.

Among the things rumored to turn dirty urine clean are soap, bleach and even pouring a vial of Visine in the sample. These may be detected, though, depending on what screening they do to the urine. Drinking tons of water is probably the safest and most natural way to dilute the sample.

You should contact the American Civil Liberties Union office in your area or a local employment lawyer to find out about the laws in your state.

We turned for advice on this issue to one of our legal eagle friends who passed on most of the above to us.

His parting advice was that if there is a situation where there is someone monitoring the giving of the sample and you know you are dirty, piss all over them because you are going down anyway and it's better to get fired for pissing on the monitor than for testing dirty.

Grunty

restricted by a collective bargaining agreement, private employers have almost unlimited authority to implement drug testing programs in their workplaces." Montana, Iowa, Vermont and Rhode Island have laws that prohibit employers from testing employees unless there is a suspicion that a particular employee might be using drugs. While most drug testing is done when there is a reason to suspect an employee may be using illegal drugs or after an accident, the American Management Association found that random and periodic testing is rising sharply. In 1996, the group reported that 33.7 percent of corporations carry out regular and random tests on their employees, up from 10.3 percent in 1990.

Drug testing not only invades the privacy of employees, say critics, but it also fails to truly do what employers say they want to accomplish through it. Instead of insuring a safe workplace, it usually serves as an intrusion into the private lives of employees away from work and seeks to punish them for having a lifestyle of which the employer may disapprove. A drug test will tell an employer that there are traces of illegal drugs in a person's body, but will not tell if someone is impaired while on the job. There are ways to measure impairment using computers to test such things as hand-eye coordination. These tests detect any kind of impairment that could affect a worker in a safety-sensitive job, whether it is drugs, illness or inability to concentrate because of a bad fight with a spouse. The American Management Association found that while 83 percent of human resource managers in organizations that use drug tests feel they are an effective way to deal with workplace drug abuse, there is no statistical evidence to support this. "The data does support, most emphatically, the deterrent effect of drug education and awareness programs, supervisory training and employee assistance programs," said the report. "Testing cannot and should not be expected to take the place of good supervision and management practices."

Through the reefer madness that allows us to piss away our civil liberties into a cup, employers have sought access to information not only about their employees' use of illegal drugs, but of prescription drugs as well. The same urine sample used to test an employee for illegal drugs can provide private information about the employer's use of prescription medications. It's not hard for an employer with that information to draw inferences about an employee's health and to make decisions based on that. As part of a drug

Feeling Pissed

I was given a container in which to urinate. I waited for the attendant to turn her back before pulling down my pants, but she told me she had to watch everything I did. I am a 40-year-old mother of three: nothing I have ever done in my life equals or deserves the humiliation and mortification I felt.

An employee quoted in an ACLU briefer on workplace drug testing.

test, employers routinely order their employees to disclose any medications they are on to insure against a false positive on a test. If employees disclose they are taking drugs associated with specific ailments, such as AZT (which is used by people who are HIV positive or who have AIDS), their employers might see them as potential liabilities who can raise the cost of their health insurance.

In a paper delivered at the 1996 National Employment Lawyers Association's annual conference, the employee rights attorney Cornish discussed the trend of employers' keeping records on their employees' legal use of prescription drugs. "Although never admitted as a goal, employers have an economic interest in minimizing the employment of individuals who either suffer from, or are predicted to suffer from, illnesses which are expensive for an employer to treat or to accommodate," Cornish said.

It might seem like a blatant invasion of privacy to most people to have their employers demand to know what prescription drugs they use, but the courts have not always seen it that way. In one case, the Tenth Circuit rejected a challenge to a policy of ConAgra Poultry Co. that required employees to disclose their prescription drug use while being tested for illegal drugs. The company said it was necessary to assure the accuracy of the test. The court ruled that since

Employees Tell Motorola to Butt Out

Motorola Inc. decided to scrap a policy that would have prohibited employees at its cellular phone plant in Libertyville, Illinois, from smoking in their vehicles on company property.

The company, which planned to fire anyone who violated the policy four times, had defended it as a way to control litter and promote employee health.

The firm bowed to public pressure following press reports about the policy. The *Chicago Tribune* reported that Motorola granted that "security guards might have more important things to do than play smoking police."

Unconfirmed reports said that the change in policy left intact a rule that required employees to brush their teeth after eating in the company cafeteria.

the information was not disclosed to others, it represented an "insignificant" invasion of privacy. As part of the *Loder* v. *City of Glendale* case, the California Supreme Court paid little attention to the issue, but as part of its ruling, it overturned a lower court decision that employers could not require prescription drug use information routinely as part of a drug test.

In other instances courts have shot down employers' attempts to gain information about their workers' prescription drug use as a violation of the Americans with Disabilities Act. The Equal Employment Opportunity Commission has taken a similar view of such policies. An enforcement guideline issued by the EEOC said prescription drug use constitutes a "disability-related inquiry" since the information is likely to provide information about a disability. Cornish notes that if employers' reason for wanting to know the prescription drug use of their employees is to discern legitimate explanations for positive drug test results, as they generally maintain, a far less invasive way of gathering the information would be to request it only if a positive drug test result occurs. "Therapeutic drug searches ignore the wall of separation which should exist between the employer and the employee's body," said Cornish. "In the absence of sound, scientific evidence and a compelling need for such information, prescription search policies, as currently manifested, are insulting to the privacy and dignity of employees."

Even when employees don't tell their employers about their prescription drug use, their blood and urine can. That employers conduct medical tests on their employees without their knowledge, once they have their blood and urine, is a workplace reality. Employees at Lawrence Berkeley Laboratory in Berkeley, California, filed a class-action suit in 1995 and charged that since the 1970s the Department of Energy lab had collected blood and urine samples from employees during mandatory medical examinations and had performed syphilis and pregnancy tests without workers' knowledge. The suit also charged that the lab singled out black employees and performed genetic testing for sickle-cell anemia. "I was horrified when I looked at my medical file and discovered they had tested me for pregnancy, syphilis and sickle-cell disease without ever telling me," said Marya Norman-Bloodsaw, a black accounting clerk at the lab and lead plaintiff in the case. "LBL has no business knowing more about my medical status than my own doctor." The trial court ruled that the invasion was not significant since the employees knew they were undergoing a medical exam even if they did not know they were being subjected to certain tests. The case is now pending before the Ninth Circuit Court of Appeals.

With the rapid expansion of medical knowledge and the falling cost of testing, genetic screening is posing new threats to privacy. As scientists map more of the human genome and identify genetic links for the onset of certain diseases, there is a real risk employers may choose to rid themselves of employees who they think could become costly liabilities, even though the presence of a gene may not mean that an employee will eventually develop the related disease. Six states have passed laws that restrict employers from requiring genetic screening of employees or job applicants. There is a belief among civil libertarians—and it is supported in part by the Equal Employment Opportunity Commission's policy guideline—that the

Broadcast News

Sometimes it's the employee and not the employer who poses the biggest threat to their own privacy. Once E-mail is sent, it can be difficult to control what happens to it. E-mail gets forwarded, printed out and posted and also gets backed up on the computer system so that even when an employee thinks he has deleted a message, a retrievable copy still may exist.

"Once you hit enter, all electronic data is out of your control," said John Jessen, managing director of Electronic Evidence Discovery Inc. in Seattle, which advises companies on the use of E-mail and often recovers deleted files for investigations. "You don't know where it's going. You don't know how it's been stored or backed up. The only thing you can control is what you type in."

Jessen said sometimes it's just a matter of being a little too fast at clicking a button, as he likes to illustrate with the story of what happened at one office with a video E-mail system where he was called in to do some training.

A camera placed on top of each computer terminal allowed employees to send video E-mail messages to each other. A woman who was having an affair with a married coworker decided to send him a spicy message. She performed a striptease and as she shook and shimmied before the camera on top of her computer monitor, she told him of the night of pleasure that awaited him when they met for their illicit rendezvous later at their favorite hotel. The problem was that when she sent the message, she clicked on the wrong distribution list. Instead of sending it to her lover as she had intended, she sent it to 480 people throughout her firm.

"I heard the hotel was sold out that night," Jessen said.

Americans with Disabilities Act would offer employees some protections. In the meantime, the cost of genetic testing is the biggest protection employees have right now. But the costs of these tests are falling dramatically and an estimated 1 percent of major corporations now use them.

While employees generally know when they are being subjected to drug, genetic, honesty or personality tests, new office technology has allowed employers unprecedented ability to monitor their workforces. Employers routinely monitor phone calls, E-mail and even the keystrokes their employees enter into their computers all day. A 1993 survey by *Macworld* magazine of a cross section of 301 companies found that nearly 22 percent engaged in electronic monitoring of their workforce. Of those, less than one-third said they gave their employees advanced warning of the monitoring. Today, the American Civil Liberties Union concludes that as many as 40 million people are monitored electronically on the job.

The law and the courts have given employers enormous leeway to monitor what goes on in their places of business. For instance, even though it is illegal to wiretap phone conversations without the consent of one of the parties, the Electronic Communications Privacy Act of 1986 permits employers to monitor E-mail and voice mail maintained on systems the employers own. They are also permitted to listen in on job-related telephone conversations of their employees. Since business and personal relationships can often intertwine, employers have significant latitude to listen in on conversations that employees might consider private. Unfortunately, since most employees wouldn't think their employers had the audacity to monitor these communications, let alone any kind of right to do so, many get an alarming wake-up call when they learn their employers' ears are bigger than Ross Perot's. One widely reported case in the early 1990s involved Rhonda Hall and Bonita Bourke, two employees with Nissan USA. The two had bad-mouthed their bosses in E-mail exchanges to each other and eventually got hauled into their supervisors' offices and chewed out. They complained to higher-ups that their privacy had been invaded,

Peekaboo

Of the 21 percent of companies in a 1993 *Macworld* survey that said they electronically monitored their employees, the percent that answered yes to monitoring the following was:

Electronic work files 73.8

E-mail 41.5

Network messages 27.7

Voice mail 15.4

but they didn't find a sympathetic ear. Instead, they were fired for misusing the company's E-mail system. They sued, charging invasion of privacy and wrongful discharge, but the company won a summary judgment.

"The only time you have privacy is when you have a reasonable expectation of privacy," said Cliff Palefsky, the plaintiffs' attorney with McGuinn, Hillsman & Palefsky in San Francisco. "I think most people have an understanding that E-mail systems are company property and retrievable. I think it's becoming more difficult to assert a reasonable expectation of privacy." That's certainly been the attitude of the courts, which have basically said that if the computer equipment is owned by a corporation, it has a right to access anything that is residing in it. In fact, some think that corporations that don't take the trouble to find out what kind of E-mail is shooting through their systems are foolish because it can create legal liabilities for them.

Just because employers have the legal right to do certain things doesn't mean it is necessarily a good idea to exercise that right. It builds distrust, kills morale and takes employees who might consider themselves part of a team or a family and lets them know it's an us-against-them relationship by robbing them of basic human dignity. "There's no way to define freedom without including in that definition a zone of privacy," said Palefsky. "It is essential to self-esteem and dignity."

That's clearly the case with a policy in the telephone industry called "adherence," a practice of

Getting to Know You

The reasons given by the 21 percent of companies in a 1993 *Macworld* survey that said they electronically monitor their workforce:

Monitor work flow	29.2
Investigate theft	29.2
Investigate espionage	21.5
Review performance	9.2
Prevent harassment	6.2
Seek missing data	3.1
Seek illegal software	3.1
Prevent personal use	3.1

monitoring the phone calls handled by service representatives and making sure workers "adhere" to a rigorous schedule in which every fifteen minutes of an employee's day is mapped out. The policy is designed to insure that staffing matches call volume at all times. This is made possible through the telephone switching equipment, which not only directs calls to the workers, but delivers reports to the supervisors simultaneously. If workers spend too much time on a call and their schedule is thrown out of adherence, they are given a demerit. At Bell Atlantic, according to a report on adherence from the Communications Workers of America union, the policy on adherence says any violation of the schedule "may result in disciplinary action, up to and including dismissal on the first offense."

"Adherence is a totalitarian control system," said the report. "It deprives employees of basic human rights to privacy, dignity and autonomy. It is especially ironic that our employers are implementing these inhumane policies at the same time that they talk about restructuring work to 'empower' employees to make decisions. It is impossible to empower employees to solve problems when Big Brother tracks every second of one's day and punishes for any deviations."

Debbie Goldman, a research economist with the union, said that adherence has created the electronic sweatshop. "In the employer's view it allows them to be efficient in a way they couldn't before. They think it's the greatest thing since sliced bread," she said. "Several years ago when this technology was happening, employees were getting

Stress for Success

"In my office of 38 reps, 5 are out on stress-related disability. Three more have colitis and another has an ulcer. We have big boxes of Motrin that we share. Not a day goes by that I don't take a Motrin for headaches. I never take them on Saturday or Sunday."

Service representative with 16 years service with Bell Atlantic in Reading, Pennsylvania, quoted in Communications Workers of America report on adherence.

adherence reports, but we were not hearing a lot about it because it was being used for scheduling, not discipline. Now it is used for the speed-up."

Goldman said the constant monitoring leads to a tremendous increase in stress for workers. Some of those workers have sought transfers to new positions to avoid the pressure, and others have just succumbed. Goldman tells of one phone worker in Pennsylvania who had been a good employee for nineteen years and one day just couldn't take any more. She rose from her terminal, got a pitcher of water and poured it over her computer. Though it cost her her job, it was a small price to pay compared with what happened to the workers at the Imperial Food Products chicken-processing plant in Hamlet, North Carolina.

7

Dying to Work

"So long as brakes cost more than trainmen we may expect the present sacrificial method of car coupling to continue."

—REVEREND LYMAN ABBOT
*speaking about the railroad industry's reluctance to use
air brakes and automatic couplers in the 1880s*

EMMET J. ROE was just being a good businessman. To guard against employee theft at Imperial Food Products, a poultry-processing plant he owned in Hamlet, North Carolina, Roe ordered doors padlocked. While that violated safety codes, it protected something far more important than workers—chicken parts with which employees might try to fly the coop. On September 3, 1991, a hydraulic line sprung a leak and spayed fluid onto gas burners beneath a fryer and began a fire. The padlocked doors prevented workers from escaping the inferno. By the time the blaze was over, 25 workers lay dead and 56 others had sustained injuries. The 150 workers employed at the plant who were unscathed got to ponder their good fortune on the unemployment line, where they could thank God they hadn't perished like their colleagues at a job that paid around $5.50 an hour.

The North Carolina Department of Labor's Occupational Health and Safety Division inspected the plant following the fire. It documented eighty-three violations of Occupational Safety and Health Administration standards, including fifty-four of them classified as "willful violations" and twenty-three as "serious," including the absence of a required sprinkler system. The department assessed more than $800,000 in penalties on the company, a record fine within the state at that time. It was the first time during the plant's eleven-year history that it had been inspected. When reporters challenged North Carolina labor commissioner John Brooks about why the state had failed to inspect the plant previously, Brooks told reporters that the OSHA program is not a universal inspection program. "We have no responsibility to periodically inspect plants."

Roe was hit with numerous lawsuits as a result of the fire, and also faced criminal prosecution. Under a plea bargain arrangement, Roe pleaded guilty to involuntary manslaughter and was sentenced to 19 years and 11 months in prison. Though that might seem harsh, particularly because it was one of the first instances of an employer's facing criminal charges for the deaths of workers caused by unsafe working conditions, survivors and family members of those killed were outraged. Had the sentence been one month longer, Roe would have found himself in the state's only maximum-security prison, but he was spared that. The plea deal also spared from prosecution Roe's twenty-nine-year-old son, who served as director of plant operations, as well as the plant manager. All three had originally faced as many as 250 years each in prison for the fire. Roe would become eligible for parole after two and a half years of his sentence.

Though the Imperial fire case has inspired prosecutors in other cases to pursue criminal charges against employers, less than a dozen employers have been jailed for workplace deaths, according to

Grunty Fun Fact

Construction workers accounted for one in six deaths on the job in 1995.

Source: Bureau of Labor Statistics

a 1997 report in the *Wall Street Journal*. For most workers, it is not the threat of criminal prosecution of employers that stands as their best protection against hazards in the workplace, but the Occupational Safety and Health Administration, or OSHA.

Every day Americans cram themselves into subway cars, buses and automobiles, brave congested roadways and bridges and roll off to work. And every day, seventeen of them don't return. They get chewed in tree shredders, flattened by construction cranes, disassembled on assembly lines, unscaffolded from scaffolds, thrown through windshields, seared by power lines, poisoned, punctured, roasted, toasted, burned, beaten, sliced, diced or presented in some other way with the ultimate in early retirement packages. Each year more than six thousand workers in the United States die from injuries sustained on the job. Another estimated fifty thousand die each year from illness caused by workplace chemical exposures. All together, more people die from work each year than the number of Americans killed during the entire Vietnam War.

The Bureau of Labor Statistics has put the cost of workplace deaths at about $120 billion a year. Highway accidents are the leading cause of work-related deaths, accounting for 21 percent of the more than 6,200 fatalities in 1995. A little more than half of the traf-

---

Flat Broke

A demolition worker at a General Motors plant in Canada was killed when the 5,000-pound bulldozer he operated rolled over him, the *Toronto Star* reported.

A 39-year-old employee of the Teperman and Sons wrecking company had gotten out of the machine to inspect its front end when it apparently slipped into gear and ploughed over him.

The employee had been moving scrap metal at the plant.

Though a coroner's inquest was scheduled, we understand the real delay was finding a 27-foot-long coffin.

8/6/88

fic deaths involved people who were either driving a truck or riding in one.

The number of people killed on the job pales next to the number of working wounded. Six million workers suffer nonfatal workplace injuries each year. And while these workplace problems seemed to have been improving since 1970, when the Occupational Safety and Health Administration was established, new workplace dangers having to do with indoor air quality, computers and the growing incidence of violence have turned seemingly benign work environments such as offices into physically hostile places for people to wile away the hours. Without a doubt, work is hazardous to your health.

Making it even more dangerous these days is an ongoing political battle over what role government should play in mitigating the dangers of the workplace. For years, OSHA has been under siege. Republicans have tried through budget cuts and legislation to take the biggest pliers it can find and yank the agency's teeth from its jaw. OSHA would still exist under Republican plans, but only as a consultant to employers. Gone would be its bite and its ability to protect workers through enforcement of the law. Labor Secretary Robert Reich described Republican efforts as nothing less than "a war on American workers."

Labor advocates say OSHA has been underfunded and ill-equipped for its fight against workplace hazards. Its budget of just more than $300 million funds a total staff

The Daily Grind

A 22-year-old worker at a wholesale meat company was killed when he was pulled head-first into a meat-grinding machine, the *Fort Worth Star-Telegram* reported.

A worker at Deen Wholesale Meat Co. in Fort Worth, was drawn into the machine while he was standing on a ladder trying to force meat through it.

Though he was pronounced dead at the scene, an autopsy was scheduled to determine the cause of death.

No doubt they wanted to rule out e. coli as the cause of death.

11/2/93

of 2,300. Its inspection staff of 1,100 is so small that by its own estimates it can visit a regulated business only once every eighty-seven years on average. "OSHA has made tremendous progress, but when you look at the needs, we have barely begun," said Joel Shufro, executive director of the New York Committee for Occupational Safety and Health, a coalition of unions, health professionals and attorneys fighting for stronger OSHA enforcement. "We've come a long way since 1970 when the act [establishing OSHA] was passed; however, we are at a situation where the amount of resources devoted to safety and health is woefully inadequate to do the job. The consequence is that we are constantly behind the curve. Employers can violate the law with relative impunity."

Though it's hard to imagine most employers ever having to run up against an inspector from OSHA, representatives of business groups portray it as a scourge on the economy armed with the stickiest brand of red tape in one hand and an arsenal of fines, paperwork and nonsensical rules in the other. "OSHA is at the center of conflict between business and government. Business wants to protect its autonomy and its ability to say what goes on in the workplace and OSHA stands right in opposition to that," said Vernon Mogensen, research associate at the Michael Harrington Center of Queens College. "Though never fully funded to the level that it could carry out its congressional mandate to assure every American a safe and healthful workplace, it's always been held up as this big, evil, insidious regulation run amok."

The fear and loathing OSHA inspires often translates into tales of small-business owners being harassed with exorbitant fines for nitpicky violations. Other times, it has given rise to a unique brand of urban mythology, with OSHA trying to prevent kids from going to the beach because it says sand is dangerous. (Though the story is not true, OSHA critics made this claim because silica has been identified as a known carcinogen by OSHA and is present in sand.) Critics contend that rather than protecting workers, OSHA just hinders business. In an August 1995 legislative summary for an OSHA reform bill before the House Subcommittee on Workforce Protection of the Economic and Educational Opportunities Committee, staff member Gary Visscher wrote:

> OSHA is well known for issuing and enforcing intrusive rules and regulations, which do little to promote safety and defy common sense. OSHA has had rules, for example, that prohibit roofers from chewing gum while roofing, that require a "hazardous substance" label on bricks, motor oil and dishwashing soap, that prohibit employers from using plastic (as compared to steel) gas cans. While some of these have been reversed since Republicans and employer groups spotlighted them, OSHA continues to work on standards, such as indoor air quality and ergonomics, which potentially impose even greater costs on employers with little proven benefit to safety of employees.

The memo goes on to question whether OSHA has done much to improve worker safety at all, arguing that while death rates for workers have fallen by more than half since OSHA's creation, it is merely continuing a pattern that got under way in 1946. "There is little evidence that OSHA has made a significant difference in the safety and health of American workers," he said.

Among the favorite OSHA horror stories detractors like to tell relates to dentists telling children they can't keep extracted teeth for the Tooth Fairy because they have blood on them and therefore must be disposed of as biohazards under OSHA regulations. Stories such as these led to charges that the demonic, childhood-stealing bureaucracy was trying to off the Tooth Fairy. OSHA officials call these stories exaggerations and lies. "Ah, the OSHA stories. You hear so many of them," said Joseph Dear, then assistant secretary of labor for OSHA, at a conference in September 1996. "OSHA killed the Tooth Fairy; OSHA thinks bricks are poison; OSHA cites teachers for blackboard chalk. The most important story and the one you are least likely to hear is this: OSHA saves lives."

Created in 1970 to assure that working people have safe and healthful working conditions, OSHA has jurisdiction over 6.5 million employers with 100 million employees. The agency boasts that since its creation nearly thirty years ago, the workplace fatality rate has been more than cut in half. In areas where it has taken direct steps to address specific workplace problems, the results have been impressive. It said strengthening of trenching protection in 1990 led to a 35 percent decline in death from trench accidents. OSHA's lead standard reduced blood poisoning in battery plant and smelter workers by two-thirds. The administration's cotton dust standard virtually eliminated brown lung disease in the textile industry. And grain handling standards helped reduced fatalities in grain facilities by 58 percent and injuries by 41 percent.

While changes in standards have helped bring about improvements in safety, OSHA inspections have also proven themselves an important and effective means of cutting down on workplace hazards. In the three years following an OSHA inspection and fine, injuries at affected work sites declined by as much as 22 percent. In the manufacturing, construction and oil and gas extraction industries, where OSHA has concentrated 84 percent of its enforcement activities since 1975, the injury and illness rate has fallen. In contrast, the wholesale, retail, health care and financial services indus-

Just Plain Tired

A construction worker died on Highway 70 in Carbon County, Utah, when a rear tire came loose from a truck, the *Salt Lake Tribune* reported.

The tire rolled across two lanes of traffic, bounced over a divider and crossed two more lanes to career into a 41-year-old worker, who was near an on ramp. The tire hit him in the face and chest and killed him instantly.

The driver was pulled over miles from the incident and was unaware what happened.

It just shows you, you've got to watch out when your employer tells you he's putting you where the rubber meets the road.

8/19/93

tries, where OSHA has been considerably less active, injury and illness rates have risen.

Two words that have been inseparable from OSHA in recent years have been "reform" if you are Republican and "reinvention" if you are part of the Clinton administration. "Reform" is a very Zen concept of reducing workplace injuries. It's kind of like asking, "If a tree falls on a worker in the forest and no one is there to hear it land on him, does it make a noise?" The thrust of reform efforts has been to try and eliminate the enforcement role of OSHA and have the agency act in a consulting capacity to businesses that want its advice. Proposals have focused on reducing penalties, requiring a cost-benefits analysis before enacting new rules, replacing punishment with incentives and, perhaps the most onerous of the ideas, requiring employees to report problems to their employers before reporting them to OSHA—a rule that could have a chilling effect on employees who might otherwise bring hazardous conditions to light.

Leading the charge has been Representative Cass Ballenger, a Republican from none other than North Carolina, home of the Imperial Foods poultry-processing plant. Ballenger, chairman of the Workforce Protection Subcommittee of the Economic and Educational Opportunities Committee, pushed for two OSHA reform bills, but both died with the 104th Congress. Ballenger's foes had referred to one bill as the "Death and Injury Enhancement, or DIE, Act of 1995." Ballenger had no immediate plans to reintroduce the bills in early 1997, but was instead planning hearings on the Clinton administration's efforts to "reinvent" OSHA.

"Reinvention" is a sign that the Clinton administration is able to out-Republican the Republicans, to steal their thunder and engage in Orwellian political-speak just as well as they do. Reinvention means turning OSHA into a kinder and gentler agency. As the Republicans want, it seeks to take away the adversarial relationship between business and OSHA and puts a greater emphasis on partnership. In the world of good cop–bad cop, the old OSHA was the bad cop and the "new" OSHA is the good cop. The administration's nod to labor is a

promise that while OSHA will cozy up a chair to business, give 'em
a cigarette and a soda and talk softly, should a business not cooperate, it will stroll down the hall for a cup of coffee while the other
OSHA roughs 'em up something fierce. "If businesses choose the
high road of trying to insure that job sites are safe and healthy, the
adversarial relationship will end, and the red tape will be history,"
said OSHA's Dear, speaking before the American Hygiene Conference in 1996. "If not, we tighten the screws with enforcement."

The shape the new and improved OSHA has taken for companies with particularly poor safety records is a program called the
Cooperative Compliance Program, which focus on high-hazard
workplaces. The program grows out of a pilot program in Maine
known as the Maine 200, a system developed there to deal with the
basket cases of health and safety that were helping to drive the state's
workers' comp system rapidly down the toilet. Under the program,
employers with high numbers of injuries were given a chance to
work with OSHA to develop safety and health programs. It puts an
emphasis on self-policing in exchange for OSHA's not penalizing
companies for violations they identify themselves and take steps to
correct.

While OSHA's been taking heat from Republicans for some
time, others have been critical of its reinvention, fearing it is doing
to itself what Republicans failed to do to it in Congress. These critics say the Clinton administration has just followed in the footsteps
of the Reagan and Bush administrations in relying on voluntary compliance rather than the threat of enforcement by offering exemptions
for those who self-report. "It creates a temptation to pad and falsify
records," said the Harrington Center's Mogensen. "If left for employers to do, there's a strong temptation to cheat. It's really a situation where the fox will be guarding the henhouse."

Such concerns are not unfounded. Consider the case of Decoster
Egg Farms, which was no little chicken-shit operation. The $40 mil-
lion Turner, Maine, egg farm, the nation's largest producer of brown
eggs, was a member of the Maine 200. But what the Department of

Labor discovered to its chagrin was that despite the positive improvements in safety and health conditions spelled out in reports from Decoster to OSHA, the company was not a good egg. In fact, according to OSHA officials, Decoster went so far as to falsify a photograph to make them think the firm was complying with the program. OSHA eventually stepped in and found stomach-turning conditions that Labor Secretary Robert Reich described as "atrocious." He stated, "The conditions at this migrant farm site are as dangerous and oppressive as any sweatshop we have seen. Fear and intimidation kept these workers in this unsafe, unhealthy atmosphere and living in totally unsanitary conditions."

Workers at Decoster labored ten to fifteen hours a day without protective gear to shield them from disease. According to OSHA, workers used their bare hands to pick up dead chickens and handled manure potentially infected with salmonella bacteria. They were exposed to life-threatening electrical hazards and when injured on the job often went without medical treatment for hours. Decoster housed its workforce in 10-by-60-foot trailers, often with twelve people in each. Overused septic tanks became full, causing toilets to back up several inches into shower tubs. "Flushing toilet paper was not allowed, so feces-covered toilet paper often overflowed from wastebaskets in the bathrooms. Without adequate and operable shower or laundry facilities, workers were often unable to clean themselves or their soiled cloths," an OSHA report said. The agency fined Decoster $3.6 million, but stepped in only after a local newspaper and state legislators created public pressure.

Stephen Gaskill, a spokesman for OSHA, said there's nothing that can be done to prevent someone from falsifying data if one wants to do that. He feels that asking about the ability to defraud OSHA under its new approach reflects the wrong question. "The question is, Are we using the limited resources we have to protect the highest number of workers in the best way possible?" he said. "We are able to target those employers that have high numbers of hazards on their work sties and work with them to fix those hazards."

Climbing the Corporate Ladder

A while ago a friend of mine was working on an office building in the San Francisco Bay Area. There was a real asshole foreman working with one crew pouring concrete for a floor. They had all this lumber they were using.

My friend didn't realize the lumber was for the forms for the floor and took some and started to climb this gang ladder and go to work on one of the upper floors. All of a sudden the foreman started yelling at him.

"You stole my two by fours! I'm going to go up there and kick your ass," the foreman said.

"Are you sure you want to do that?" my friend said.

"I'm going to kick your ass," the foreman said as he climbed the ladder.

The gang ladder was this heavy wood about 32 feet high and it was nailed at the top. My friend started taking the nails out.

"You're sure you want to do this?"

The foreman was still yelling as he climbed. My friend pushed the ladder and the foreman fell about 20 feet and broke both of his legs. The general contractor came running out. Everyone was nervous. He told my friend, "Don't worry about it. We've been trying to get rid of that asshole. Nobody saw anything. The ladder just fell over."

Tom B.

While OSHA can point to places it is having an impact despite its limited resources, it has been slow to focus on new workplace hazards that reflect changes in the culture, the way people work and the technology in the workplace. Much of OSHA's existing rules are aimed at an industrial economy led by a manufacturing sector. But the workplace in today's service sector economy is different. The introduction of desktop computers, the development of office buildings with sealed windows and recirculating air after the oil crisis of the 1970s and the potential for violence represent new hazards that OSHA is still struggling to address. It's not that OSHA is ignoring these problems; it's just that anytime a new class of regulations is introduced the agency becomes deeply bogged down in politics. The fight to establish standards for workers who use desktop computers has been under way since the early 1980s.

So today, tucked snugly in downtown office cubicles, workers may not fear losing a few fingers to an improperly shielded machine, but they do have plenty of other hazards to worry about. They can worry about losing use of their hands to repetitive stress injuries caused by poorly designed computer workstations. They can worry about the threat that some deranged psycho who didn't like the way someone sounded on his voice mail is going to walk in with an AK-47 and redecorate the office in a lead motif. And they can worry about contracting Legionnaires' disease and other types of illness from improperly designed and maintained ventilation systems.

Workers who do find their nose runs, their chest tightens and their head aches when they return to the office after a good weekend outdoors may be suffering from more than a case of the Monday morning blues. It may well be they are allergic to work—or at least the office in which they work. The problem could be what is known as "Sick Building Syndrome," a term used to describe a range of maladies caused by poor indoor air quality. A 1984 report from the World Health Organization suggested that as many as 30 percent of all new and remodeled buildings have significant indoor air quality problems. Separately, OSHA estimates that of the 70 million employees who work indoors in the United States, 21 million are exposed to poor indoor air and millions more to environmental tobacco smoke. All of this carries a hefty price tag. The National Institution for Occupational Safety and Health (NIOSH) estimates that the problem costs in the tens of billions of dollars when related health care, absenteeism, reduced worker productivity, building investigations and building improvements are taken into account. "It's very real and very widespread," said Richard Byrd, director of indoor air quality investigations for Machado Environmental Corp. in Glendale, California. "Most of the effects are not very serious, but there are a lot of sick days caused by this and a lot of people who are not working as well as they could because of this."

Sick Building Syndrome remains a bit of a controversy, with some experts saying no such thing exists. Part of the problem is that

Office Air Pollution

Biological Agents: These include bacteria, viruses, fungi, pollen, dust mites and other insects, animal dander and molds. They can cause sneezing, allergic reaction, rashes, watery eyes, hoarseness, coughing, dizziness, lethargy, breathing problems and digestive problems.

Carbon Monoxide: Garages and loading docks can be a major source. Improper ventilation of leaky ductwork can allow the gas to seep into an office. It can produce fatigue, confusion, headache, dizziness and nausea, impede coordination, worsen heart problems and, in high exposure, cause death.

Formaldehyde: Found in as many as three thousand building products, including fiberboard, plywood, glues, furniture and upholstery. It can cause headaches, sore throats, fatigue, rashes, nausea, dizziness, and eye and respiratory tract irritation. Formaldehyde is a carcinogen.

Secondhand Tobacco Smoke: Contains more than four thousand chemicals, including formaldehyde, carbon monoxide and other cancer-causing agents. It can cause headaches and nausea. Prolonged exposure can cause cancer and heart disease.

Volatile Organic Compounds: These are released at room temperature from certain solids, gases and liquids. They include a variety of chemicals (benzene, carbon tetrachloride and styrene), which can have both short- and long-term health effects. They can cause eye, nose and throat irritation; headaches and nausea. High-level exposure can produce damage to the liver, kidney and central nervous system.

Other Pollutants: Copying machines can emit ozone, which causes coughing, choking, headaches and fatigue and lowers the body's resistance to infection. Ceiling and floor tiles can contain asbestos. When asbestos fibers are inhaled, they can cause scarring of the lung, asbestosis and cancer.

Source: American Lung Association

there is not a single cause that has been identified and the ailments it causes are a collection of cold- and flulike symptoms that could be unrelated to the workplace, such as headaches; eye, nose or throat irritation; dry cough; dry or itchy skin; dizziness and nausea; poor concentration; and fatigue. Nevertheless, the issue of indoor air quality in the workplace is being taken seriously by more and more people who have come to recognize it as a multibillion-dollar workplace issue.

The rule proposed by OSHA in 1994 would apply to more than 4.5 million nonindustrial workplaces, including offices, schools and training centers, commercial establishments, health care facilities, cafeterias and factory break rooms. Among other things, the rule would require affected employers to write up and implement indoor air quality compliance plans, including inspection and maintenance of current building systems to insure they are functioning as designed. OSHA held hearings on its proposed indoor air quality regulations in 1994; three years and seventy-seven hearings later, it was still working through the 115,000 letters from the public the effort has generated.

While there may be no single cause of Sick Building Syndrome, there are several well-known indoor air pollutants. Among the chief ones listed by the American Lung Association are biological agents such as bacteria, mold and fungi; carbon monoxide; formaldehyde, which is present in furniture, adhesives, upholstery and building material; secondhand tobacco smoke; volatile organic compounds such as benzene and styrene that are released into the air by certain solids, liquids and gases and ozone, which is produced by copiers. However, experts say the biggest culprits behind indoor air quality problems are not the pollutants themselves, but poor ventilation and improperly maintained ventilation systems. Architectural trends have exacerbated the problem, thanks to the construction of energy-efficient buildings with windows that don't open and the use of multiple rather than single ventilation systems. The multiple systems are cheaper to install, but much harder to clean and maintain. "It's always been a problem, but it really only hit the fan since the Arab oil embargo of the early 1970s," said David Dyjack, professor of public health at Loma Linda University in Loma Linda, California. "Architects are becoming a little more conscious of indoor air and taking it into account more, but in the last twenty years, architects haven't helped us out that much."

The clearest indication that a building might be suffering from an indoor air quality problem is if workers experience symptoms that disappear when they are away from the workplace. "Sick Building Syndrome" is the term generally used to describe the situation if more than 20 percent of the people in the building complain of symptoms. Calling the problem to the attention of management is one thing; getting them to do something, other then sticking the complaint in the round file, is another. If it is a serious problem that causes a medically diagnosable illness, such as Legionnaires' disease, OSHA will get involved. Otherwise, it is generally up to state regulators to act on employee complaints. The reactions can vary widely, but this can be an effective way to get an otherwise unwilling employer to act. In California, CalOSHA will send a letter to the employer saying it has received a complaint about the company's indoor air quality and giving the employer fifteen days to respond with an explanation of steps taken to correct the problem. If the answer is unsatisfactory, CalOSHA could initiate an investigation, a certain nightmare for an employer.

Even when an employer wants to cure a problem, finding the source of it may not always be easy. Machado's Byrd tells of one case at a computer company headquarters in Southern California. He was called in to investigate a problem that was affecting workers in two areas of a 100,000-square-foot building. The source was eventually found—a single box of papers that had grown moldy after a fire sprinkler was triggered during an earthquake. Though the building had been carefully cleaned and wet papers thrown out, one employee had packed away the contaminated box among some four hundred other boxes. "The problems are always curable," said Byrd. "The question is how far you have to go to get to the bottom of them."

Unlike air quality problems, ergonomic ones don't generally require much effort to remedy. Nevertheless, repetitive stress injuries represent the fastest-growing type of ailment in the workplace, accounting for three of every five new injuries. In 1993 there were 2.73 million workers' compensation claims involving repetitive stress injuries for a total of $20 billion—a third of all money paid out in claims that year. The surge in the problem has been attributed to the rapid growth of computer-based jobs involving intensive data entry, as well as a speedup of the poultry-processing workforce and the automation of that industry.

The problem, in many instances, is that the worker has been forced to fit the workplace rather than the workplace being designed to fit the worker. In the case of computer data entry workers, the National Institute of Occupational Safety and Health has made recommendations for protecting workers. These include adjusting office lighting to reduce glare; providing chairs with adjustable height, backrest and tension, using adjustable tables and offering a minimum of a fifteen-minute break every two hours (every one hour after intensive work). As simple as such proposals might seem, OSHA and NIOSH have been fought every step of the way by business groups, which have lobbied to prevent important research into the risks workers face from such equipment. The researcher Mogensen, in his book *Office Politics: Computers and the Fight for Safety and Health,*

Carpal Tunneling His Way to Poverty

My story is an example of how things can change so fast. What started as minor hand cramps a few years ago, has ended up with me being in too much pain to work.

I am a healthy 32-year-old male. I have worked in the electrical field for 18 years. I started complaining of hand cramps about four years ago.

After two carpal tunnel surgeries, I can't even write. The Ontario Workers' Compensation Board has screwed with this for two years, saying that this is not work-related, despite the opinion of several doctors.

So from $50,000 a year, I'm now less than ninety days away from a welfare claim.

Rick S.

shows how business interests successfully reframed the debate over ergonomic standards in Congress from one of health and safety to merely one about worker comfort.

While repetitive stress injuries have turned seemingly benign work environments into hazardous places where workers run the risk of suffering crippling and career-ending injuries, violence has turned these workplaces into potentially lethal arenas. Where once employees might have expected to have work slowly suck the life from their being over a forty-year career in an office, today there is the possibility that a customer, coworker or former coworker will burst into the office with firearms blazing.

In July 1993, mortgage banker Gian-Luigi Ferri walked into 101 California Street. The granite and glass skyscraper, set back on a plaza, is prominent in San Francisco's financial district. Ferri got in the elevator wheeling a black canvass bag on a cart and rode to the thirty-fourth floor. He entered the offices of the law firm Pettit & Martin and removed two 9mm semiautomatic pistols and a .45-caliber semiautomatic handgun and opened fire with some of the more than four hundred rounds of ammunition he was carrying. He continued to work his way down the building until he was confronted by police on a stairwell between the thirtieth and twenty-ninth floors and took his own life. By then, he had killed eight people and wounded six. It was not known why Ferri selected Pettit & Martin. He hadn't had any dealings with the firm since 1981. Though police found a list of names on his body, none of the people killed were on that list.

That such things happen is a reality of today's workplace. Homicide represents the second most prevalent cause of death on the job, behind highway accidents. In 1995 violent acts accounted for 16 percent of all workplace deaths. Contrary to popular belief that working at a post office with a deranged coworker represents the greatest risk of workplace homicide, robbery is the most common motive, with two-fifths of the workplace homicide victims working in retail establishments, such as convenience stores, bars and restaurants. While women accounted for just 9 percent of all workplace fatalities, they represented 46 percent of workplace homicide victims.

But homicide is an extreme example of workplace violence. Thousands of workers encounter milder shades of violence every day. Between 1987 and 1992, there were approximately one million assaults a year on people at work, including more than 600,000 simple assaults, more than 250,000 aggravated assaults, nearly 80,000 robberies and more than 13,000 rapes. Recognizing that the workplace had changed since OSHA's founding, in 1996 the agency introduced its first national guidelines for preventing assaults on workers. OSHA tailored those first guidelines to cover 8 million workers in the health care and social service fields, which suffer nearly two-thirds of all nonfatal assaults in private industry. The guidelines have four basic components: work site analysis, hazard prevention and control, training and education and management commitment and employee involvement. OSHA is working to develop similar guidelines for other selected industries.

While these new hazards are starting to be addressed, others caused by the changes in the way people work are only just getting some attention as a problem. Notably, the rise of contract and temporary labor as a significant component of the workforce is creating concern over safety risks caused by the lack of familiarity with equipment and work practices that characterizes many of these workers. An article in the winter 1997 edition of *California Management Review* examined two studies of contingent workers in high-risk environments. The authors, Denise Rousseau and Carolyn Libuser, note that safety risks have been associated with workers' having less than one year of experience on the job and being strangers to the site and to each other. This problem, they said, is exacerbated by the increasing use of temporary and contract labor, as a result of which marginally skilled laborers are regularly brought to work sites. "When the use of contingent workers increases due to downsizing, the resulting work setting can be particularly hazardous," they wrote. "There is little evidence at this time that organizations have significantly altered their management practices to more effectively coordinate, integrate and manage contingent labor." And that's something it appears everyone is going to have to get used to, because more and more people are losing their employee IDs and getting a contract instead. And, like San Francisco cabdriver John Coleman, we're getting pretty badly screwed in the process.

8

Temporary Insanity

"People need to look at themselves as self-employed, as vendors who come to this company to sell their skills. In AT&T, we have to promote the concept of the whole workforce being contingent though most of our contingent workers are inside our walls. 'Jobs' are being replaced by 'projects' and our 'fields of work,' giving rise to a society that is increasingly 'jobless but not workless.'"

—JAMES MEADOWS
Vice president for human resources for AT&T
Quoted in the New York Times, *Feb. 13, 1996*

IT WAS 1:40 A.M., March 20, 1989, when John Coleman took his last call of the night. San Francisco prohibits cabdrivers from honking their horns after 10 P.M., so when he pulled up to the address at Farragut and Mission Streets to pick up his fare, he got out of the car to ring the doorbell. He never made it. Two men were waiting for him, and they delivered a single blow to his head with a large wooden board. The thieves stole his wallet, which contained $43. It's one thing to get bored on the job, but quite another to get board. Coleman crashed to the ground and lay unconscious. He remained in that state for a month before complications caused permanent brain damage to set in. The thirty-nine-year-old cabdriver, who was also a musician and actor, spent nearly a year in a coma at the hospital before being sent home, where his wife cared for him. He remained an invalid, unable to speak and needing to be fed through a tube the rest of his life. He died in 1993 at the age of forty-three.

That cab driving is a dangerous job is not news. The on-the-job death rate of cabbies actually exceeded the on-the-job death rate of police officers. The insult, though, that was delivered along with Coleman's injury was the fact that cabdrivers in San Francisco were not considered employees, but independent contractors. As such, Coleman and his wife, Carol Gahagan, lacked the safety net many people don't think about until it is too late. "No one is going to be able to take away the danger of driving a cab, but there is a line of responsibility," said Gahagan. "There is social responsibility, the responsibility of family and there is the responsibility of the employer, and that last one was failed to be met."

How do independent contractors get screwed? Let me count the ways. Since they are not "employed" (they are contracted), they cannot collect unemployment insurance or workers' compensation. Instead of their employers picking up half the tab for Social Security taxes, as is done for employees, contractors bear the sole responsibility. Vacation time and sick leave are merely something that other people get. Laws such as the Family and Medical Leave Act and the Americans with Disabilities Act don't protect contractors, and contractors can't bring actions under Title VII for em-

Stuck Down in the Valley

I have worked in Silicon Valley for 14 years. I have seen the decline in worker living standards despite the fact business is booming. If you are an assembler or technician, most of the jobs are temp jobs with no benefits.

The companies tell you that if things work out they will hire you as a regular employee. Typically that takes six months to a year if you are lucky. The ball is in the employer's court. If a boss does not like you, it is easy to fire you if you're a temp. I see a lot of temps working despite being ill and spreading their germs because they are so afraid of being canned.

Lynn W.

ployment discrimination. The labor laws that are supposed to protect people haven't quite caught up to the changing way more and more people are working—whether they like it or not. "The traditional institutions and mechanisms for protecting workers' rights in this country are inadequate for dealing with these new employment relations," said a 1996 report by Working Partnership USA, a group developed out of the South Bay AFL-CIO Labor Council in San Jose, California. The report, which looked at the rise of contingent labor in Silicon Valley, went on: "Without secure employment, or permanent full-time employers, most contingent workers are not adequately covered in a labor system that is based on the premise of full-time employment with a single employer, and depends on collective bargaining as the basis for worker protection."

Whether someone is an employee or an independent contractor has become an increasing concern for employers and employees as

Communications Breakdown

I was hired as an interpreter by the court system almost two years ago in response to a newspaper ad. I was just out of college and needed a job. I was thrilled when it was offered.

It was not until a couple of weeks into the job that I found out I had been shafted. The position I thought I was applying for was not the one I got. I thought I was applying for a full-time position with benefits. The position I got, and still am currently stuck in, is officially titled "temporary part-time."

Strangely enough, I still work more than 40 hours a week and have retirement taken from my check. However, I don't get benefits and get paid one-third less than the lowest full-time person. I am required to perform the exact same job as every other full-time employee, and I do mean exact.

I have gone to both of my supervisors several times asking if a position was going to be made available. One of them out and out lied to me. She said that a request had been made, and was in the approval process. Four months later she told me that there was never even tentative approval given to consider a new position.

Andy

an era of corporate downsizing has created a swelling of the ranks of legitimate independent contractors while also enticing employers to wrongfully reclassify their existing employees as such. Independent contractors, some 8.3 million Americans, according to a 1995 Bureau of Labor Statistics study, represent just one component of a larger group of workers included in the sweeping term "contingent workers." This term has been used to include independent contractors, temporary employees, part-time workers, seasonal workers, on-call workers, leased employees and the self-employed.

The Bureau of Labor Statistics only recently began tracking this segment. The problem, though, is that no one has quite agreed on what exactly is meant by the term "contingent worker," who exactly is included in this category and how to count them. On the low side, estimates from the Bureau of Labor Statistics have placed contingent workers at as little as 5 percent of the entire workforce. At the other end, Richard Belous, director of research at the National Planning Association, a private nonprofit public interest research group, argued that by 1988 as much as one-third of the total workforce was contingent and that the number was growing. That estimate, though, has been criticized for overstating the true numbers because it double-counted some workers.

While there is disagreement as to how widespread the phenomenon is, there is little dispute that it is among the most dramatic changes in today's world of work. These workers embody the dissolution of the bonds that traditionally existed between employer and employee. They are Bic workers, easily disposed of like a lighter, razor or ballpoint pen after they have served their use. These workers look like a duck, walk like a duck, swim like a duck, quack like a duck and work like a duck; they just don't get the job security, benefits or legal protections of a duck.

Once merely a way to fill gaps created by sick or vacationing employees, contingent workers now serve critical functions at all levels of a corporation and are built into the staffing strategies companies pursue. Why buy the cow when you can hire it on an hourly

Grunty Fun Fact

The average number of daily employees working through temporary service companies hit 2.2 million in 1995, up from 708,000 ten years before. During the same time the payroll of the temporary help industry reached $27.9 billion, up from $6.3 billion in 1985.

basis with no strings attached? The Conference Board, a New York–based business association, found that 35 percent of members surveyed in 1995 expected that contingent workers would account for at least 10 percent of their workforce by the year 2000. That compared with just 12 percent who answered the same way five years before that. The number one reason cited by these companies for why they use contingent workers is the flexibility it gives them. "Much has been said about the changing nature of the social contract between business organizations and workers—so much so that to talk about 'employer-employee relationships' today is not an accurate label of the current situation," wrote Bruce Steinberg, director of research of the National Association of Temporary and Staffing Services in the organization's winter 1995 issue of *ContemporaryTimes*. "The concept of cradle-to-grave employment, which was used to describe the arrangement in which an employee would move through the ranks of their entire professional career at one company, is certainly considered archaic today."

Contingent arrangements can be positive for both employers and workers. For employers, the arrangement provides the freedom to shrink and expand their staffs rapidly in changing business environments. They can help control expenses and also allow employers to bring in specialists for projects that demand them when in-house expertise is not enough. For employees, contingent work can be a good way into the workforce, a way to build experience for a first full-time job or to reenter the job market after an extended absence. It is a way to gain experience, to try out a corporation by whom they might be offered a full-time job or to see if a type of work suits them. It also allows far greater freedom to employees who want more control over their work and work schedules. "The bottom line is that contingent workers are here to stay," said Stanley Nollen, a professor of business at Georgetown University and coauthor of the book *Managing Contingent Workers.* "They are good for companies. They help solve real business problems. They let businesses achieve flexibility and make them more cost-effective."

Too often, though, these contingent workers are little more than surrogate employees, working side by side with their full-time counterparts, doing the same tasks, but having the status of second-class

Temporary Setback

I just got home from work to find that my paycheck hadn't arrived as promised. This is serious. I only have $5.79 in my checking account.

I started this job two weeks ago through a temp agency as a customer service representative/tech support for the Department of Education. I'm on a 90-day trial basis. Today I was supposed to receive my first paycheck.

An employer has an obligation to pay its employees on time. Treat them like shit, work them to death, even underpay them, so long as you do it on time. When I talked to my agent/handler, whatever you want to call the person, she said, "I'm very sorry, but there isn't anything I can do."

I asked her how she'd like it if she didn't get paid when she was supposed to. She replied, "Well gee, I guess I wouldn't like it too much." No shit, Sherlock! I was amazed at the self-control I showed in not cursing her out.

All this is made worse by the fact that I sent out $200 worth of checks on Wednesday morning, thinking when I got home from work that afternoon there would be a nice check in my mailbox.

In conclusion, I say to anyone from this temporary service or anyone else who doesn't feel that they have to pay their employees on time: You diarrhea-gargling, hemorrhoid-chewing, douche-swilling worthless piece of shit . . . (editor's note: The author went on to wish ill-health on the descendants and descendants of the descendants of the temporary service agency in a rather graphic manner.)

Ken J.

citizens. Nollen said that when contingent workers are used in the same way as full-time employees, problems arise. The regular employees want perks, privileges and benefits to offset themselves from the lowly contract workers. It could be higher wages or benefits, or sometimes something small and seemingly insignificant, such as a parking space, access to a company store or a company picnic. When contingent workers have been doing the same work as full-time employees but sense differences in the way they are treated, they start to ask why it is happening and why they should be denied benefits and perks others get routinely. "It's easy to make them both unhappy," said Nollen. "It's volatile, explosive and fraught with peril."

In some instances, companies that have downsized people out of a job have turned around and brought them back as contract workers, often having them work for the same supervisor in the same location and even performing the same tasks. This reduces liabilities and cuts expenses for employers, but doesn't do much for the worker. The Bureau of Labor Statistics has not compiled data to determine how widespread the practice of bringing downsized workers back in this way is, but in 1995 it did find that 17 percent of contingent workers overall and 22.3 percent of independent contractors were working in nontraditional arrangements for previous employers. The study did not include people who described themselves as "self-employed."

Georgetown's Nollen said that taking back downsized workers as contractors rather than reinstating them as employees is a "bad idea" if they are being asked to do the same job. "It's simply a bad way to treat people," he said. "Maybe you made a mistake. You downsized too far. But to correct it, you really ought to take back the people as employees rather than contractors. It says to the community, 'I can't manage my people very well. I'm making mistakes.' "

Though it seems oxymoronic (or just plain moronic), these days it's not unusual to see companies simultaneously laying off and hiring workers. In fact, a 1996 American Management Association survey found that 30 percent of companies concurrently eliminated and created jobs. That survey noted that these companies rehired or

No Longer Going Down with the Ship

I'm a temp. Yes, I'm one of those disposable heroes that companies on a precarious perch like to have around to make a fast profit increase when hacked.

I worked for a medical supplies company that made CPR (cardiopulmonary resuscitation) manikins and defibrillators, based on ten-year-old technology (a good sign to bail out, eh? A la IBM). A usual office grunt was, "I need two million copies of this in collated binders." I also had to design an in-house library for them—a huge undertaking.

After six months, I decided I really needed to get away. So, with everyone's blessing, I took a week off, and went sailing down the Hudson on a 106-foot traditional sloop. Having had a great ol' time, I came back to work the following Monday, and got called into the dreaded office—the one I'm sure many of you out there know all too well.

I got axed because of the usual reorganizing and not fitting nonsense. The only good side is that I left on good terms with reference letters and a phone reference from the human resources director. I just wish they'd told me before I went, so I could've stayed on the damn boat!

Doug

brought back workers who had been downsized, though it did not make a distinction in workers who returned as employees and those who returned as contractors.

Among the companies that had been doing this was Pacific Bell, the San Francisco–based Baby Bell that merged with SBC Communications in 1997. Though the company shed some 1,640 managers from 1991 through 1995, it brought on 1,700 workers through new hires and contract workers, according to Mark Thierman, an attorney representing former Pacific Bell managers in a class-action lawsuit over the company's elimination of a written job guarantee. Among other things, the suit alleges that Pacific Bell illegally terminated the managers and defrauded them out of their jobs, pensions and health benefits. The former employees suffered blows in round one: The judge threw out much of the suit and granted a summary judgment to the company for 1,600 of the employees who signed releases to get their severance pay. The judge said, however, that the company could not just tear up its job guarantee without a significant business justi-fication. That left Pacific Bell potentially liable in the case of any manager who did not sign a release—about 40 people, according to Thierman. Both sides are appealing parts of the ruling. "We're ex-tremely pleased with this decision," said Mary Lu Christie, senior counsel for the company, speaking at the time of the decision. "We believe that few companies have tried as hard as we have over the years to offer fair severance programs and other benefits designed to reduce the size of our workforce."

What's intriguing about the way Pacific Bell went about its job cuts is that it often brought back the same workers to do essentially the same jobs, Thierman said. In fact, he said, about a thousand of them have returned as contract workers and about 23 percent are doing what they were doing before they were laid off. In so doing, former employees said, Pacific Bell went from representing the best of the old to the worst of the new.

When Dick, a onetime plant engineer, joined the company in 1973, he said he thought he had died and gone to heaven. "It was a great job—a dream job," said Dick, who did not want to use his full name. "Everybody hung with each other after work and at lunchtime. You would drive down the street and wave to the other guys. It was just a blast. Your bosses would join you. It was absolutely the great-est job." By the time he left, he said, it had become "the most miser-able place in the world."

Back when he joined the company, Dick said, there was an under-standing that a Pacific Bell job was a job for life. By 1986, in order to retain employees following the breakup of AT&T, Pacific Bell took that promise of lifetime employment and set it in writing. Though unionized workers had already gotten such a clause in their contract, managers now gained an employment security agreement. The agreement stayed in place until the company felt pressure to reduce its head count and an-nounced that on April 1, 1992, it would cancel the employment security agreement. At the time, Dick said, he didn't think much about it because

TEMPer, TEMPer

Temp agencies are undermining the very foundations of the lower echelon workplace. In today's job market, entry level employment is all but nonexistent.

Temp agencies, like rats and other scavengers, fill a purpose in the corporate food chain. In catering to the profit motive of the companies, both large and small, they provide warm bodies at premium rates and expect punctuality, hard work and intelligence.

The losers are the companies themselves and those searching for entry level positions. The latter are forced to make do with less pay, no benefits and no real security or voice in the workplace environment.

Those with half a brain cell in their heads will realize that they are being screwed from both ends and will respond in kind. They will provide precisely the amount of work required to get by while scrambling furiously for a way out and into a better position. (Lots of God-damn luck!)

The corporations, like spoiled, greedy children, want intelligent, hardworking people to fill the shit details that collect in the bilge, but do not want to pay the price. This creates a "cattle car" mentality that builds losers wherever it takes hold. The company loses, over the long run, due to apathy and a rot at the "unimportant" foundations. A saying from a Tom Clancy novel has taken particular root in my office: "As long as the bastards pretend to pay us, we will pretend to work!"

The office manager may improve his or her bottom line a little over the short term but they are really only cutting their own throats. The temps lose due to the facilitation of an already cruel and demeaning entry level job market, no real training, no real pay, no chance for advancement and a savaged self esteem.

I swear to God, if Communism hadn't already self-destructed I'd scream "up with the worker, down with the capitalist, corporate pigs!" It's enough to make you sick!

Narifa1

he had always received excellent reviews, but no one was safe. In October 1995, as he was approaching his twenty-third anniversary with the company, his supervisor came up to him and broke the bad news—he was going to be terminated.

He was so stunned he said that he momentarily lost his eyesight and his mind went blank. "I went blind. I immediately thought of my kids, house, mortgage and kids' college. It all flashed before me," he said. "I said, 'You've got to be kidding me.'" She wasn't. Had he stayed another seven years, he would have walked away with a pension in excess of $300,000 and lifetime medical benefits. Instead, he received a lump sum payment of less than $100,000 and found himself without medical benefits. For signing a waiver to any claims, he got a pretax severance of around $30,000, which amounted to about $14,000 after taxes. "I was fucked, and never kissed," he said.

Then began what he described as the longest three months of his life. He had no money in the bank because he and his family had always lived at the level of what they made. He took his retirement savings and kids' college fund and paid off his mortgage, but he soon used up what severance he had. He sat around and cried during the day and suffered anxiety attacks at night. "I was just a basket case." His search for a new job wasn't turning up any leads, but then he got a call from a firm that was looking for engineers who would work on a contract basis. The caller told Dick he heard that he had recently retired and that he was good at what he did and people thought highly of him. He wondered if Dick would like to work on a contract basis.

He was open to the idea and asked where he would be working. The city where the assignment was turned out to be the same city in which he had worked for Pacific Bell. The man from the contracting firm told him what the job was and explained that the position was recently vacated and the company was looking for someone to fill it. Dick then asked the name of the person for whom he'd be working. When the caller gave him the name of his former boss, Dick interrupted him. "That was my job," he said. "You are trying to replace me with me."

Dick never went back. Instead, he took an electronics sales job, earning a third of what he made for Pacific Bell and getting only a fraction of the benefits. Many other downsized workers who got similar calls, though, have returned on a contract basis or seen their jobs filled by other people. That has led these former employees to charge that Pacific Bell wasn't downsizing, but was just getting rid of em-

Permanent Temporary

If you'd asked me three years ago if I thought that today I'd be working part-time as a temp slave for Smelly Temporary Services, obtaining reduced premium health insurance, receiving food stamps, energy or food bank assistance, and living in low income subsidized housing, I would've said, "No way!"

"Who, me? White college graduate on the Dean's List, hard worker all his life, son of successful, middle-class, Jewish parents? No way a change in our economy could affect me," I would have replied.

Yet after faxing 234 resumes in the last three months for positions as an administrative assistant, interviewing for seven of them and receiving no offers (I have better odds on getting laid on my personal ad dates.), I reluctantly accepted a temporary part-time administrative assistant position. It paid $9.80 an hour for 15–20 hours a week, so I could pay my rent and pay off student loans. The client-employer pays $16.10 an hour for my skills.

That's the problem. The money I make ($700–800) is barely enough to live on. Thus, I now qualify to pay $10 a month for health insurance. The remainder of my bill is paid by the state. I also get food stamps, energy assistance, telephone credit and subsidized housing.

Neither "employer" pays for any of these benefits. They're paid by the rest of us, the taxpayers in the amount of $5,800+ a year—the price of a year of private education, rent on an average one bedroom apartment or car payments.

If I were paid more—say $12–13 an hour—I wouldn't be eligible for any "corporate welfare" secondary benefits. And the temp body shop could still earn a profit.

So, if you're an employer using one of the temp slave companies or reducing your worker's hours to save costs ("Whose?" I might ask), you might want to ask yourself in a rare moral moment why taxpayers ought to pay for your "money-saving" efforts.

When temp slave companies and their clients won't pay a living wage or provide enough hours, the rest of us have to make up the economic difference.

Middle-class employee on welfare

ployees who were becoming or who could become too expensive and was making Wall Street happy by cutting its head count on paper.

In a 1996 article in the *New York Times* that examined the growing phenomenon of former employees returning to their previous employers as contractors, Michael Rodriguez, Pacific Bell's vice president for human resources, explained it by saying, "There were jobs that we hoped would go away when those in them did, but some of the work did not go away as quickly as we would have liked." The attorney Thierman said that the workers booted out tended to be ones who would likely cost the company big dollars, either because of medical conditions, because they were in the final years before retirement and their pensions were growing rapidly or because they had angered people above them by complaining of internal wrongdoings. Once they were out, though, Pacific Bell was very willing to bring many of them back as contractors.

Cathy Maltese was one of the former employees who returned as a contractor. Maltese originally went to work for Pacific Bell in 1979 at the age of twenty-seven in its San Jose, California, office. She rose through the ranks to become a sales support manager. Maltese put in for a transfer to Pacific Bell's Napa office, located in the heart of the wine country of Northern California. She beat out five others for the position and put her house in San Jose up for sale. About a year and a half later, she cut the price on her house by $15,000 and finally sold it. Then, two weeks later, her boss called her and told her she was sorry, but Maltese was being terminated. Like the other employees who fell victim to Pacific Bell cuts, she had sixty days to find a new position with the company, she could sign a voluntary separation agreement and get an enhanced severance package or she could be fired. Unable to find a job in-house, she took a $27,000 buyout, which amounted to $14,500 after taxes. Had she stayed with the company until retirement she would have had a pension worth about $350,000 and lifetime medical benefits. Instead, she had to cash out her pension plan and roll it over into an IRA. It was valued at $37,000.

"I was pretty devastated at that point. Not only did I not have a job, I didn't have a home and I had a teenage son to take care of," she said. "I kind of went off the deep end. I really wasn't capable of working. I was on disability." Within nine months the money she had was gone. Then she accepted an offer that she had turned down a few months earlier and returned to Pacific Bell as a contract worker. "It was the same job I had before," she said. "It was the same group and the same office in Napa. I actually was getting a little more money, but I was paying my own medical and dental, and I had no pension. It didn't compare."

Though she returned to work with the same people, things were very different as a contractor. When the group she worked in was rewarded with a trip to Disneyland for doing a good job, she was excluded. Though she had shared in the responsibility for the group's success, contractors didn't get the perks of employees. When the company provided training to employees, Maltese said, she was excluded because she was a contractor and Pacific Bell considers its

---

When Green and Pink Are Christmas Colors

I had spent nearly six months with a company, having missed the temporary layoff ax several times. It was fast approaching the end of the year and company profit reports were rolling in.

A message was sent out through the office Intranet notifying everyone of a company meeting the week of December 8th, where profit reports for the year would be announced. These company meetings happen on a regular basis so no one was at all prepared for what was about to happen.

Product line A made massive amounts of profit, just as it had for the last several years. A similar line B was making some very promising leaps and bounds. All other product lines, the ones on which the company swore their eternal loyalty to, were not performing as expected and would be dropped.

This in and of itself makes rather wise business sense. However, upon handing out the year-end bonuses to everyone, it was announced that all personnel associated with these product lines were being laid off. This amounted to about 30 or so people out of about 300. What was not so delicately put was that all temporary contract employees, whether associated or not with these lines, were also being "revoked."

Ho, Ho, Ho, Merry Christmas, now get the hell out!

Tim

training "proprietary information." She recalled, "I felt isolated and angry. I wasn't an employee." According to Maltese, "I don't have any loyalty toward them. I do a good job because they are paying me to do a good job. If I was offered a job making decent pay somewhere else and had a reasonable commute, I'd take it."

Pacific Bell's choosing to bring in contractors should not come as a surprise, given what upper management was telling supervisors to do. Though department heads had budgets to work with to bring in contractors, they were told to get their head counts down even though the work was increasing. And former employees returning as contractors not only didn't affect the head count, but didn't require training. "What do you do?" said Norm Garcia, a former Pacific Bell human resources administrator who is part of the group suing the company. "You need the work done. You can't hire employees, but you can have contractors. What better person was there to hire but a former employee who knew how to do the job?"

Pacific Bell is certainly not alone. Large and small companies alike have made use of contract employees to cut costs, but they are being challenged along the way by workers who know they are being shafted. Contract workers at Microsoft sued the company, which they said wrongly deprived them of benefits. In 1996, Judge Stephen Reinhardt of the Ninth Circuit Court of Appeals told the software giant that the misclassified workers, as many as one thousand people ranging from proofreaders to software testers, must be allowed to participate in the company's 401(k) plan and to purchase company stock at a discount, the same way other employees at the company are allowed. "Large corporations have increasingly adopted the practice of hiring temporary employees or independent contractors as a means of avoiding payment of employee benefits, and thereby increasing their profits," wrote Reinhardt in the majority opinion. "This practice has understandably led to a number of problems, legal and otherwise." Though the company argued it had done nothing wrong, the court pointed to an Internal Revenue Service ruling on

Grunty's 10-Part Test

The Internal Revenue Service uses a 20-point common-law test to determine whether someone is an independent contractor or an employee, but Grunty uses a 10-point, commonsense test.

1. Employers don't cheat you out of overtime because you are entitled to none.
2. You don't call in sick when you feel like having a day off.
3. You don't call in when you are sick, but go to work.
4. You don't get sick because you can't afford health insurance.
5. You work 7.5 percent harder to make up for the portion of the Social Security tax your employer used to pay.
6. When people talk about "paid vacation" you think they mean charging it with a travel agent before you go.
7. When you walk by the unemployment line you think, "Wow, those guys are lucky."
8. You don't worry about substantiating a workers' compensation claim because you are not covered.
9. Raiding the supply cabinet is no fun because they are your supplies.
10. You've got a contract, stupid!

Microsoft from 1990 that found the workers in question were employees under its common-law tests.

Ironically, the IRS and not the courts is most likely to be a misclassified worker's best friend—not that the IRS is particularly concerned about advocating the rights of employees. It's simply a matter of math. "The top reason why we care is that the single, least compliant portion of American society is the sole proprietor-independent contractor, especially in a cash business," said Larry Wright, spokesman for the Internal Revenue Service's Northern California region. "If the person is an employee, it makes them subject to income tax withholding. Where there is withholding, there is compliance with the tax laws."

If the IRS finds that a company wrongfully classified its workers, the firm can be held liable not only for back taxes, but penalties and interests. Though the IRS can go back longer, it usually focuses on the past three years in examining a company. It uses a 20-point common-law test to determine whether a worker is an employee or an independent contractor. The importance or applicability of any of the points will vary from situation to situation. At the heart of these determinants are two basic issues. The first is, Who has control over the worker? Independent contractors generally have control over the hours they work and how the job gets done. Once companies dictate these types of issues, they start to cross the line. The other key determinant is whether the worker works for more than one company or has more than one customer. Independent contractors are usually free to offer their services to whomever they want.

Other factors that are looked at are whether the worker can quit or be fired (something a contractor can't do); whether the person is paid by the hour, week or month (like an employee) or by the job (like a contractor); and whether the person can suffer a profit or loss—something a contractor can do, but an employee can't. Most often what alerts the IRS to a case is a complaint from a disgruntled employee. This usually is prompted by his going to his accountant for the first time and discovering he is taking an extra 7.5 percent hit because of the self-employment tax, the portion of Social Security payment normally picked up by the employer. Sometimes, though, it takes longer.

One case the IRS is investigating centers on a San Francisco beauty parlor that more than ten years ago changed the status of all the beauticians it employed to make them independent contractors. One woman approaching retirement came to understand what it meant only when she went down to the Social Security office to find out about her benefits. To her shock, she learned that for the past ten years, no money had been paid into her Social Security account. Though she had gotten a Form 1099 from the beauty shop each year—the form used for independent contractors—she hadn't understood what it was and had treated it like a W2. All along, she'd filed her taxes without paying the self-employment tax.

Workers who think they may be getting a raw deal can tell their employers they think they are misclassified, but if that does no good, there is always form SS-8. The IRS form is a request for determination, which workers can file to get a ruling on their status. When the form is filed, it might trigger visits not only from the IRS, but also from the Social Security Administration and the Department of Labor. "It depends on how much pain you want to create for the employer," said Wright of the IRS. "That's kind of the opposite end of the spectrum from talking to your employer about it."

While such steps to enforce rights in the workplace may help workers in isolated instances, they will do little to stop the transformation of work that is under way. Ultimately, though, the joke may be on employers. By pushing workers into a new world of contract work they are making workers less dependent on them. As workers find new independence it could force employers to compete more aggressively in the marketplace for the skills they require. What is missing today are laws, tax codes, retirement plans and health insurance to allow workers to exist in this new world of work without being penalized for it.

There are several groups that are working to address this problem. The answer, they say, is not to try to end the trend (which they don't see as possible), but to deal with the new realities. In 1997, Working Today, a nonprofit organization based in New York City that

> **Attitude Adjustment**
>
> This doesn't immediately solve any problems, but it's a necessary step:
> Even while we can't change an employer's attitudes, we can change our own. One attitude is "I'm just part-time/seasonal/temporary/etc., so I don't deserve much and I'll be happy with low pay and benefits." Employers hire temps or part-timers precisely because they know such employees accept being underpaid. We have to stop accepting that.
>
> Eric F.

acts as an employees' lobby, launched its "Campaign for Good Jobs in the New Economy." The effort is an outreach to build a network of organizations representing the new mobile workforce of consultants, freelancers and the self-employed—"anyone," explained the group, "smart enough to know a job doesn't last a lifetime." The group is trying to bring together a constituency of independent workers so they can have a voice in the public policy debate.

Sarah Horowitz, executive director of Working Today, said the rise of "independent workers"—a term she thinks more accurately characterizes what is often meant by the term "contingent workers"—is by no means an American phenomenon. She points to Germany, which has one of the strongest trade union movements and one of the strongest social welfare systems and yet is experiencing the same changes in its workforce. "The nature of work itself is changing. That companies can take advantage of that is undoubtedly true," Horowitz said. "But to say things have not changed, let's go back to

Why Not Organize

Some of us don't do temp work because we are pampered housewives trying to get a little more money to afford luxury items. A good deal of us temp because it's the only way we can get work, and pay, when we need it. At least with a temp agency, they don't string you along for a couple of weeks or months after you interview.

When they say you can start working tomorrow, you work tomorrow. I'll take that, although I'd like to get paid more. Temps are, as one article put it, the forgotten workers of modern America. Why not organize? I have sometimes thought that a guide to frequent employers and agencies, plus helpful tips and other resources, would be an excellent idea.

But even better is something a guy I was working with at one temp job suggested. Why not get together with some of your friends and start your own temping cooperative? Most temp agencies are charging the client twice what you're making in an hour. If you and your fellow worker-owners went out on all the jobs and did all the administrative functions, as well as sharing all the profits, you could both charge less than the agency and make more money yourselves! Seize the means of production!

Dan C.

the old social order, is a mistake. There's a mobile workforce, and we need a new type of safety net that allows people to move from job to job."

The group is focusing on the need to create portable health and pension benefits so that as workers jump from employer to employer they carry their benefits with them. The group also wants to change the tax code so these independent workers no longer take a double hit on Social Security taxes and get the same types of tax breaks that employers get for pensions. Working Today also wants to see unemployment benefits expanded so they cover more than just the 32 percent of people eligible today. "You can come up with a new type of safety net that protects this new kind of workforce," Horowitz said.

The mobility of contingent workers poses particular challenges for unions, which have had enough problems maintaining their membership let alone trying to bring into their fold new types of workers who don't seem to stay in any one place long enough to build an allegiance to a union. Amy Dean, executive director of the South Bay AFL-CIO Labor Council in San Jose, California, has been looking at new ways of organizing so that unions can better address the new ways people work today. For unions, said Dean, that means making a bit of a return to the past in order to move forward. "In many respects we are returning back to the future to a kind of occupational version of the guild society where the goal in this kind of new, fluid labor market is to create some level of permanence in the new environment," she said, adding that unions will in many ways overlap today's temporary agencies. "Temporary agencies essentially control the supply of labor. The next generation of labor organizations will function very similarly. They will supply labor, but instead of being a for-profit organization that takes 45 percent off the top, they are going to be an organization that reinvests back in skill training and other kinds of professional and occupational needs and social needs that people have. Employee-owned and employee-run: That's what a labor union is."

The first experiment in this direction that Dean is working on involves a collaboration between Working Partnership USA, West Valley Community College District and SEIU Local 715 to create a representation structure within that union for temporary workers. The goal is to create a working model of a union that establishes multi-employer relationships, can dispatch workers out of a hiring hall or through a registry and provides a secure benefits structure for its members.

The experiment reflects a greater effort on the part of unions to do something they haven't been able to do for decades. They are trying to lift themselves off their badly kicked asses and get relevant again. But, as Daymon Hartley found out, employers have some thoughts of their own on what the future of unions should be.

9

Union Hall

"The rights and interests of the labor man will be protected and cared for—not by the labor agitators—but by the Christian men to whom God in his infinite wisdom has given control of the property interests of this county."

—GEORGE BAER
Mine owner who refused to negotiate with the
United Mine Workers of America during a 1901 strike

DAYMON **H**ARTLEY **HAD** found himself in war zones before. As a five-time Pulitzer Prize–nominated photographer for the *Detroit Free Press,* his work took him to such places as Nicaragua, El Salvador and Israel's West Bank at times when bullets screamed, clubs swung and rocks flew through the air. None of it, though, quite prepared him for the black-shirted storm troopers who marched in and occupied his office on that July day in 1995. That's because he never expected it to happen in Detroit.

On July 13, 1995, six unions representing twenty-five hundred workers at Gannett's *Detroit News* and Knight-Ridder's *Detroit Free Press* walked out on strike over what they said were the companies' unfair labor practices. The newspapers dismissed the claims as nothing more than "union rhetoric" and said that the strike was really over economic issues: Before the strike, the newspapers had tossed out the existing pay scale that provided cost-of-living increases and imposed a merit system for determining raises. The companies had also pushed to replace union jobs with nonunion ones.

In June 1997, nearly two years after the strike began, federal administrative law judge Thomas Wilks, in a National Labor Relations Board decision, ruled that management of the newspapers had indeed failed to negotiate in good faith, unlawfully implemented terms of employment, unlawfully threatened to permanently replace employees and committed other illegal acts that caused and prolonged the strike. Because the newspapers had failed to reinstate workers after the unions offered to unconditionally return to work in February 1997, they could be held liable for millions of dollars in back pay and benefits owed to more than two thousand striking employees. The newspapers appealed the decision, which could leave the dispute tied up in the courts for another few years. "Our attorneys advise us that we have a very strong legal case, and we expect our position to be upheld," Detroit newspaper officials said after the ruling. "It is, of course, our opinion that this was not an unfair labor practices strike. As we have said over and over again, we bargained in good faith at all times."

Union officials say the Detroit newspaper strike was a clear example of the great American pastime of union busting. They say it is a reflection of the orchestrated efforts that employers make to strip employees of their rights, protections and strength by either breaking apart their unions or rendering those unions completely impotent. They point to what they see as the newspapers' bad-faith bargaining that forced the strike, to the newspapers' preparations, made months before the strike began, and to the great expense they were willing to endure to achieve their goal. At the time of the NLRB decision, union representatives estimated the strike had cost the two newspapers $300 million in actual expenses and lost revenue.

The first visible sign of the newspapers' preparation for the strike was provided when the *Detroit Free Press* closed off employee access to the second floor of its building to set up barracks for the

Power Outage

It seems pretty clear and obvious that the power remains entirely in the hands of employers, supported by government, enforced by the known economic needs of the entire workforce and enhanced by the maintained fragmentation of employees.

Sure, the unions have gotten too cozy with management. That was the way they were ultimately co-opted, when management realized that the heavy-handedness of union busting simply raised the ante, and the backs of the workforce. Every kind of manipulative and propaganda tool was used against the power of the union, and people eventually forgot (as they always do) the reasons for what they had built. Another generation came along, without the awareness, and let itself get fragmented.

The unions fell out of favor, and maybe deservedly for the mistakes they made. Reagan's heavy-handed bust of the air traffic controller's union was the final deathblow . . . and not enough people really cared, in the grand love affair with Old Teflon that the country was going through, in those years.

So, face it, employees are simply powerless until they rebuild their unions. However, it has to be done. It is the only force (other than reinventing the same wheel) capable of a massive representation for workers rights. But it must, of course, be guided by an involved and aware workforce—the lack of which is what led to the 50-year decline and demise of the last great union movement.

Irv T.

security forces it was bringing in for the strike that eventually came about. Workers say the security guards started appearing in the hallways and elevators wearing street clothes around May, a few months before the strike. The regular employees had little contact with them until the start of the strike. When workers said they were walking out, the security guards appeared throughout the building in black shirts, gray pants and jackboots and marched them out of the building. Some of the workers were so terrified by these menacing figures that had stormed into the newsroom that they broke down in tears. "You're dealing with a lot of journalists who covered stuff like this all over the world, but never dealt with it on a personal basis," said the photographer Hartley. "It was a rude awakening. People couldn't believe this company could do that to them."

As early as January union representatives say the newspapers had contacted the Sterling Heights Police Department and arranged to fund special riot training and the purchase of riot gear so the police department could be used to insure that a printing plant in that suburb north of Detroit avoided any disruption from striking workers. In all, the newspapers forked out $2.1 million to the Sterling Heights police through the strike, according to Solidarity, a publication of the UAW.

In addition to paying the Sterling Heights and other police departments for special security, the newspapers contracted with firms that provide replacement workers (or "scabs," in union parlance) and security (or "goon squads"). Among the security firms retained by the newspapers was Asset Protection Team, Inc., a subsidiary of Oakton, Virginia–based Vance International, a collection of security guards in riot gear with a notorious reputation within the labor community. Pressman Vito Sciuto was left with a lasting impression of Vance when his head managed to sample the company's unique brand of employee relations. Sciuto had been demonstrating peacefully when a V-shaped battalion marched into a crowd of demonstrators, including women and children, outside a distribution center, according to testimony before the Michigan House Labor and Occupational Safety Committee in hearings on the need for legislation regulating the use of private security companies. Sciuto required brain surgery after the incident and still suffers from seizures as a result of it. A representative of Vance denied that the company had played any role in the injury to Sciuto and said that despite the striking union's characterization of the company, it sees its role as one of peacekeeper.

The *Detroit Journal,* a daily newspaper published by striking newspaper workers, reported it had obtained a video of Vance guards being trained. The videotapes, made by the company during the Caterpillar strike, had come to the *Journal* from the UAW, the pub-

Hardball Requires a Big Bat

I've been a member of a union for 21 years now, the latter half being targeted by this ongoing harassment campaign by the same couple of supervisors. I consider this a personal attack. Along with myself, there are several other employees who are in the line of fire as well. I believe this a prime example of management abusing their authority. Not only are the threats, actions and verbal abuse immoral, they are illegal.

They're not hesitant or shy to inform you that you'll be sorry if you happen to exercise your seniority in the wrong place or clique, even though you are totally qualified to do so. This kind of arrogance resulted in me being pulled out of service within one or two days after making my "bump." The company continues to back up the manager's false accusations and support only one side of the story.

Being bound by the bylaws of the union, I have only one avenue of representation, an elected union official that was a machine operator. I'm confident in his ability to represent all of us fairly, but when dealing in good faith with people who insist on playing hardball, despite the issues, I believe we should take it one step further as well. In a court of law, one is usually presumed innocent until proven guilty, but I will let the facts speak for themselves. My experience has proven to be quite to the contrary.

Upper management and the laborers, I think, have the same professional, safety orientated train of thought. But, when middle management is involved, a fudge factor appears. An "I'm the fuckin' boss" kind of attitude. There's no way an honest, hardworking, away-from-home employee or union representative can deal with these matters and people in a faithful manner.

We need experienced litigators, or civil lawyers to not only resolve this "blackball" problem, but to expunge it as well.

I've wanted to voice my opinion for some time now, refraining only in hopes of change. Unfortunately this has been to no avail.

Name withheld

lication said. The *Journal* reported that the guards would spend hours training to learn "how to club people with riot batons without being detected by video cameras." The instructor on the tape apparently demonstrates how to use short, snapping motions to deliver hard blows. He explains to the guards he is training that the company will have video cameras everywhere there are guards. Because of that, he reportedly tells them, it is critical to use the technique in case the tapes make it into court, the judge won't ask, "Why'd you have to beat him so hard?" The instructor explains, "That doesn't look good for us and it doesn't look good for you." The Vance representative said that he had not seen the tapes, but that the company does not use such tapes in its training. While Vance does instruct its employees in basic self-defense training and the use of baton, he continued, it by no means teaches them how to hit people in a way that it would be undetectable.

The newspaper strike became bigger than a mere labor dispute because it happened in Detroit, a city with a long and rich labor history. This was the Motor City, birthplace of the industrial labor movement. It was one of the most heavily unionized towns in the country and chances are anyone who wasn't a union member probably was immediately related to someone who was. Mike Zielinski, a field representative for the International Brotherhood of Teamsters, one of the striking unions, said, "For the companies to draw a line here in Detroit says something significant about their ideologies. For them, it wasn't just about wanting to bust the unions to save money. I think it's sending a signal on behalf of corporate America and the rest of the newspaper industry that they want a union-free environment, and they decided to take the unions on in what's been their stronghold and wage an all-out war."

Despite the strong ruling in favor of the unions by the NLRB administrative law judge, the dispute is far from over. The newspapers' appeal of the decision could leave the issue unresolved in the courts for several years, and that doesn't even take into account the question of a new contract. In addition, some two hundred striking workers received notices during the dispute that they were being fired for "strike misconduct." The photographer Hartley said he was fired five times during the strike. To get their jobs back, the fired workers will have to go through separate NLRB hearings. "The basic approach here is violate and litigate," said the Teamsters' Zielinski. "Go out and violate federal labor laws and litigate it for years."

That is a favorite strategy for busting unions. Employers use the labor laws as a way to diffuse union drives, wear down support and drain organizers of money. "The labor laws are stacked against working people and the machinery is best manipulated by the bosses," said the Teamsters' Zielinsky. "There have to be some changes. There's not a just system in place when working people have to wait years and years for a court to decide their fate. Companies and their corporate lawyers can just tie this up in circles. In the meantime you're out in the street without your job. Nobody can afford to be out of their job for five years while a court vindicates them."

Of course, the labor laws were meant to protect workers, but things change. In 1935, Congress passed the National Labor Relations Act, also known as the Wagner Act, which gave workers the right to organize and bargain collectively.

Grunty Fun Fact

Even though it's illegal, about 10,000 people a year are fired in retaliation for their efforts to organize a union.

Source: AFL-CIO

Among other things, it set the ground rules for labor negotiations, protected workers from being fired for organizing or participating in union activities and created the National Labor Relations Board to see that the act was enforced. Employers weren't originally part of the process in which employees decide whether or not they want to join a union. Because of the economic control employers exert over their workers' lives, lawmakers feared that their role in that process would be inherently coercive.

Many people look to Ronald Reagan's decision to call in replacement workers during the air traffic controllers' strike in 1981 and his subsequent decision to disband the union as the beginning of the end of the labor movement. Reagan certainly made union busting fashionable, fueling a trend among employers to replace striking workers and gutting what had been perhaps the most powerful threat unions had against an employer. But unions' troubles date back to 1947, when Congress passed an amendment to the National Labor Relations Act known as the Taft-Hartley Act. Until then, unions had been rising in strength. By 1945, union membership as a percentage of the civilian labor force had reached 26.6 percent, up from just 5.9 percent in 1934, the last year before the passage of the National Labor Relations Act. After a few years of decline, union membership reached its peak in 1953 at 26.9 percent, but fell fairly steadily through 1996, when it hit 14.5 percent, its lowest level in nearly fifty years.

Taft-Hartley turned the tide on the growing labor movement. It pared back the types of employees eligible for unions, enabled employers to charge unions with unfair labor practices, expanded rights for employers to campaign against union organizing drives, banned "closed shops" that made union membership a precondition of employment and gave the president the right to order strikers back to work for a cooling-off period if the situation was deemed a national emergency. It encouraged and gave rise to so-called "right to work" legislation at the state level, which further undermined unions. Nelson Lichtenstein, professor of history at the University of Virginia, wrote in the American Social History Project's "Who Built America?" that Taft-Hartley "signaled a major shift" in the tenor of class relations in the United States. "To survive," he wrote, "the unions would have to function less as a social movement and more as interest groups protecting their own turf."

Elaine Bernard, executive director of the Harvard Trade Union Program, an executive program for union leaders at Harvard University, said thanks to its amendment, the National Labor Relations Act has "become a barrier to union organizing." She said, "Labor and capital is Bambi versus Godzilla in our law. We look around and wonder why employers play like Godzilla. It's because our laws empower them to." In addition to requiring an absolute majority rather than a simple majority, something that would have kept Bill Clinton out of the White

House, the amendment opened the door for employers to actively campaign on the "no" side of a union election. "Isn't this decision something workers should be making on their own?" asks Bernard. She said Taft-Hartley continued to evolve by "some of the most atrocious court decisions," leaving the labor laws such that the right to strike means a worker can't be fired, but can be replaced. "You can't explain that to an intelligent person," she added.

Waiting for the Payoff

I was a union member in an aerospace plant for 17 years. During this time the company worked a seven-day, 24-hour-a-day schedule.

When layoffs started in the late '70s, the union kept telling us with each contract that layoffs would be eliminated. As we foolishly voted for each contract, the layoffs became bigger and more frequent.

When the plant finally closed in 1992, the last 150 workers got generous pensions. The other 1,000 of us got "promises" of pensions when we reached retirement age. I don't expect to see any pension from the company or the union.

Fuck the company and the union!

G.

By giving employers a right to a voice in organizing campaigns in their workplaces, it allowed them to do the most effective form of union busting—killing a union before it starts. In his book *Confessions of a Union Buster,* management consultant Martin Jay Levitt, who had been among the fiercest hired guns brought in to fight organizing campaigns, came clean on the dirty business. At the time the book was published in 1993, Levitt said there were more than seven thousand attorneys and consultants who made their living busting unions, making up a billion-dollar-a-year industry. Levitt, who planned and ran more than 250 union-busting campaigns across the country before renouncing the profession, described in detail the manipulation, dirty tricks, abuse of the law and disregard for lives of people involved in the fight that are all part of a corporate campaign against a union drive.

"Some corporate executives I encountered liked to think of their

Catering to Employees

The National Labor Relations Board ruled that Caterpillar, Inc., violated federal law when it gave popcorn, pizza, ice cream and other perks to replacement workers and workers who crossed the picket line during a seventeen-and-a-half-month strike started in 1994.

The board said that the perks, which included not only snacks, but steaks, catered meals and T-shirts, represented a significant benefit and by not giving it to the strikers the company discriminated. It ordered the company to pay a cash equivalent to the strikers, according to a report in the *Peoria Journal Star.*

Caterpillar called the ruling "incredible" and "ridiculous" and said it served as further evidence of the board's bias. They planned to appeal the decision. The United Auto Workers said the perks were used to lure people across the picket line and that it was "further evidence of the patterns of lawbreaking by Caterpillar."

The company is said to have been willing to settle the case by paying the former strikers peanuts.

12/25/96

anti-union consultants as generals. But really the consultants are terrorists. Like political terrorists, the consultants' attacks are intensely personal," he wrote. "Terrorists do not make factories and air strips their victims; they choose instead crippled old men and school children. Likewise, as the consultants go about the business of destroying unions, they invade people's lives, demolish their friendships, crush their will and shatter their families." Levitt's standard operating procedures included not only investigating police records, personnel files, medical records and the family lives of union proponents to find a way to discredit them, but, in the absence of any good ammunition, simply concocting something to do the job. "To fell the sturdiest union supporters in the 1970s, I frequently launched rumors that the target worker was gay or was cheating on his wife," he wrote. "It was a very effective technique, particularly in blue-collar towns."

One way Levitt and other union-busting firms found clients was by holding "union avoidance" seminars for companies. These gatherings seem as much about advising corporations on what to do during an organizing drive as scaring the living bejesus out of them so they will cough up the hefty fees necessary to retain a firm's consulting services. Matt Bates, associate editor of the *IAM Journal,* a publication of the machinists union, de-

Organizer Needs a Union

I recently pursued a position as union organizer. I was fired up and wanted to organize. I felt that the only way to save the country was to organize and educate working people.

I couldn't afford the salary. Health benefits were only available after three months! What are we fighting for?

Teresa C.

cided to see for himself what goes on behind the doors at these seminars. Bates put on a suit and signed up for a seminar offered by Executive Enterprises of New York and led by the law firm Jackson, Lewis, Schnitzler & Krupman, a national outfit that is regarded in the labor community as one of the leading firms retained by businesses that want to bust a union.

Though the ads for the two-day seminar expressly warned that people affiliated with unions were not eligible for registration, Bates went undercover to get the skinny on what is really said at these meetings. For two days at the Hilton Hotel in Atlanta, Bates played the paranoid businessman, blending in with the fifty or so executives and human resource directors in attendance. His cost of admission was $1,000, about the cost of a one-day fee for a mid-priced union-busting consultant. He said the scare tactics began before the seminar with the ads, which had headlines that read, "New AFL-CIO Leadership Committed to Massive Organizing Drive!"; "Mega-Unions Forming to Increase Membership! Is Your Company Vulnerable?"

"It used to be back in the 1930s you'd have your windows shot out or getting your legs broken by goons. By and large, that's not the way they play now," said Bates. "They crippled the law enough that

Heal Thyself

I couldn't agree more that much improved upon labor movement is "an" answer. It's just not "the" answer. When unions bow to management, what good are they? They become middlepersons keeping a closer eye on their coffers and positions than improving/protecting the lot of workers. Unfortunately, as with many other things in life, unions are not what they used to be.

I can't see workers continuing to put their futures and fate in the hands of second (employers) and third (unions) parties, when it is the workers themselves who have the value. The point is for employees to strive for a more powerful position by extricating themselves from the effects of poor management and the whims of self-serving unions and/or employers.

Rx

they don't need to do the wet work anymore. They can get their blow-dried, tanned attorneys to do the deed. They've become more sophisticated, but underlying it all is still the brute force that says, 'I can put you and your family out on the street and see you never work in this town.'"

During the conference, Bates said, the audience was told to shift employees' focus away from the company and its profits and turn it to the dangers of getting involved with a union. They were told to let their employees know the terrible things—dues, assessments and strikes—that can happen if they sign a card authorizing a union election. And they were told how to threaten employees without violating the law. It's illegal to tell employees that if they authorize a union the plant will close, but there is nothing illegal about posting new clips about strikes and plant closings to subtly suggest what may be in store for a unionized company. In fact, a 1996 study by Kate Bronfenbrener, director of Labor Education Research at the New York State School of Industrial Labor Relations at Cornell University, found that the majority of employers threaten to close a plant during organizing drives and 12 percent follow through on the threat when the union wins the election. "One of the most effective components of employer threats were the photos, newspaper clippings and video footage of plants that shut down in the aftermath of a union campaign," she wrote. "Thus the impact of plant closings and threats of plant closings during organizing campaigns goes well beyond the individual workers in the unit being organized."

Of course, employers don't always use threats and force. Sometimes they simply try to buy the loyalty of employees during union drives. In Atlanta, two managers of Coca-Cola Enterprises Inc. found themselves indicted in federal court in 1997, charged with attempting to bribe a worker at the company in order to defeat a union-organizing effort. According to accounts in the *Atlanta Journal,* managers Jimmy Wardlaw and Eric Turpin bribed truck driver Jeffrey Wright with $10,000 and a promotion to defeat an organizing drive by the Bakery, Confectionery and Tobacco Workers Union at the company's plant in Decatur, Georgia. Wright had secretly recorded the meeting with the managers. Both pleaded not guilty and their attorney has sought to throw the tapes out as evidence, saying they had been edited. Richard Bensinger, organizing director of the AFL-CIO, said that what is startling about the case is not that an employer would take such steps to defeat an organizing drive—he said he's never seen a campaign where someone wasn't bribed—but that someone is willing to prosecute them as they should be under the law.

Striking Numbers

The number of work stoppages involving a thousand workers or more rose in 1996 after hitting an all-time low in 1995.

There were 37 major work stoppages begun in 1996 that idled 273,000 workers and resulted in 4.9 million days of idleness. That compared with 31 stoppages in 1995 that idled 192,000 workers for a total of 5.8 million days of idleness.

In 1952, there were 470 work stoppages that idled 2.75 million workers, a record since the Bureau of Labor Statistics began to track these numbers in 1947.

Source: Bureau of Labor Statistics

Partner Against the Partners

Law firm employees should organize a union to support the nonowners of the firm.

Associates, paralegals and secretaries are underpaid, overworked and highly stressed out in an industry that is making billions and paying the peons nominal pennies.

TMC

While there are many illegal things that employers do to keep unions from forming in their workplaces and to render them ineffective if they are there, Bensinger said the sad truth is that it's not the illegal stuff that's scandalous. The scandal, he said, is what's legal. "You don't have to break the law today to win," he said. "The law gives employers no equal time requirement, total access, total control, the ability to order workers into meetings and force them to listen every day, whether it's one-on-one meetings or group meetings. They have the right to order union supporters out of the room. If you refuse to leave, you're fired. If you refuse to go to the meeting, you're fired."

To illustrate his point, Bensinger compares the campaign for a union to electoral politics. Were the presidential election run the same way, he said, Clinton would never have defeated Bush in 1992. "Bush would still be in office because he would have filed an objection to the conduct of the election and would have litigated it for years," he said. "Clinton would have had to stand on the Mexican or Canadian border and leaflet people as they drove into the country."

The other thing employers are increasingly doing to stave off unions is to short-circuit demand for them by creating internal grievance procedures and organizing employee involvement programs. Though such programs seem benign on their surface and employers hail them as "employee empowerment," unions criticize these efforts as "sham unions" and "paternalism" that exert a type of mind control on employees by having them view their interests as being aligned with those of their employers rather than of their fellow workers. While these programs appear to give a voice to employees, critics

All We've Got to Save Us from Shifty Employers

Unions are not perfect, never were, never will be. But they are all there is to protect workers.

At the aircraft company where I work, we are battling over the four-day workweek. It can be nice if it is your choice to work that shift. But there are companies trying to implement four, 10-hours-a-day weeks or three, 12-hours-a-day weeks. They call it voluntary, insinuating that if I don't want to work this schedule, I don't have to.

I run a machine at work. If they put that machine on the four day 10-hour workweek schedule, and I refuse the schedule, I will be transferred to another machine. By seniority rank, I will end up working three days a week, 12 hours a day. Fine for some people, I suppose, but not for weekend fathers or people whose significant others work a regular workweek.

Peatree

say the employer stays in control and has done nothing to truly share power with workers over how the company is run. In fact, one of the things companies were told to do at the Jackson, Lewis seminar on union avoidance attended by Bates of the machinists union was to create channels for employees to voice legitimate concerns and create mechanisms for dealing with them, such as ombudsmen, appeals processes, internal mediation and peer review. "You can't have a true partnership between people with unequal power," said Bates. "It is a way of disenfranchising people under the guise of empowering them. It's very insidious."

The use of such mechanisms—in some instances sincere, in others not—came into sharp focus in the case of Electromation Inc., an electronics manufacturer in Elkhart, Indiana. After the company told workers there would be no raises, it established committees consisting of managers and workers to address workplace issues, including wages and working conditions. In 1992, the National Labor Relations Board found that the company violated the National Labor Relations Act in establishing the committees because it had created, structured and dominated the committees in violation of the law. A federal appeals court upheld the ruling two years later, saying that because the employer created the committees and their continued existence depended on the employer, they "lacked the independence of action and free choice" guaranteed by law.

The decision shook up the business community, which has increasingly embraced so-called employee involvement programs. It feared that these programs would be considered illegal in light of the Electromation case. In 1996, hoping to once again strip away protections of the National Labor Relations Act, employers pushed hard for the Teamwork for Employees and Management, or TEAM, Act. The

Union Blues

Unfortunately, due to globalization, it has become necessary for some union offices to downsize their staff. The loss of unionized jobs within the workforce has become difficult for us all, including staff working for unions.

I have had a very difficult experience. The most difficult part has been that I feel I cannot express my negative feelings about being downsized. Within the labor movement, there seems to be no place for disgruntled ex-union staff to appeal for support.

I will continue to be an active union member, but will never again be a staff member for a union. It is my personal opinion, based on my own experience, that all union staff should be elected so members are assured that no staff in the office will remain silent on issues important to the members by virtue of the fact that they may lose their jobs.

I worked as a senior staff person in a union. Working within this middle management position, I not only lost my job, but also had to lay off other staff. This was a very difficult position for me to be in. I knew I would soon lose my job after the layoffs, but I was told not to share these details with the staff. The end result has been laid off staff taking staff jobs with another union, which is raiding our membership.

There are many gritty details to this story about what I feel was the abuse of power and mismanagement. Nonetheless, I will continue to believe in the importance of solidarity within the labor movement. The problem I have is the silence from the labor movement concerning the downsizing within our organization. I would have received more support from my brothers and sisters in the labor movement if I had been working for the private sector rather than the union movement.

Name withheld

legislation won approval in Congress, but President Clinton vetoed it. Despite employer claims that the TEAM Act was needed to keep America globally competitive, he saw it as little more than an effort to undo more than sixty years of protection for workers and to undermine unions. It would seem unions could change their lot by fighting for labor law reform that would restore the National Labor Relations Act to a state where it would once again protect workers' rights and encourage collective bargaining. But the AFL-CIO's Bensinger thinks that's the mistake unions have made for years as their memberships have dwindled. "I've been hearing that for twenty years," he said. "The main answer for unions is to rededicate themselves to organizing. We shouldn't be sitting around complaining about the law." According to Bensinger, the number of National Labor Relations Board elections had fallen to 2,700 in 1996 from nearly 9,000 in 1973. "If we won 100 percent of our elections today, we still wouldn't organize what we did in the 1970s," he said. "It's not the win-loss percentage that's the problem, it's the lack of organizing activity."

Bensinger argues that unions need to hire organizers in unprecedented numbers and involve members in a way that labor hasn't done in decades. Along these lines, the AFL-CIO raised its organizing budget to $30 million in 1997, up from just $2.5 million the year before. There are unions following that lead and doing likewise, shifting 30 to 40 percent of their budgets into organizing efforts. Bensinger said it is not a complicated plan, but a necessary one because the labor laws are so unfair. While such an emphasis on organizing may not seem like a radical plan, it does represent a significant change in the posture of unions.

Bensinger said that during the late 1960s, employers embarked on a philosophical change and developed deunionizing strategies to bring about union-free environments. This effort included such things as moving abroad, heading south to states that were hostile toward unions or simply fighting unions where they existed. Unions' response to all of this, according to Bensinger, "was pretty pathetic." Unions were "incredibly complacent" on the organizing front and

His Career Went Up in Smoke

I was a temp for a year and then was offered a permanent clerical job covered by the Oil, Chemical and Atomic Workers Union. It was a wonderful job with great pay, benefits and job security.

I climbed the ladder until one day they said, "Oh, do we have a deal for you—a manager's position."

So I took the job, which required me to work a twelve-hour shift with no overtime. Then the union went on strike, and I had to cross the picket line. Yes, go right through the friendly coworkers I knew so well, who were out there with no pay, fighting for company benefits, which I would also get.

The strike ended and I suddenly had no friends, only enemies. My coworkers, like myself, were hard-working Americans trying to make a living to support themselves and their families. Suddenly, though, they put me on the shit list.

I continued to work as supervisor for more than six union clerks until 1989 when a non-union temporary without adequate training failed to padlock a valve. *Bang! Boom! Booom booom! Pow! Pow!* EXPLOSION!!!!!!!! It registered an eight on the Richter scale twenty-five miles away. People within seventy miles felt it. Car tires in the neighborhood exploded, slabs of houses, light fixtures and ceiling fans fell down. A total of twenty-three people were killed and hundreds were injured running for their lives as they tried to flee from flying debris. Huge chunks of storage tanks flew into the air and fireballs lit up the sky. Suddenly the noon sun was darkness. The air filled with chemicals, black smoke and who knows what else. Birds fell from the sky dead.

An investigation found that the company was told numerous times this would happen if they didn't enforce safety procedures and make certain improvements. Instead of listening, the company increased its work stoppage insurance so they'd be covered when it happened.

Now it's 1997. I am forty-nine and on Social Security disability. I suffered through neck and two back surgeries. Sure, you say, "Lucky to be alive." I have no savings, no benefits, no income, no friends, major depression, no activities, no ESOP, no annual reviews for praise to raise my income, no home (lost due to expenses of medical), no monthly shopping sprees for work clothes, no schedule of meetings. You get the picture yet?

I was thrown out like a number. I never got an "I'm sorry"—nothing. But the union employees are still employed and making a living for themselves and their families.

We must all fight for our rights. GO UNIONS!!!

L.J.W.

simply tried to defend the membership they had from attack. "We've had this theory for decades if you did a good job servicing the members you have somehow nonunion workers would come rolling through the door. That theory has cost us power," he said. "And that loss of power means we can't even represent the members we have because we don't represent a high enough percent of the workers in the industries they are in."

Bernard of the Harvard Trade Union Program calls this "Mc-Donald's unionism"—a "we do it all for you" attitude that makes joining a union more like purchasing a service than becoming a part of some greater social movement and feeling solidarity with other working people. As a result, by failing to broaden for all working people through political action gains won at the bargaining table, the better wages and working conditions of unionized workers have helped to distance them from other workers. Also, since those gains have not been widespread, it has inspired greater antagonism from employers because of the premium union workers represent. As an example she points to Canada, where the rate of unionization is twice that in America and employers feel far less threatened. When workers lose their jobs, they don't lose their health care because Canada has socialized medicine, something first won through collective bargaining, then extended to all workers through political action.

The focus on members rather than the broader pool of workers and workers' issues took its toll on unions and, Bernard argues, on democratic society. In her essay "Why We Need Unions," she writes workers learn about the relations of power and the rights they have to participate in making decisions in the workplace. "As power is presently distributed, workplaces are factories of authoritarianism polluting our democracy," she writes. "It is no surprise that citizens who spend eight or more hours a day obeying orders with no rights, legal or otherwise, to participate in crucial decisions that affect them, do not then engage in robust, critical dialogue about the structure of our society. Eventually the strain of being deferential servants from nine to five diminishes our after-hours liberty and sense of civic entitlement and responsibility."

The purpose of the National Labor Relations Act, she said, was not just to encourage collective bargaining and create harmony between employers and employees in the workplace, but to bring about industrial democracy. Promoting industrial democracy is not part of the agenda for today's politicians, but Bernard thinks it must be for unions. While unions make passing reference to this in their rhetoric, talking of such things as "workplace democracy," she said that in recent years they have failed to draw the connection between democracy within and outside of the workplace. Rather than speaking of workplace democracy as an abstract and long-term goal, Bernard said, unions must make this a centerpiece of their goals if they are to develop a greater following. "Unfortunately, American workers are schooled every day at work to believe that democracy stops at the factory or office door. But democracy is not an extracurricular activity that can be relegated to evenings and weekends. And citizens' rights should not be subject to suspension at the whim of one's employer. The labor movement is the natural vehicle to lead the struggle for basic democratic rights inside and outside the workplace."

Then again, those not patient enough to wait for unions to solve their problems may find it better to take matters into their own hands.

PART 3

Getting Gruntled

10

The Planning Department

> "I don't know of anything that can be applied that will bring as much satisfaction to you, and as much anguish to the boss, as a little sabotage in the right place at the right time."
>
> —"BIG" BILL HAYWOOD
> *Industrial Workers of the World*

IN THE EARLY 1970s a computer programmer named John was working to create customer and personnel databases for a Fortune 500 company on the West Coast. As he progressed toward the end of the project John began to fear once he was done he would be fired. So he decided to write an insurance policy in the form of a computer program, explained Ethan Winning, an employee relations consultant in Walnut Creek, California, who likes to tell the story to illustrate the problems companies can run into when they put too much power in a single employee's hands. The program essentially told the computer that if John's name was deleted from the personnel database, it should delete the customer database.

John's instincts were good. So were his programming skills. Two years after he began the project he finished it. Soon after that, he was given a poor performance review and was fired. "They canned him without much fanfare," said Winning. "No severance pay." Within a matter of weeks somebody removed his name from the personnel database and like magic, the customer database vanished. It didn't take long for the company to suspect John had done something, and even if he hadn't, there weren't too many places for them to turn to for help at the time. So the company finally called him and he fessed up to what he had done. It took about six months of negotiations, but the company, which took no action against him, brought him back as a consultant to rebuild the databases. Before he was fired, Winning said, John was making $26,000 a year. Afterward, he was making $60,000 a year working for the company part-time. "It scared people, because one person could take the system down," said Winning.

That was back at a time when computers were still relatively new and the concept of computer crime was virtually nonexistent. While it points out the vulnerability corporations can be to computer-savvy employees who feel wronged, the computer just puts a new twist on something employees have been doing for as long as there have been employers. It goes on every day all over the world and represents a great leveler in the often skewed playing field on which employers and employees find themselves. In simple terms, what John did was an act of sabotage.

Within the employer's lexicon, sabotage has a notorious meaning that stirs images of terrorism, violence and destruction. In reality, though, sabotage takes many forms and many employees already practice it without ever dreaming that they are committing anything so nefarious. They foolishly think sabotage is something done only by bomb-throwing anarchists and that if they add a few hours to their time cards, help themselves to some company supplies or sit around the office making personal phone calls, they are merely taking that to which they are entitled.

Ron DiBattista, professor of management at Bryant College in Smithfield, Rhode Island, examined data collected from 44 human resource professionals and 164 supervisors at ten companies and catalogued them for an article in *Public Personnel Management* in September 1991. He placed the different types of sabotage into three

Survey Says

In 1993, Ron DiBattista, professor of Management at Bryant College in Smithfield, Rhode Island, asked 120 human resource managers from small, medium and large companies in the Northeast to rate thirty different types of sabotage that rate the highest on the barometer he developed in terms of probability of occurrence and potential for harm. Reporting the findings in the spring 1996 issue of *Public Personnel Management*, the events listed were:

- Stealing to compensate for low pay and poor work conditions.
- Snipping cables on word processors.
- Turning on a machine and walking away, knowing it will crash.
- Altering or deleting data stored in computer databases.
- Disclosing secret information to competitors.
- Lying to management about important data.
- Altering company records.

Of actual sabotage events these human resource professionals experienced, 82 percent interfered with normal business operations; 62 percent damaged the company's bottom line and 18 percent damaged the company's public image.

categories: sabotage aimed at destroying goods or machinery; sabotage where the goal is to stop production without destroying things; and sabotage aimed at reducing the workload.

"In general, sabotage seems to hit a different industry every five years or so. A couple of years ago the computer viruses were going wild. Before that, there were more machines jamming at manufacturers. Now it's more the white-collar stuff, things going on in banks and credit unions and on Wall Street," said DiBattista, who added that there seems to be a correlation between industries downsizing and the level of sabotage they experience. "You can't always prove a cause and effect, but the relationship is pretty high. These employees have reached a real high level of frustration. They may have done some job hunting and know they are going to leave the company."

Early in the century, Elizabeth Gurley Flynn defined sabotage another way. Writing in 1916 in a pamphlet for the Industrial Workers of the World, Flynn wrote, "Sabotage means primarily: the withdrawal of efficiency. Sabotage means either to slacken up and interfere with the quantity, or to botch in your skill and interfere with the quality of work, of capitalist production or to give poor service." Flynn's pamphlet has been withdrawn from the official union literature of the Wobblies. Apparently even a union determined to do away with the wage system and bring capitalism to its knees harbors concerns about its image. Instead of "sabatoge," the union today uses the safer term "direct action," meaning those things employees can do on their own, without turning to government agencies, unions or lawyers to improve their working lives.

Sabotage was officially adopted in 1897 by the General Federa-

Getting Steamed

I was training the new dishwasher. A cook and I decided to have some fun as it was a little slow. The trainee was very eager to please. We were working the steam table. A steam table is a large metal table with a deep dish heater in the middle. You pour water in to the deep square dish and it heats the water, creating steam, which keeps the food warm.

About a block away from our restaurant is another restaurant. We grabbed a large garbage bag and set the prank up. The cook ran frantically into the dish pit where the newbie and I were working. He blurted out that the steam table was out of steam, handed him the bag and told him to run as fast as he could to the nearby restaurant to ask for steam. I put my best shocked face on and told him to go. He ran at full speed to the restaurant and asked for steam. He ran back looking disappointed and said, "They're all out." We laughed for three weeks. What a sucker!

Another sucker was also eager to please. We sent him to the store to get a packet of ice mix as we were out of ice. He was in the store for 45 minutes, looking for it without the presence of mind to ask a clerk who would have told him there is no such thing. He came back disappointed and said they didn't have any. Then he asked what ice mix was anyway. All I said was, "Water."

tion of Labor of France as a weapon in their workers' arsenals. Though there is some dispute on the precise origin of the word, it seems to involve the fancy footwork of French laborers. In one popular version, the term was given life after a French laborer took his wooden shoe, known as a "sabot," and wedged it into machinery to grind it to a halt. Another explanation relates to the slow and cloppy way people are made to walk when they wear the wooden shoes.

While the French may have given sabotage its name, they by no means invented it. In one of the earliest writings about sabotage, which was translated from French into English in 1912, Emile Pouget offers a Scottish example from Glasgow dockworkers in 1889. Instead of the word "sabotage," the Scottish used the term "go cannie," meaning to work slowly. The dockworkers had just failed to win a two-cent-an-hour raise through a strike. The strike was ineffective because the employer went to great expense to bring in replacement workers from farms throughout the surrounding countryside. Though these farmhands lacked the skills of the dockworkers, they were able to break the strike. Before returning to the same jobs at the same wages, Pouget writes, a union official told the dockworkers:

> The contractors have expressed and repeated all their satisfaction for the work done by the farmers who have scabbed on us during these last weeks. We have seen them at work and know full well what kind of satisfactory work was theirs—we saw indeed that they could not even keep their balance on the bridges and saw how they dropped in the sea half the cargo they loaded and unloaded. In one word, we have seen that two of them could not do as much work as one of us. Nevertheless, the bosses said they were satisfied with their labor, therefore, we have one thing left yet; let us give them the same kind of labor. Work them just like the farmhands did—they often pushed their incapacity to the point of falling overboard, but it is not necessary for you to do this, of course.

A few days after the longshoremen began "going cannie," the contractors agreed to give them the wages they demanded in exchange for having them work as they had before the strike.

It wasn't long after the introduction of the word "sabotage" that its meaning took on evil connotations. As early as 1919, the economist and social critic Thorstein Veblen, in his essay "On the Nature and Uses of Sabotage," addressed the coloring of the word in the United States: "The sinister meaning which is often attached to the word in American usage, as denoting violence and disorder, appears to be due to the fact that the American usage has been shaped chiefly by persons and newspapers who have aimed to discredit the use of sabotage by organized workmen, and who have therefore laid stress on its less amiable manifestations," wrote Veblen. "This is unfortunate. It lessens the usefulness of the word by making it a means of denunciation rather than of understanding."

Evil or not, sabotage has an ever-present role in the American workplace. There are no comprehensive numbers that put an annual price tag on the losses corporations suffer every year from employee sabotage, but employee theft alone in the retail industry has been estimated to be as much as $27 billion by the National Retail Federation. Numbers are impossible to calculate. Businesses usually don't like to disclose when they are victims

> **Kids Get the Last Laugh**
>
> The American Seed Co. closed its doors following five consecutive years of losses, the *Wall Street Journal* reported.
>
> The Lancaster, Pennsylvania, company served as the gateway to the free enterprise system for elementary school–aged children who went door-to-door selling packs of seeds.
>
> Children were supposed to sell the seeds for 60 cents a pack and send back 40 cents a pack to the company. The kids did some of that fancy new math and decided to pocket all the money themselves. That cost American Seed $600,000 its last year alone.
>
> *It's nice to see kids discovering truly free enterprise.*
>
> **9/30/81**

of employee sabotage and oftentimes don't even know with certainty. Employers concerned about their vulnerability to angry workers often search out expensive and elaborate means of protecting themselves through surveillance systems, antitheft devices and sophisticated computer firewalls. "If you have an incompetent programer and you fire the guy, you hope," said Peter G. Neumann, principal scientist of the computer science lab at SRI International, a nonprofit think tank in Menlo Park, California. "If you don't hustle him off as you speak and seal off all the trapdoors he stuck in the system, how do you protect yourself? Firing anybody is a risk."

What seems to be the most effective defense against sabotage is simply to treat employees well. It's what's known in the vernacular as a no-brainer: happy employees don't commit sabotage. Consider a 1996 study conducted by the University of Florida's National Retail Loss Survey Project and the Winter Park, Florida, consulting firm Loss Security Prevention, Inc. The survey queried 350 retail companies from all fifty states in twenty-two different types of retailing. The study is unusual because it examined the relationship between the way companies treat their employees and the level of employee theft they experienced. What it found was that companies that pay and treat their employees better have low worker and manager turnover levels, promote from within, have profit-sharing throughout the company, maintain a high ratio of full-time employees to part-time employ-

> ### Managers on the Run
>
> In one of my previous workplaces, a colleague and I pulled the ultimate office prank. Just before a major 3 P.M. meeting of all the high level dick-smackers, we were kind enough to replenish the office coffeepot with an extra special ingredient—half a box of Smooth Move Laxative Tea.
>
> We were on the floor laughing as they all filed in for their cup of Java. This was the ultimate prank since none of these fine gentlemen and ladies would ever admit that they shit their pants driving home during rush hour.
>
> The Anonymous Prankster

ees and suffer fewer problems of theft than retailers who rate badly in these areas. "It seemed to show the more positively we treat our employees, the lower the inventory losses," said Read Hayes, a senior consultant with the security firm.

In the meantime, companies that continue to assault their workers with degradation, poor wages and mistreatment run the risk of finding themselves the victims of the workplace equivalent of guerrilla warfare. At a time when management gurus like to talk about "empowering" employees by flattening out the organizational chart, introducing total quality management and team workgroups, employees embrace sabotage as a way to accomplish instant empowerment without the hefty consulting fees and nauseating jargon. Certainly there is nothing more empowering than pouring a cup of coffee into the back of a computer, intentionally misfiling an important document or putting a little Krazy Glue into the lock of a critical file cabinet. Only the boss might be able to crack the whip, but anyone can pull a plug. "It can help people make a situation better. It lets people take matters into their own hands, blow off steam or make work a little more interesting," said Martin Sprouse, author of *Sabotage in the American Workplace*. "That's very important."

Employees who feel powerless often think their only choice is either to accept what their employer dishes out or to go on strike, and that's not much of a choice. Strikes are ineffective. They cost employees a loss of wages that is usually harder on them than the

A Pot to Piss In

Several years ago I was security manager for a famous national retail outlet. The store manager was a regular tyrant with short persons' syndrome. He got great satisfaction from belittling everyone under him.

I found a good way for me to cope was to enter the store after closing hours and urinate on all the prized and pampered plants he kept in his office. Funny how they all eventually turned yellow and died!

Mr. B.

financial pain they inflict on the employer. In recent years, as employers have become increasingly emboldened to bring in replacement workers, strikes have become even less effective. In addition, workers who are not organized have significant and obvious impediments to calling a strike. Some employees have found sabotage a viable alternative to strikes (a form of sabotage itself) as a way to bring about constructive change. Sabotage allows workers to bring pressure to bear on an employer without their having to sacrifice much-needed paychecks.

One example Sprouse likes to refer to happened in 1986 at a bike messenger service across the water from Seattle in Bellevue, Washington. The service had recently had a change in management. The new management told the messengers that the company was going to raise its image now that it was dealing with bigger businesses. Instead of the shorts and T-shirts with the sleeves cut off that the messengers liked to sport, the boss told the messengers they had to wear long pants and shirts made of a heavy material. "Try biking ten miles up hills, up massive hills with heavy packages as fast as you can, in

Former Kodak Employee Exposed

Eastman Kodak Co. filed a lawsuit against former employee Harold Worden, who the company charged had stolen trade secrets he hoped to sell to the company's competitors, the *Wall Street Journal* reported.

A Federal Bureau of Investigation search of Worden's home reportedly turned up nearly 40,000 documents, many relevant to the lawsuit. The company charged Worden, through his consulting company, enlisted about 63 former Kodak employees over a three-year period to get documents the company called proprietary.

The company said Worden was also getting and selling confidential information about such companies as Xerox Corp., Polaroid Corp. and DuPont Co. Worden was nailed in a sting operation set up by the company.

It is nice that coworkers can get together after work and do their own special projects.

11/8/96

long pants," said Mike, one of the former messengers who now works as an animator in San Francisco.

The messengers decided they needed to take action. The plan they agreed upon was a simple one. They wouldn't wash their uniforms. To add to the effect, they also started to eat special diets consisting of such combustible delicacies as bean burritos in order to create volatile releases from their intestinal tracts. "There was a big health food store nearby with all kinds of nasty things to do to your intestines," said Mike. "Whenever we were in a big office building, we farted. You can imagine what it was like when one of us was in an elevator with ten businesspeople in suits. Our clothes were stinking, our bodies were stinking and within a month the company had enough complaints to let us wear shorts again."

In another instance, Sprouse said, workers have been able to achieve through sabotage things their union could not successfully obtain through bargaining. Workers at a cannery in Alaska had a contract that allowed just one fifteen-minute break every four hours. Though the job paid well, it was monotonous and dreary and the working conditions were poor. The cannery's conveyor belt frequently broke down. A mere wayward lid that flipped upside down would jam the machinery and grind the operation to a halt. Each time that happened, mechanics would have to come in and clear it out. It would take about fifteen minutes and during that time all of the workers just stood idle.

The lids came in a stack and the only way for a lid to flip upside down was for someone to reach in and place it that way. As workers milled

Getting E-nailed

We broke into the company president's E-mail account and sent a coworker an invitation to take a jump in the sack. We made it worse by sending her a key to his house with an "I'll expect you naked in my bed" note attached to it.

Yes, she showed up. And so did he and his wife.

Beaner

Teledelinquents

Phones can be a lot of fun. I once had a coworker who would run out of the bathroom to grab his phone if it rang. The bathroom was right next to his office. One day, I glued his handset to the cradle, and made sure that everyone in the office called his number over and over. He went nuts!

He got me back, but good. I had a private line that had call-forwarding on it. He knew that I always came in around 10 A.M. or 11 A.M. on Fridays. So one Friday morning, he got to work really early and forwarded my line to a phone sex service. I heard about that one for weeks afterward.

Several weeks later in retaliation I removed the microphone from his handset and screwed the thing back together. When people called, he could hear them just fine, but they couldn't hear a word he said.

Continuing, he responded by removing the "4" key from my phone's keyboard, hiding it and then telling me it was somewhere in my office. I spent about two hours before I found it, taped to the underside of my desk.

The last prank: I changed the programming in the switch for his extension, so that every call he made was routed to a local flower shop. He told me he bought his wife flowers twice a week, so I thought I'd help him out.

Nicetry

about and talked, they realized that without telling each other, everyone at one time or another was intentionally jamming the line when he or she wanted to take a break. Because the shutdowns happened in different lines and at different places, management just accepted it as part of the process. "Every time we shut down the line we got some satisfaction out of the fact that we were spitting back at management in some way," David, a worker at the plant, told Sprouse. "The whole thing just seemed so alienating that I could justify doing practically anything. It was probably one of the most miserable experiences of my life, and somehow what I did helped make it a little more livable."

In other cases, employees have turned to sabotage as a way to get things that they openly demanded. In longshoring, with the advent of automation, most cargo is placed into truck-sized boxes that would be stacked on container ships. Once they are in port, huge cranes lift the boxes off the ships and place them on truck chassis. With automation, said Reg Theriault, a former San Francisco Bay Area longshoreman and author of *How to Tell When You're Tired: A Brief Examination of Work,* longshoreman could control their work through the slowdown. "There is only one way on the job that the worker can have any influence on the work, and that is by slowing the operation down. And it's deliberate and it's done. I've been a part of it," said Theriault. "Only in really dire circumstances would we shut it down. We discovered that slowing it down was much more effective."

An advantage longshoremen have is the high cost of keeping a ship in port. The ships are on tight schedules and expect to turn around quickly. If a ship has to burn extra fuel to make up for lost time, it costs lots of money. A good crane driver, who loads and unloads the container ships, can perform 30 moves of the crane in an hour. That's the equivalent of unloading fifteen, forty-foot containers an hour. Typically, when a ship comes in, there will be 240 to 250 moves. If things go well, and not too many things get in the way, that will represent a full eight-hour day of work. When unavoidable problems happen and there are delays, the longshoremen are allowed to work two hours overtime.

One night, though, according to Theriault, he and his crew were "hard-timed," so they "hard-timed 'em right back." Normally, a

The Check's in the Basement

Theodis Lofton, a mailman for ten years, said he stole more than fifteen thousand pieces of mail, the *San Francisco Chronicle* reported.

Lofton, a letter carrier in St. Louis, pleaded guilty to possession of stolen mail.

The mail was stored in the basement of his home.

No wonder you haven't won the Publishers Clearing House sweepstakes yet.

9/16/95

crane driver has a crew of six moving the containers to or from the crane. But instead of ordering six longshoremen that night, the company thought it would try to save a little money by ordering just five, since it was not a full ship and there were only 165 moves to make. Though that might have seemed reasonable, it violated an unwritten understanding on the waterfront. Basically, if the longshoremen bust their asses to get a job done, they get to go home when it's finished.

We Got His Number

I am an Air Force technician who works with electronics. We work closely with engineers of a major aerospace firm.

One day we set up an engineer, John, who wanted a "failed" electronics flight package for a display toy in his office. John had a reputation for being a serious prankster, so we really had to do it right.

The stage was set. We took the old serial number plate off of the failed unit and glued another one in its place. Then we called John and told him to come and pick it up. He came out to our shop and was like a kid in a candy store. That's what we banked on.

In his zeal to take his prize, John didn't read the serial number plate which we swapped. He took the $1.2 million piece of hardware and dumped it into his van, then dragged it across the carpet into his office cubicle. (Dragging the item across the carpet is very bad for the electronics.)

About an hour later, my boss called John at his office and really laid on the worried tone. He told John that the unit we gave him was the actual flight article for the next launch and that we had to get it back right away before anyone found out about it.

John nearly had a stroke! He explained that he had probably damaged the unit with the rough handling and the static of dragging it over the carpet. "No problem," my boss said. "Just switch the serial number plates."

"What!!" John said. "You can't do that!" My boss, feeling John had had enough, said, "Why not, we did it before." John didn't catch on. He just swore we were nuts and continued to stew in the sweat of his anxiety.

We decided to see him in person. When we got to his office, he was smiling, but had obviously been shaken. My boss had finally gotten through to him. He told us nobody had ever gotten him like that before and he promised to get us back. We're still waiting, John!

Julie O.

By short-staffing the crew, it meant it would take the full shift to un-load the ship and would necessitate overtime if anything went wrong.

Like their Scottish predecessors who used the go cannie, long-shoremen today use the slowdown. When longshoremen normally slow down the work, they drop from about 30 moves an hour to 25. That night, Theriault said, they took the operation down to 5 moves an hour. The walking boss came down and hung on to Theriault's trailer and said, "Okay, Reg, what do you want?" Theriault told him he wanted a full crew. "We slowed them on that situation, and it's tough. You've got to find things to do. You take a lot of heat," he said. "I'm pulling this thing under the crane and trying to screw it up. I pull forward and the crane can't pick it up and the hatch tender says, 'Back up.' So I back up too far. Everybody who works a job knows how to fuck it up."

What works in one industry, though, does not always translate easily to others. Service sector workers are faced with a dilemma. They may want to do something that puts pressure on their employer, but at the same time they don't want to hurt the people who are their clients or customers. It's here that a technique known as a "good work strike" can be particularly effective. In a good work strike, as described by the Bay Area IWW's Bossbusters project, workers give better and cheaper service at their bosses' expense. In one case where restaurant workers in New York City had lost a strike, they were later able to win some of their demands by following the union's advice to "pile up the plates, give 'em double helpings and figure the checks on the low side."

Another example of this technique cited by Bossbusters was used at Mercy Hospital in France, where workers, reasoning that a strike would hurt patients, gave the patients their care, but refused to process billing slips for drugs, lab tests and doctor visits. The IWW said the hospital's income was cut in half and the administration caved in to all of the workers' demands in three days.

Sometimes, instead of not following the rules, the best way to get an employer to respond to employee demands is by following the

A Real Cutup

I used to work with a woman who had to be in on everything going on. At Halloween time, I asked the village idiot of the company to assist in a prank.

With the band saw buzzing away, I poured fake blood all over the kid's hand, wrist and arm, then yelled, "Oh my God!!" The idiot and I ran to the bathroom and closed the door and waited.

I think it took about ten seconds for her to burst into the john. We were already on the floor laughing. What fun!

Eliza

rules a little too well. In most work situations, employees know, if they stick to the letter of a contract or the rules of their workplace, everything can get clogged up. While "working-to-rule" has been used as a tactic by unions, even individuals in nonunion work settings can find it a useful approach at times.

That's what Eric, a thirty-five-year-old civil engineer at a mid-sized firm in California, realized. He was working as a design engineer on a project and had been asked by a municipality involved in the project to submit some proposed changes. He forwarded the plans along with some requested changes and marked them "proposal." When the client saw the drawings, he went ballistic and chewed out the project manager, Eric's boss. The client was concerned about the added cost of the proposed changes. The project manager felt blindsided, because he'd never seen the drawings—though there were cost implications, the changes weren't significant enough that the project manager would have reviewed them under normal procedures. Nevertheless, embarrassed, the project manager lashed into Eric and told him that if he ever did anything like that again he would be fired.

From that point on, the project manager insisted on seeing everything before it went out the door. Eric thought the response was inappropriate and was angered at having his job threatened. So, he decided to follow his boss's instructions, and made sure the boss saw everything before it went out the door. The most insignificant memos, communications and responses to clients wound up on the project manager's chair or in his in box with a little yellow Post-it note politely reading, "Please review, initial and forward." Explained Eric, "It was a way to tell him to back off. He needed to be taught a lesson." Eric has continued to bombard his boss with paper for two solid months. "I think I've gained more respect from him. He appreciates what I do and what I can do if needed. He hasn't fucked with me since then."

Compensatory Damages

CS First Boston Corp. withdrew a lawsuit against an unknown prankster who E-mailed confidential salary information to hundreds of employees, the Dow Jones News Service reported.

The company would not say whether it ever identified the anonymous sender of the message, only that the matter had been resolved.

The message had been sent out after there were complaints about 1995 bonuses and a defection of executives unhappy with them.

I guess it was no longer an issue since the information was no longer confidential.

6/12/96

Of course, sabotage is not without risk. Depending on the nature of the activity, saboteurs can lose their jobs and a lot more. Though computer crimes did not exists on the books in the early 1970s, when the Fortune 500 programmer John was able to compute a little job security for himself, many who followed in his footsteps have not fared as well. In one notable case Michael John Lauffenburger, a former General Dynamics worker, found himself charged with one count of computer tampering and one count of attempted computer fraud for planting a logic bomb in a computer designed to destroy information relating to the Atlas missile program. Prosecutors charged Lauffenburger was disgruntled because he hadn't won the recognition he felt he deserved. The indictment said his plan was to offer himself to General Dynamics as a high-priced consultant and the only one capable of restoring the lost data. Another employee discovered the file before it was able to trigger. General Dynamics said the program would have caused $100,000 in damages. Lauffenburger pleaded guilty to reduced charges of computer tampering, a misdemeanor.

A Little Shit Eats Little Shits

About 15 years ago, I worked for a newspaper. We had a company refrigerator where employees kept their lunches. One woman really liked to bring trail mix. She kept having problems with people stealing it.

Sometimes they would just take some of it. Sometimes they would take the whole thing.

She got really pissed about it. So one day she mixed the trail mix with fresh rabbit turds. They looked just like carob or chocolate peanuts. After she told us about it, we waited. It turned out the thief was the publisher's grandson. He wasn't even too ashamed to ask people, "Hey, who put the rabbit shit in the trail mix?" I thought that was great revenge.

Judy M.

In another case, programmer Donald Gene Burleson was convicted of harmful access to a computer for writing a program that deleted 168,000 payroll records at USPA and IRA Co., a Fort Worth, Texas–based insurance and brokerage firm where he had worked. The program triggered two days after he was fired. The incident delayed paychecks at the firm for more than a month.

While some sabotage is done merely for revenge, and other sabotage is done with the hopes of winning concessions from the boss, a final form has no goal other than the perpetrator's own amusement. The Internet has provided a continual opportunity for employees to fuck off from the comfort of their own desks. The beauty of this is that as they surf websites, wander through chat rooms and fire off E-mail to their friends, they appear to their boss to be slaving away at their computer terminals.

John McAfee, the computer security expert who founded the antivirus software firm that bears his name, is now heading a company called Tribal Voices in Woodland Park, Colorado. The company makes communications software called PowWow that allows up to seventy-five people to chat with each other on-line. McAfee said 7 million connections are made each day with the software, half of those—3.5 million—by people with Internet addresses indicating they work at such places as AT&T, General Motors and the federal government. "They are using our tax dollars to have fun and games all day," he said. Instead of using the technology for such things as finding solutions to engineering problems they might be having, McAfee said, they are spending time in such chat groups as "married and cheating." Of course, it's a reasonable assumption that people who cheat on their spouses probably have no qualms about cheating on their employers with a little stolen time to goof around on-line.

For those who like to goof off with a little style and thought, there is the office prank. Pranks not only provide a break from the stress and boredom of work, but also provide one of the few opportunities these days for a worker to conceive of a project and oversee it from conception to execution, giving a level of satisfaction that is often hard to come by elsewhere in the workplace. Though pranksters usually construct their practical jokes for their own amusement or a small audience of coworkers, pranks are sometimes done on a grand scale.

At Maxis, a Walnut Creek, California, software company that produces games, including its flagship SimCity, programmer Jacques Servin worked on a new helicopter simulation game called SimCopter. The player flies the helicopter on a variety of rescue missions and tries to save people. Servin, who is gay, decided he would take some liberties. Instead of programming animated bikini-clad bimbos who would greet the heroic pilots, he inserted male hunks in swimsuits who would kiss each other. As a player progressed through the game, and on the birthdays of Servin and a former boyfriend of his, the ani-

Nailed with a Stapler

My favorite slightly vicious prank is to come into the office late, get a box and go around the entire department collecting staplers, leaving behind little sticky notes saying, "I borrowed your stapler, I'll return it tomorrow—Joe." Stash the box under Joe's desk and laugh. Watch as he spends the next day returning staplers one-by-one as people show up.

Steven O.

mated male figures got wilder. Maxis had delivered nearly eighty thousand copies of the program before it became aware of the problem and offered a software patch to circumvent Servin's handiwork. Though the bit of rogue programming cost Servin his job, it did make him an international cause célèbre. The gay community held him up as a brave activist, a role he downplays.

"Me a brave activist? I'd done nothing active to speak of— maybe two hours of giggling in a drab and temperate office, shirt on, not sweating—and I'd had just about no agenda, nothing to recite, no belief construct to squat in, barely a brainwave aforethought," he wrote in a 1997 article scheduled to be published in *Cursor* magazine. "I could see it called whimsy, peskiness, play, mischief—or, with a stretch, subversion, sabotage, fucking shit up. For all the amusement it brought me, I'd just call it a fabulous deal." Servin later acknowledged that the prank wasn't entirely spontaneous, but that he had been enlisted into the project and accepted $5,000 to do the deed from a group calling itself ArtMark, which funds nonviolent sabotage aimed at the consumer culture.

Though sabotage is often maligned, there is one exception today in which the worker who makes use of the practice is often held up as a hero and offered special protections and sometimes even rewards from the government. It's too bad the coworkers of these brave souls often ostracize rather than support them. Walker C. Smith, in an IWW newspaper editorial he wrote in 1913, called the practice "open mouth sabotage," but today it has a more familiar name.

11

Blowing It

> "There is not a single portion of the commerce of the entire world where exact truthfulness would not spell financial ruin under the present conditions."
>
> —WALKER C. SMITH
> *Editor of the* Industrial Worker
> *On "Open Mouth Sabotage" in 1913 editorial*

RICHARD LUNDWALL FELT betrayed. After thirty-one years of loyal service to his employer, the fifty-five-year-old executive found himself out of work. According to a profile in the *New York Times,* a week before Lundwall took off for a Christmas vacation in 1995, his boss gave him a bon voyage present: He called him into his office and told Lundwall he would be terminated in six months. In January of 1996, Lundwall cleaned out his desk in the finance department and was given a new desk in human resources and little to do as he waited for the clock to wind down on his tenure with the company. He received no organized send-off from his coworkers or boss. A month later, Lundwall suffered kidney failure and lay in a hospital bed after emergency surgery. He was upset that the company had failed to even extend the courtesy of a personal note while he was there. The *Times*'s Kurt Eichenwald writes, "As his long career seemed to be dwindling to a depressing end at age 55, the bedridden executive felt powerless for the first time in his life. And then it hit him: The tapes."

The tapes Eichenwald refers to were the smoking gun that led to the largest settlement of a discrimination suit ever when Texaco forked over $176.1 million to resolve a class-action suit that charged the company had discriminated against blacks. Lundwall had secretly made the tapes on a handheld, microcassette recorder concealed in his pocket during a meeting at which executives allegedly discussed destroying evidence in the case and used racial epithets. The oil giant not only suffered a hefty financial blow in order to bring an end to the suit, but had a public relations crisis on its hands and found itself the subject of a criminal investigation for possibly destroying evidence as well.

Whether it was revenge or outrage over the company's behavior toward minorities that pushed Lundwall to turn over the tapes is not entirely clear. Though Lundwall said he felt that coming forward was "the right thing to do," reports of the tapes' contents indicate that the executives at the meeting not only discussed destroying documents possibly relevant to the case but that Lundwall was a willing participant. Nevertheless, Lundwall's action put pressure on Texaco to compensate workers who may have been deprived of advancement and forced the company to address the question of diversity with more than lip service. The tapes also sparked a national debate about racism in corporate America and the underrepresentation of minorities in senior management ranks.

What happened to Lundwall next, though, represents the types of rewards bestowed on whistle-blowers for their efforts and is a reminder that no good deed goes unpunished. For doing this, Lundwall found himself accused by his former employer of violating company rules about destroying documents and had his benefits cut off. As if that were not enough, he found himself the first Texaco executive indicted in the case, on one count of obstruction of justice, which carries a maximum ten-year prison term. He was later acquitted.

Sending His Regrets

Whistle-blowing, like going to war, is a young person's activity, preferably a young person who has no dependents who look to him or her for emotional or financial support. It is also an activity that will inevitably test the vitality of even the strongest marital commitment, particularly if in the end the battle goes sour, which is to say, nearly all the time.

If you are a family person, however strong your personal conscience may be about the immorality which you see taking place under your nose in the workplace, rest assured. That emotion of indignity, if you follow through upon it with open action, will eventually be dwarfed to the nth magnitude by the guilt and the sadness and the despair you will eventually experience when you finally realize what a terrible price you have paid for your so-called expression of conscience.

Like fast motorcycles and late hours and other private pleasures, any person with dependents should regard the assertion of personal conscience as a basically selfish personal indulgence. Why?

Because in the current employment climate in this country, and no matter how obviously appropriate your whistle-blowing contentions may be, you and your ability to make a living are highly likely to be severely hobbled if not altogether destroyed by the venomous counterattack which you will inevitably encounter from your employers and yes, your "friends."

I am no scholar on the subject, but I have done a lot of research on the topic of whistle-blowers. The failed marriages, ruined careers, suicides and mental disorders which accompany whistle-blowing are so consistently in evidence that I suspect that the institutional hostility encountered by all whistle-blowers is fueled by some kind of biological, human species imperative.

It is no exaggeration to say that going against organizational trends as a whistle-blower is a family-destroying and potentially life-threatening activity. Conscience and personal scruples are a good thing, but sacrificing the future of your children to satisfy your personal needs, however noble, is something that I myself did without sufficient forethought. I know that both my family and I (assuming it stays together) will continue to pay the price for this self-indulgence of conscience. And while my children may possibly in the future be inspired by my actions, I know that the bone-deep guilt which I feel right now tells me already that it will not have been worth it.

Name withheld

Whether it's moral concern for the greater public good or merely a hunger to bite the hand that feeds, whistle-blowing is one of the most powerful weapons in the employee's arsenal to bring about change—although it can work a little like a volatile explosive. Employees who are not careful can find themselves in the way of the blast or at least the target of an unrelenting return of fire from their employer.

Myron and Penina Glazer, in their 1989 study *The Whistleblowers: Exposing Corruption in Government and Industry,* call whistleblowers a "historically new group." The two argue that only since the 1960s has there been a continual stream of employees "who do not act primarily out of self-interest, but concentrate on exposing policies that could endanger or defraud the public." They point to several social and political factors that together have laid fertile ground from which whistle-blowers could rise. These include new regulations relating to public health and safety, legal protections for whistleblowers and an atmosphere of public cynicism toward government. The Glazers refer to the whistle-blowers they write about as "ethical resisters . . . to denote their commitment to the principles we all espouse—honesty, individual responsibility and active concern for the public good."

Ethical resisters may represent a modern phenomenon to the extent that public policy has been put in place to foster whistleblowing. Employees today, in our post-Watergate and post-Vietnam society, may be more inclined to question authority. And, the loyalty employees once felt toward employers is now little more than a quaint memory. But long before Daniel Ellsberg pulled his all-nighter at the Xerox machine and Deep Throat played Twenty Questions in a Washington, D.C., garage, "open mouth sabotage," as the Wobblies called it, was seen as a perfectly dandy way to cut an employer off at the knees. Whether it was telling customers how they were being cheated, tipping off competitors to trade secrets or making public disclosures about industry-wide practices that endangered public health, the open mouth has always been available to an employee interested in improving the workplace or just wreaking a little havoc in the lives of the whip-crackers. "In the foodstuffs industry, open mouth sabotage is particularly potent," wrote Walker C. Smith, editor of the Industrial Workers of the World's newspaper, *Industrial Worker,* in a 1913 editorial. "Its use will at once enlist the support of a large portion of the public. It becomes one of the highest social acts. Let the workers, instead of striking, or even when on strike, expose the methods of manufacture and the boss will soon come to terms."

On a small scale, the practice of open mouthing can be as simple as employees letting customers know when they are being billed for work not done or not needed. On the grand scale, it usually involves turning to government authorities, public interest groups or the media to expose large-scale fraud and corruption, as Department of Defense cost analyst Ernest Fitzgerald did when he went before Congress in 1968 to expose cost overruns on defense projects and in the process became a model for a generation of whistle-blowers to follow.

The United States government may be stupid enough to pay $439 for a $7 hammer (as Fitzgerald called to congressional attention), but it is also smart enough to know that the motivation for whistle-blowers doesn't have to be pure. In fact, Uncle Sam offers would-be whistle-blowers a more reliable motive than morality—a piece of the action. In 1986, Congress amended the False Claims Act to entice whistle-blowers. Though the law dates back to the Civil War and the government's desire to prosecute companies that delivered shoddy goods or charged excessive prices for war supplies, in more recent times it was going largely unused—and not because our corporate citizens had suddenly become exceedingly forthright and honest.

To help shake things up a bit, the amendments allow anyone aware of fraud against the government to bring a lawsuit in his own name on behalf of the United States. The government generally has sixty days to decide whether or not it will join the suit. If it does, the

Mutiny for the Bounty

Since the False Claims Act was amended in 1986 to allow whistle-blowers to bring suits on behalf of the government and share in a portion of the recoveries, it has led to cumulative settlements in excess of $1 billion.

	Cases	Recoveries
1987	33	—
1988	60	$ 2 million
1989	95	$ 32 million
1990	82	$ 40 million
1991	90	$ 36 million
1992	119	$124 million
1993	131	$193 million
1994	221	$379 million
1995	274	$243 million

Source: U.S. Department of Justice

person who filed the case gets between 15 and 25 percent of what the government is able to collect. Cases the government chooses not to join can still be pursued by whistle-blowers. In those instances, the whistle-blower gets between 25 and 30 percent of what is recovered. Employees who avail themselves of the False Claims Act are protected against retaliation. The law entitles any employee who is harassed, demoted, fired or punished in any other way to collect damages, including twice the amount of any lost wages.

The financial motivation might dull the glow on the halo normally afforded to whistle-blowers, but so what? It's helped uncover fraud. Total recoveries under the False Claims Act since it was amended topped the $1 billion mark in 1995, according to the U.S. Department of Justice. The number of cases had grown to 274 in 1995 from just 33 in 1987. Among the biggest cases to come under the False Claims Act was a 1997 settlement with SmithKline Beecham Clinical Laboratories Inc., which agreed to pay $325 million to settle claims that it billed the government for lab tests that were unnecessary or never performed. The settlement came after two former employees and two employees of a competitor had filed lawsuits.

Some whistle-blowers have deservedly earned heroic status for risking their own careers and personal safety for the greater good, but whistle-blowing by no means requires or earns the sporting of wings and a harp. Pissed-off, jilted or money-hungry employees can be just as effective as any saint, as long as they speak the truth. Employers might try to dismiss the whistle-blower's public disclosures as little more than the rantings of a disgruntled employee, but revelations of fraud, waste and hazards to the public often have a way of withstanding such assaults. As the saying goes, "Sunlight is the best disinfectant."

It is standard operating procedure for the offending company to challenge the whistle-blower's credibility and motives, but it is often those who have less than pure motives who are in the best position to have access to the most damning information. A company man who has risen high enough through the ranks during years of loyal service will get a key not only to the executive washroom, but also to the closet where the skeletons lie. And one need not feel a sense of betrayal to make the plunge. Sometimes something as simple as the instinct for self-preservation may be enough of a motivator. It certainly seems it was for Archer Daniels Midland Corp.'s Mark Whitacre.

Whitacre, thirty-eight, was not just some bagboy at the so-called supermarket for the world. He served as president of the bioproducts division of ADM and was heir apparent to the throne of the agricultural giant. He first found himself in the spotlight in July 1995 when the *Wall Street Journal* reported that he had been a mole for the FBI, secretly recording and videotaping top ADM executives and competitors during a two-and-a-half year period as part of an antitrust investigation by the government.

By his own account, Whitacre became a whistle-blower only after the company called in federal investigators to look into possible sabotage at the bioproducts division. The company was having problems with the production of lysine, a corn derivative that is added to feedstock to promote lean muscle growth in animals. The company suspected that contamination of the lysine at the plant was possibly the work of a foreign competitor. In a first-person piece that appeared in *Fortune* magazine in 1995, Whitacre said he decided to spill the beans about price-fixing because he knew his phones at work and at home would be tapped and because he trusted the FBI agent who had come to interview him. Whitacre said blowing the whistle cost him his job, subjected him to death threats and made him the target of fraud and embezzlement allegations by his former employer. ADM accused Whitacre of using phony contracts and invoices to steal as much as $9 million from the company. Whitacre has acknowledged receipt of off-the-books money, but said the company knew about it and used it as a way to compensate top executives through offshore accounts to avoid taxes and tracing. ADM agreed to pay $100 million to settle charges that it had fixed prices in two commodities, lysine and citric acid, the largest fines ever levied in a case of this kind.

Like most whistle-blowers, Whitacre didn't seem prepared for the reaction from his former employer once it became known what he had done. "It amazes me how just a few weeks ago I was potentially the next president of the company, and now it's pure character assassination," Whitacre wrote in *Fortune*. "Here's what's being said about me. That I wasn't a good manager, that I wasn't good with people, that the feds caught me price-fixing." Weeks after being fired, Whitacre had reportedly attempted suicide by leaving his car running in the garage of his home. Legal battles with his former employer, as well as the feds continued. In March 1988 he was sentenced to nine years in prison after he pled guilty to embezzling $9 million from ADM.

Whitacre might not seem like a typical whistle-blower, but the fact is there is no such thing, according to Marcia Miceli, professor of management and human resources at Ohio State University and

Remembering a Former Employer

An aviation security company I used to work for has a CEO who is an absolute prick. He rips off his customers, pays his employees shit and strings his vendors out for 120 days. He was constantly changing departmental bonus plans in order to keep more money for himself.

His shenanigans personally cost me more than $3,000. Plus they stiffed me for six days vacation pay. When I left the company to hook up with a former vice president who had been stiffed on $10,000, we decided to make things a bit unpleasant for the owner.

We started by getting in touch with a former information systems director, who had been trying to get the company "legal" with all of its software. The CEO had told this guy that the governing groups didn't know what they were doing and they would never be caught.

We took this audit information to the Business Software Alliance and the antipiracy group. They threatened to come in and shut down all of the company's computers and perform an audit. If only these groups had been stronger or more insistent, they could have made the company go under. Instead, the offending company has spent $30,000 to try to get everything legal.

A nice start, but we've only just begun to torment this guy.

Name withheld

coauthor of *Blowing the Whistle: The Organizational & Legal Implications for Companies & Employees.* "Even the best studies still have a lot of unexplained variance," she said. Nevertheless, Miceli notes there still are some "statistically significant" characteristics of whistle-blowers. Whistle-blowers do not generally fit the stereotype of the "disgruntled" employee. They aren't newcomers. They have slightly higher self-reported performance. And they feel "morally compelled" to report the wrongdoing. Miceli also points out that despite the moral compulsion they feel, whistle-blowers do not necessarily have higher moral codes than those who remain quiet. In fact, she said, one study suggested just the opposite. Whistle-blowers who go outside their companies to call attention to what is going on within them tend to work in organizations that have climates that are more retaliatory. Whistle-blowers also believe the public or their coworkers are being harmed by the wrongdoing when they decide to go outside their companies.

How effective whistle-blowers are at improving their workplace and working lives varies. It depends on the culture of an organization, the nature of the offense and who the guilty parties are. As one whistle-blower remarked about a failed ethics policy at the California defense contractor for which he had worked, "If it was some guy stealing parts from the supply room, the company was very quick to respond to the whistle-blower, but when it came to allegations of conflicts of interest against members of senior management, the whistle-blower quickly became a persona non grata."

As a means of improving the workplace, whistle-blowing can be a selfless approach. Whistle-blowers can be effective in bringing about change for coworkers—Texaco is probably a better place for minorities to work today than before Lundwall shared his tapes with attorneys—but about all it does for the whistle-blowers themselves is force them to come to terms with the reality that there exists a deep and irreparable rift between them and their employers. In many cases, whistle-blowers are mercilessly driven out of the organization or simply leave because they find they can no longer work for their employers in good conscience. Though family, financial and career trauma often results, in a strange way whistle-blowers improve their working life by simply acknowledging and respecting their own values. "Some consider it a benefit to find out the truth about their organizations, coworkers or friends, even though it may be painful at the time, and it is likely that some then move on to organizations that they find truly share their values," said Ohio State's Miceli. "Many gain respect for themselves and their courage."

Some, though, say it's just not worth it. Bill Bush, who regularly counsels would-be whistle-blowers, is blunt about it. "I ask them, 'Are you a masochist?' If you are, hell, go forward and speak the truth," he said. "If you are a sensitive person and don't want to lose every dime you saved, hell, don't do it." Bush, a former engineer at

NASA's George C. Marshall Space Flight Center in Huntsville, Alabama, blew the whistle on several problems in the mid-1970s, including the fact that he and other employees sat around all day getting paid with nothing to do. He said that when supervisors ignored his complaints, he took them to the press.

NASA fired back at him with fourteen pages of complaints about his work and demoted him. Instead of having engineering responsibilities, he was assigned clerical work and his $32,000 salary was cut by $10,000. Though a civil service appeals board eventually reinstated him, it was just the start of more than ten years of harassment and legal battles with the space agency, which took a harsh toll on Bush. He was isolated from coworkers, a private investigator probed his personal life and he continues to suffer from three stress-related illnesses he attributes to his whistle-blowing experiences. "It's ruined my health, it's ruined my financial condition and it's ruined my marriage," he said. "I'm lucky in the respect that I still have my mind. Many of my friends who have spoken up have ended up in an insane asylum."

Insane asylums are actually a favorite place government agencies and the military like to send whistle-blowers, although that's become a bit tougher thanks to Dr. Donald Soeken, a former government psychiatrist who went before Congress in 1978 to blow the whistle on the practice of harassing whistle-blowers by questioning their sanity and subjecting them to needless psychiatric examinations. "I would see that most people they sent were not mentally ill. They were whistle-blowers or 'troublemakers' or people who had trouble with their bosses," he said. "You can't get it out of your file. It sticks with you your whole life." He succeeded in getting legislation passed that prohibits the use of psychiatric examinations by government agencies in personnel actions, except where public safety is an issue. Soeken eventually left the Public Health Service after a second round of whistle-blowing and founded Integrity International, a Laurel, Maryland–based counseling service for whistle-blowers.

In 1987, Soeken conducted a study of ninety whistle-blowers

and found some rather grim results that quantified the general health, family and financial problems that can go hand in hand with whistle-blowing. Of those queried, 10 percent said they had attempted suicide, 17 percent had lost their homes, 15 percent got divorced, 20 percent lost their job and more than half said their peers had harassed them. Coworkers often feel threatened when a colleague turns whistle-blower for basic economic reasons. They fear that the revelations made by the whistle-blower can cost the company vital contracts, important customers or big fines that jeopardize their jobs. Even when they know the whistle-blowers' claims to be true, rather than embrace them as heroes, more often they ostracize them and label them "squealers," "finks" and "troublemakers." Soeken said, "It tears your moral guts out. Many whistle-blowers say, 'I'm stronger now. I can sleep at nights.' But they don't eat well and their family may be all broken up."

Experts such as Soeken say there are ways whistle-blowers can protect themselves in going public with their allegations. The best way to blow the whistle is to not let anyone know you are doing it. One means of doing this is to anonymously deliver documentation to the proper authorities or to do it through a third party. As Federal Aviation Administration whistle-blower Jim Pope remarked to the Glazers in their book *The Whistleblowers,* the Watergate scandal's Deep Throat is perhaps the ideal whistle-blower. "Deep Throat's revelations were all covert, provocative, suspenseful, serialized, accurate and documentable," Pope told the Glazers. "As far as is known, Deep Throat is the only whistle-blower to have successfully accomplished the two major objectives of any whistle-blower: one, to suffer no repercussions for his revelations and two, to successfully accomplish his mission."

Anonymity, however, is not always possible. Frequently the whistle-blower will have complained internally about the problems and may be the only one with access to the relevant information. If that's so, then the more noise the whistle-blower makes the safer the whistle-blower will likely be. "It's much easier to kill you in the dark," said Ann Medlock, president of the Giraffe Project, a Langley, Washington–based nonprofit organization that tries to call media attention to "people who stick their necks out" in order to make the world a better place. "We try to shine as much light as possible."

Publicity helps level the playing field between the employer and whistle-blower. "You've got to make all the noise you can," said the researcher Myron Glazer. "You need to get protection." He said it is crucial to bring in allies, which includes not only the press, but also public interest groups that might take on the case. He said once the allegations are made public, employers will do whatever they can to undermine the whistle-blower. "If there is anything in your past that can come out to undermine your credibility as a witness, it will come out," said Glazer. But the first thing the experts advise before one goes public is to speak with family and friends who will be affected by the decision so they will know what to expect and be there to offer support.

No matter how well the whistle-blower plans, nothing is going to guarantee them full protection. Because of that, whistle-blowers would be wise to consider if they are ready and willing to leave their job, if the information they are going to make public is significant enough to garner attention and whether the information is verifiable. Before going public it is best to accumulate or record whatever documentation will help substantiate the case. Relevant documents have a nasty way of becoming inaccessible to the whistle-blower or vanishing once the allegations are made. It is also a good idea to line up the support and corroboration of coworkers before actually making the disclosure. Last, consider using internal mechanisms before going outside the company. Experts say that while this will make anonymity nearly impossible, it will help prevent allegations that the disclosures are part of an effort to bring someone down or that the company was unaware of the problem and would have corrected it if only it knew.

When Michael Lissack raised concerns to his bosses that the firm was overcharging municipalities for treasury securities, he said

Making the She-Ape Roar

I am finding out just how horrendous whistle-blowing can get, especially when one blows the proverbial whistle on an ape-boss who is lying her hiney off to everyone from OSHA, the Department of Health, the IRS, the Labor Board, the Liquor Control Board, the property management company, employees and others. She's a very famous chef who owns a lot of restaurants.

To keep my job of 18 months as manager-slave for her restaurants, I tolerated a lot of illegal, immoral and filthy conditions and situations. I have a handicapped seven-year-old, so I was easy to manipulate—a workaholic when promised future opportunities in the business like franchises and specialty food businesses.

When the ape-owner persisted in removing the soap and sanitizer from the dishwasher, as well as 40 other health violations, I called the health department, anonymously, so she wouldn't fire me.

Well she did. It's been a month and a half now. No one will hire me even though I have an excellent work record and a lot of skill. I'd love to know the law. She has sent people to offer money to shut me up, and has threatened employees still in her clutches, should they witness against her.

OSHA is here, getting them to sign forced, perjured statements about my termination. I can't believe they're willing to lie for her. Once this is over and I succeed in forcing her to admit what she's been doing, I'd like to help other people not end up as hostages of conscience.

Amy R.

he was told to "shut up and do my job." A managing director in Smith Barney's public finance department, Lissack said he grew frustrated over being silenced. At the end of 1993, Lissack began to anonymously supply information to the FBI about the practice known as "yield burning." Since he exposed the practice, which he said goes on throughout the industry, reports have estimated that local governments have overpaid more than $1 billion for treasury securities from their investment bankers since the early 1990s, when falling interest rates began a wave of refinancing. Unlike refinancing a mortgage, where a homeowner can retire high interest debt with new, lower-interest debt, municipalities usually have to wait at least ten years before they can pay off bondholders because of the way deals are structured. If interest rates fall, municipalities will refinance their debt and purchase treasury securities with the proceeds and hold them in an escrow account until the higher-interest bonds can be retired. Under law, though, they are prohibited from profiting on those escrow accounts. So, Lissack said, the investment firms decided to capture that profit for themselves by marking up the treasury securities and then getting opinions from friendly competitors that the securities were being sold at fair market price.

The FBI wanted to know who their anonymous informant was, but Lissack told agents, "I value my job. I like getting a paycheck. I will get fired if I tell you who I am." Lissack knew he would not be able to keep his anonymity forever, but he wanted to control when his employer found out. In February 1995, fourteen months after he first contacted the FBI and one New York Minute after his annual bonus check cleared, Lissack sent a memo to his bosses, along with copies to the FBI, Department of Justice and Securities and Exchange Commission. As he recalls it, the memo said, "I am no longer willing to follow your instructions to not talk about this." He was fired the next day, ending thirteen years with the firm and abruptly cutting off his "high, six-figure salary." A month later, he took his story to the *New York Times,* which in March 1995 exposed the practice of yield burning. The investment banking firm has denied any wrongdoing relating to Lissack's allegations.

To a large extent, Lissack's story fits the pattern of many other whistle-blowers. He experienced a severe reduction of income, was unable to get employment in his profession, was ostracized, got divorced, suffered a nervous breakdown and attempted suicide. "But all in all," he said, "I'd say it was worth it."

What gives Lissack's case an added touch of genius was his use of the Internet. Just about any schlub with access to a computer can set up a web page. With a little knowledge and a modest amount of money, whistle-blowers can gain instant access to an international audience and offer unfiltered disclosures about their employers. Web pages targeting employers are increasingly cropping up. They range from gripe pages, such as the Wal-Mart Employee Abuse Forum, where people are told that "not every employee has a smile on their face like in the commercial," to more sophisticated attempts to reveal abuses and organize employees, such as the Former and Current Employees of Intel or FACE Intel page.

Seven months after going public, Lissack launched his "Municipal Bond Scandals" web page. He has since struck the site because he said it has served its purpose, but for fourteen months the website tracked news accounts of various wrongdoings in the public finance arena. He said bond scandals had usually been treated as local occurrences. The web page with so much information gathered in a single place, allowed government regulators and members of the news media to understand that it was a pervasive national problem.

The website also featured "The Smith Barney Page," which included a drawing of a pickpocket at work next to text that read, "Making money the 'old-fashioned way,'" a play on the company's slogan. Smith Barney was none too amused by it all. Attorneys for the investment firm sent letters to Lissack, accusing him of infringing on the trademarks of Smith Barney and its parent Travelers Group, Inc. Lissack believes that Smith Barney's big concern was that as the company pushed forward on building its presence on the World Wide Web, people who use search engines—websites that allow someone to enter key words to find web pages of interest—would find Lissack's page when they went looking for Smith Barney. In fact, that is a concern that Smith Barney's attorneys at Orrick, Herrington & Sutcliffe make clear in their letters. They wanted Lissack to strike all references to Smith Barney. They accused him of repeatedly using the firm's name to cause search engines to find his page "as one of the most relevant on the subject of the 'Smith Barney.'" That points to the beauty of the Internet to whistle-blowers. It allows them to speak as loudly as the multibillion-dollars targets of their alarms.

Lissack's Safer Way to Net Results

Smith Barney whistle-blower Michael Lissack offers some suggestions to any would-be whistle-blowers who would like to avoid putting their careers, family and finances at significant risk. "This will do the trick," he said. "It's an interesting way to spend a Saturday. You would have done your bit, feel good about yourself and won't wreck your life."

1. Buy an inexpensive second hard disk for your home computer—the cheapest you can find—and install it.
2. Build a website that says what you think needs to be said. (All you need to do this is a word processor and a basic guide to HTML or a web page editing program, such as Netscape Gold, Microsoft Front Page or other such program.)
3. After it is all built, copy the website to floppy diskettes. Remove the second hard drive from the machine and run it by a strong industrial magnet several times, take a hammer to it, take it apart and dispose of the pieces. This is to make sure the data is not recoverable.
4. Drive at least fifty miles away with the floppies and find an Internet café. Pay cash and get on-line.
5. Open a hotmail account (it's free and anonymous) for E-mail.
6. Go to Geocities, Tripod or any other website that offers a free home page.
7. Take out the floppies and post it to the site.
8. Notify search engines and relevant news groups through the hotmail account.
9. Take scissors to floppies and throw them away.
10. Go have a pleasant lunch or dinner, drive home and smile knowing that havoc will proceed as you go about your business as usual.

Smith Barney eventually backed off on its trademark infringement claims, but is still embroiled in legal wranglings with Lissack. Lissack's whistle-blowing has led to more than a dozen civil and criminal investigations by the SEC, the Internal Revenue Service and the U.S. Department of Justice. Lissack is seeking $200 million in a wrongful termination case against Smith Barney. Smith Barney has filed a counterclaim seeking $15 million in damages for libel. Separately, Lissack paid $30,000 and accepted a 5-year ban from the Securities and Exchange Commission to settle fraud charges relating to allegations he misrepresented savings for Dade County, Florida, in a bond transaction.

Lissack is working on a Ph.D. in management and no longer has the time or feels the need to maintain the page now that investigations are under way. As for his whistle-blowing and all of the fallout he has endured, Lissack said it was a matter of integrity and self-respect and he would do it again if he had it to do all over. However, he wouldn't recommend it for others. He said he was lucky enough to have the means and not have to worry about children. "The reality is," he said, "if it isn't a major league scale, it's probably not worth wrecking your life over."

Then again, there are those like Wendy Siegel who take it one step further. They have decided work itself is not worth wrecking your life over.

12

Quitting Time

"People will farm in the morning, make music in the afternoon and fuck wherever and whenever they want to."

—JERRY RUBIN
Do It

WENDY **S**IEGEL **LIKED** her job, as unlikely a job as it might have been for her. Originally, she worked as a special education art teacher, but her position lost funding as a result of Reagan-era budget cuts. In 1982, she wound up as an account executive for the Dreyfus mutual fund family in Garden City, New York. The pay was modest, but was better than she made as a schoolteacher. Within six months she began moving up the ladder. She became a training instructor, then a supervisor, then rose to become an assistant vice president in charge of all of the training for the entire corporation. Not bad for a woman who just a few years before was teaching art to kids with problems. In the process, she tripled her salary—and her workload. "I was upwardly mobile. I was doing well. It was a good job," said Siegel. "I loved learning. I loved having to design courses. I loved the job."

Siegel said eventually she was managing 230 people and was responsible for teaching all levels of the corporation about new products that the company was introducing. When new executives

It Is a Far, Far Better Thing I Do

I turned my back on the whole damned business world (after twenty years of it), and just dropped out. I'm not going to say it's an easy way. It is a magnificent challenge to one's wit and courage, but it is a glorious adventure and filled with unique learning. The point being, however, that it *can* be done, and is far better, in my estimation, than either throwing in with the bastards or living a hollowed-out life for the remainder of one's years. (Which may be one and the same thing.)

Irv

were hired, they sat down with Siegel to learn about the company and its offerings. But what began as a nine-to-five job had grown into something far more demanding. As an assistant vice president, Siegel would arrive at the office around 7 A.M. and leave at 9:30 P.M. with a briefcaseful of work to do at home. "There were days I was writing training manuals until two or three in the morning," she said. "I would try to take at least one weekend day off. Frequently, I didn't."

Siegel studied art in college and considered herself a painter, but with the hours her job demanded she no longer had time to paint—except for one day each year. Though vacations often had to be canceled, Siegel would take her birthday off and spend the day painting. Because she had always lived simply, not increasing her expenses as her salary grew, she was able to squirrel away a fair bit of money—roughly two-thirds of what she was making as an assistant vice president.

After about six years with the company, Siegel said, the stress was starting to get to her. She felt she had "too much responsibility and not enough support." On Labor Day 1988, she made a promise to herself that within two years she would quit her job and paint full-time. A year later, at the age of thirty-five, she resigned. She was fully vested in the company's retirement plan, debt-free and, because she had always lived modestly, had managed to tuck away five years' worth of living expenses in the bank. "I realized that what I wanted more than anything else was to be painting and doing artwork. By keeping the corporate job, I was denying my true love of artwork," she said. "If I didn't do it then, I don't know when I would have done it."

What Siegel did is becoming common enough in today's working world that it has gotten a name: "downshifting." In basic terms, she merely did what many people would do if they could only figure out a way to do it. She opted out of the rat race. After Siegel gave up working, she rose with the sun, would start her day by meditating and then paint until lunch. Depending on how involved she was with a painting, she might take a walk during the afternoon or just paint straight through. In the evening she socialized, although the longer she was away from work the less important socializing became to her. The main difference was that the daily stress she had come to accept as part of life was gone. "I would play music and dance while I would paint," she said. "There was so much joy in my life. The more I painted, the more joy there was."

Increasingly, work-weary people like Siegel are realizing that time is more valuable to them than money. They are trading in their standard of living for quality of life, learning to give up their new and improved, turbocharged, deluxe, consumer ways for greater freedom and control over their lives. They are avoiding debt, buying things they need instead of things they want and enjoying their lives more.

Gerald Celente of the Trends Research Institute in Rhinebeck, New York, said that about 5 percent of baby boomers have already simplified their lives in some way in order to work less, and he

Kill the Messenger

The average person watches more than four hours of television each day. At that rate, in a sixty-five-year life, he will have spent nine years in front of a television set, according to the Washington, D.C.–based nonprofit organization TV-Free Nation. The group said the average child sees twenty thousand, thirty-second television commercials a year. By the time a person reaches sixty-five, he will have seen 2 million commercials.

expects that number to grow to about 15 percent by the end of the
year 2000. Some of these people, he said, are not practicing "voluntary simplicity," as it is known, but what he calls "involuntary simplicity"—changing their lives only after they have found themselves
downsized out of a job. Celente compares many of these people to
heart attack victims who survived their ordeals to find that their new
lives of exercise and healthy diets were better than their sedentary,
artery-clogging ways. "People are giving up conspicuous consumption items—the Sharper Image stuff; things you don't need but
would like to have," he said. "They are giving up gadgets and excess
clothing and overindulgence in entertainment. Instead of spending
five thousand dollars to go to Disney World, they pack up the family
and go camping. It's the simple pleasures."

Though it would be hard to tell from watching television—especially a nice, new, 32-inch set with stereo sound and a satellite dish—
there appears to be a certain uneasiness among Americans about their
values and the way they live. The old American dream was rooted in
materialism. It was the promise of a home and a car, explained Ellen
Furnari, executive director of the Center for a New American Dream,
in Burlington, Vermont, a nonprofit organization that helps people
examine the consequences of consumerism and materialism. "We'd
like to think there's a new American dream about community and
family and enjoying the outdoors," she said. "It's not about power
and money. These are the values people say they have. But when you
ask them are they doing anything different, they say, 'No.' There's a
gap between what people say they value and what their plans are."

While the American passion for material goods doesn't seem to
have waned much, Americans are saying they think their priorities
are out of whack, according to a 1995 study commissioned by the
Merck Family Fund as part of an effort to address the consequences
of our culture of consumerism. The report, *Yearning for Balance,*
which involved a series of focus groups and a national survey, concluded that people of all backgrounds share fundamental concerns
about the values driving society and complain that the American

Dream is "spinning out of control as the compulsion to keep up with the Joneses is becoming increasingly unhealthy and destructive." "They believe materialism, greed and selfishness increasingly dominate American life, crowding out a more meaningful set of values centered on family, responsibility and community," the report said. "People express a strong desire for a greater sense of balance in their lives—not to repudiate material gain, but to bring it more into proportion with the nonmaterial rewards of life."

Breaking free of the consumer lifestyle may seem like it requires a 12-step program—"My name is Danny and I'm a consumer"—but Joe Dominguez and Vicki Robin say it only takes nine. In their book *Your Money or Your Life,* they outline a way for people to free themselves of work by gaining control over their financial lives. At the heart of the approach is changing the relationship people have with money by having them do a little soul-searching to figure out what their values and needs are. One of the first steps is to come to an understanding of how much time and money they put into work. Once people understand the actual amount of time it takes them to earn a spendable dollar—the amount of life they are trading for it—they can start to make intelligent choices about whether the things they are spending their money on are really worthwhile to them.

To calculate what someone really makes an hour, the two argue, people need to consider all the additional time they lose to the job, such as commuting, decompressing, preparing and seeking distractions from work, and to add that to the hours they actually work. At the same time, they need to deduct from the money they earn at work all of the expenses they incur that they would not have if they didn't work, such as suits or uniforms, dry cleaning and eating out because they are too tired from having worked to cook. In a hypothetical example of someone who works a forty-hour week and earns $440, that person would appear to earn $11 an hour. But when Dominguez and Robin calculate in all of the other time needs and job-related expenses, the person loses another thirty hours a week to work and spends $160 because of the job. All of a sudden, his workweek grows to seventy hours and his pay falls to $280 a week, or just $4 dollar an hour—about enough to pay for a large latte and blueberry muffin on the way to the office in the morning.

"Some people have no sense that their life is about anything more than being a wage slave. It's very hard to motivate yourself to do anything other than drive back and forth to the office," said Robin. "Some people have a sense that their life is about something more: having friends, raising a family, contributing to a community, doing art, surfing—anything. They feel there is a larger them that deserves expression."

Those who view themselves as greater than their work are finding ways to cut back. The Merck survey found that 28 percent of those queried said that within the past five years they had scaled back on their salaries and lifestyle to "reflect a different set of priorities." Some took work that paid less, some reduced the hours of their jobs and others quit outright to stay at home. The most frequent reasons cited for these changes were wanting a more balanced life (68 percent), wanting more time (66 percent) and wanting a less stressful life (63 percent). A little more than half of these people downshifted to care for their children. Overall, 87 percent say they are happy with the change they made, although 30 percent said they did miss the extra income.

Patrick Schlesinger is someone who decided to trade job status and income for more time with his family and a life with less stress. It wasn't long ago that Schlesinger looked like he had been in an auto wreck. In need of sleep, the environmental attorney walked around at a weekend gathering for his son's nursery school wearing a cervical collar that made him look like the classic whiplash victim. Another parent turned to his wife and said, "My God, what happened to Patrick?" His wife casually responded, "Oh, it's just stress from work." Schlesinger said stress was a contributor, but that his neck problems also had to do with marathon conference calls without the aid of a speakerphone. Unable to sleep because of the neck pain, he would get up at 3 A.M. and just work. "I figured I might as well be billing if I'm going to be up," he said.

After three years with the Environmental Protection Agency, Schlesinger joined Landels, Riply & Diamond, a mid-sized law firm in San Francisco with a growing environmental practice. Though Schlesinger said he loved being a lawyer, work began to change. As the economy tanked, clients became more sophisticated consumers of legal services and demanded more for their money. The financial pressure started to take its toll on the culture of the firm. Known as one of the more relaxed and liberal firms in the city, it became more "businesslike," he said. In 1993, Schlesinger became a partner and suddenly found that, in addition to his existing workload, he was expected to serve on committees and take on new responsibilities, such as marketing the firm. On a typical day, he would begin work at 9 A.M. and leave between 6:30 and 7 P.M. and then put in a couple of more hours of work at home.

But as demands at work were building, so too were demands at home. His wife, Esther, worked as well and their second son was

Firmly Back Down to Earth

After working for a large aerospace company for more than five years, I was getting tired of the mindless procedures and blundering management. I had been hired to do mechanical design. (I am an engineer.)

Yet, I spent most of my time trying to get around the company bureaucracy—a thankless, nonproductive job. Thoughts of quitting had frequently crossed my mind, but the job paid very well, it was familiar and my coworkers were fun to be with.

One day I was riding down the elevator with an older engineer whom I'll call Joe. Joe was retiring after 30 years with the company. This was his last day.

I asked Joe what the highlight of his career was. He stared at me for a solid minute over the box of personal belongings he carried. He looked away. His face got cloudy. As he walked out of the door for the very last time, he shook his head and mumbled, "What a waste, what a waste!"

I quit the next day.

James K.

Brother Can You Spare a Dime an Hour

I poured my heart and soul into the company for $5.00 an hour. I loved the work so much, money was not an issue. After three years, I asked for a 10 cent per hour raise, but I didn't really want the money.

I wanted one week paid at Christmas to be with my daughter who lives with her mom. I figured it out and one week with pay was the equivalent of a 10 cents per hour raise for one year.

My boss, who had kids too, denied my request. So I suggested that he take one paid week one year and I get it the next. "No way!" he replied. "If I have to work that week, I get time and a half. No way."

Of course, my attitude went in the toilet. I quit in April; they went bankrupt in December. I can't count how many times customers assumed I was a partner in the business because my attitude was that good. It's comforting to know that business has a self-cleansing nature if the owners are stupid enough long enough.

After this experience, and a couple of similar ones, I have decided that as long as I can eke out some level of survivable existence, I will never work for anyone other than myself again.

Jim P.

born in 1995. Soon after, Schlesinger found himself embroiled in a case that he was preparing for trial while his newborn son was up through the night. "It was putting a strain on the marriage," he said. "Something had to give, and it was not going to be my marriage."

Schlesinger tried some unusual approaches at the office to ease the time demands. During the annual ritual at the law firm when the compensation committee would meet to review salaries, each of the lawyers would argue over his or her value to the firm in memoranda known as "brag sheets." They would spell out why they were God's gift to the firm and why they deserved the raises they were proposing. Schlesinger would go in and say, "I don't want more money. I want more time"—an exercise that would leave some partners wondering whether he was sane, on drugs or simply from Mars. "Some of them didn't take me seriously," he said. "To their credit, they gave

Bye Bye Birdie

Unfortunately I spent four years of my young life slaving away at various sites of a famous pizza chain. At one particular restaurant, I encountered many problems with the power-hungry manager. I would come home from school at 2:15 P.M., sleep for two-and-a-half hours and then go into work for the 5 P.M. shift. I'd leave work around 11 P.M., go home to do homework until about 2 A.M., get up by 7 A.M. for school the next morning. My sleep schedule was weird, but I was used to it.

As a consequence of this schedule, I would show up for work at 5 P.M. with reddish eyes because that's how my eyes always are soon after waking up. I was treated weirdly for a while until I found out from one of the manager trainees that my boss thought I was coming into work stoned. I had never tried illegal drugs in my life. He didn't even have the nerve to ask me. He just started spreading rumors.

After I confronted him politely about it, I eventually was "promoted" to day shift manager, meaning that I would open up the store on weekends and would run it until the night manager got there. Then I would balance the books, do the day's paperwork and leave by 5:30 P.M.

One Saturday afternoon I received a phone call from a friend telling me that a friend of ours had been accidentally shot and was in intensive care at the nearby hospital. When the same manager as above came in to run the evening shift, I did my paperwork and asked him if I could leave, explaining that a friend of mine was terribly hurt and I needed to see him and his family at the hospital.

He refused and kept me there until I finally walked out at 8 P.M. The store was slow. There were enough workers to cover the evening rush. He was just power-tripping. After asking him again and again and listening to him say, "Just stay twenty more minutes" and "Oh, I'll need you to stay for another hour," I didn't bother to ask. I calmly walked to the back, changed out of my uniform and headed toward the door. When he asked where I was going, I told him I was going to the hospital to see my friend who had been shot and that I didn't appreciate his inflexibility. With customers in the store, he hollered, "If you walk out that door, don't come back!" I said, "Fine!" shot him a bird and left.

Cat

me a raise every year, but everyone had to crank to make the firm profitable."

Then, in 1996, a friend of Schlesinger's who worked as a staff attorney for the University of California told him she was leaving her job and asked if he would like to take her place as a university counsel. The work was interesting: handling environmental law issues for the university statewide. The job meant a 25 percent pay cut, but he took it anyway and his life changed. In exchange for accepting less pay, he has cut his commute in half, his workday runs from 9 A.M. to 6 P.M. and he now has dinner with his children every night, something that was not possible before. For the most part, he never works on weekends anymore. And, instead of spending time discussing billing with clients, filling out time sheets and performing committee work, he spends his whole day working on legal issues. "The biggest adjustment was dealing with the unremitting joy of not filling out time sheets," he said.

There were financial pressures. He and his wife drive cars that are eight years old, they no longer take the two annual trips back to his wife's parents' home in North Carolina and now they budget their expenses, something they never needed to do before. "When you start to budget," he said, "you realize you spent a lot of money on stupid things."

It's through helping people avoid spending on stupid things that Amy Dacyczyn was able to retire at the age of forty-one and raise her six children full-time. Her husband had already retired from the military to be a full-time father. For six years from her home in Leeds, Maine, Dacyczyn published *The Tightwad Gazette,* a newsletter through which she preached the virtues of penny-pinching. She said that for the most part, the downshifters she is seeing are people in two-income households who are making a conscious decision to scale back in order to reduce stress in their lives. But rather than using the term "downshifting" or "voluntary simplicity," Dacyczyn calls it a return to frugality. That's because what people do in cutting back on work and spending less often requires learning new skills and doesn't necessarily mean a simplification. For instance, in many ways it's "simpler" to buy a loaf of bread than to bake one, especially if you are making bread for the first time. The real simplification of life comes from removing pressure and demands on time. "In the big picture of life, it is simpler to be a one-income family than a two-income family," said Dacyczyn. "When you are trying to balance the needs of your children with the needs of your employer it's hard. These are two groups that want to have their needs fulfilled right now."

It's not hard to understand how the competing demands of work and family create stress. Just imagine a woman at work who gets a call from the elementary school that her son is sick and she must take him home right now. At the same time, her boss is demanding that she attend a meeting—right now. "Downshifting is simpler because it is not competitive," she said. "If your child is hurt, you can put down the gardening."

Living more frugally doesn't mean you have to go Dumpster-diving for dinner, just that you be a little smarter and live a little more deliberately. In a two-income family, time is scarce. Instead of making dinner, people eat out. Instead of fixing something around the house themselves, a repairman is called in to do it. Dacyczyn said she and her husband turned around their financial lives when they realized they were spending a lot of their money on "temporary pleasures"—eating out, going to movies—and nothing on the long-term things, such as furniture. She just reversed that. In buying food, she keeps it simple, stocking up on basics when they are on sale, but she will spend real money on a piece of furniture that the family will live with the rest of their lives. "We just stopped wasting money on things that didn't matter in the long run," she said. And while doing it yourself is cheaper, it's even cheaper and easier to do without or to keep it simple, such as exchanging a few small gifts and enjoying each other's company.

Some people may try to take it to extremes at times. Marc Eisenson, an electrical engineer and contractor, decided he'd had enough with work in 1972. When he was twenty-nine, he and his brother sold the business they had built and decided to live more simply. Of course, times were a little different then. When he first gave up work he wanted to see how far he could take it. He spent six months in a ramshackle barn on an abandoned commune in upstate New York during the winter. The barn had no heat when he moved in to it. "I wasn't a genius at the time," he said. "The next day we had to buy a woodstove." Even with the woodstove he would wake up in the morning to find that the glass of water by his bed had turned to solid ice. He said he and his companion were able to get by on about $15 each a month for food. "I learned a lot about myself. I like a few more amenities," he said. "I can live a simple life, but I like electricity, I like indoor plumbing, a car, a telephone."

Today he lives with his partner, Nancy Castleman, in less Spartan surroundings and publishes a newsletter called the *Pocket Change Investor*, which teaches people how to free themselves of debt and live simply. For the last sixteen years he has rented a house on a 375-acre farm in Elizaville, New York, in Columbia County on the Dutchess County border. He pays in rent what taxes alone for a small house in a nearby town would cost him. They maintain a 10,000-square-foot garden where they grow "everything except rutabagas," including fifteen varieties of tomatoes. "Even when I was a successful businessperson, it didn't make any sense to me to buy things I didn't need and essentially waste money that at some point could buy me my freedom," said Eisenson. "Once you have manageable debt or no debt, you are relatively free."

That's what Max Blackwood has found out. Blackwood graduated with an MBA from the Wharton School of Business in 1971 and walked into a job at the Bank of America. In 1991, after working in various capacities at the bank, he and BofA mutually agreed the two were no longer meant for each other. "They didn't think much of my output," he said. "We reached an agreement for me to leave." He was working in the bank's leasing department at the time. It was then that the forty-six-year-old Blackwood discovered something important about himself. "Looking back on it," he said, "I realized I didn't like working all that much then and still don't."

Instead of taking another job in the leasing business, he went to work for his brother selling roofing materials. It represented a cut in income, but he didn't have to work too hard. He negotiated a deal where he could have the freedom to go to a baseball game during an afternoon or play a round of golf if he wanted to do that. Eventually

Checkout Time

I was the head of housekeeping for a hotel undergoing a complete renovation.

For two months I'd been putting in ten- to twelve-hour days. Suddenly my staff and I find ourselves working sixteen-hour days for a week straight.

The night before the hotel was due to open much of the room furniture had not arrived.

Trouper that I was, I stayed until the very last of what little furniture we had was installed in the rooms. At 2 A.M., the rooms manager called me into his office and immediately began berating me, belittling me and treating me like shit. He said, and I quote, "A complete moron could have accomplished more in the last two months than you have."

It got worse. I went home that night (morning!), extremely exhausted and fed up. I returned to work at 9 A.M., determined to do the right thing. I typed up a resignation letter and put it on the director of human resources' desk. I thought it would be only right to give them two weeks to fill my position.

But after a few hours consideration, I changed my mind. At noon, I walked into the human resource director's office, and said, "I've rethought that resignation letter I gave you this morning."

"Oh," she responded, "would you like me to give it back to you?" smirking at me as if I still wanted this shitty job.

"No," I said. "I'd like you to shove it up the room manager's ass. I don't know what I was thinking, giving you two weeks to replace me. You don't deserve two minutes more of my time. You know where you can send my final check. Don't call me, I'll call you."

It felt great!

Baldty

he was on a straight commission basis and, he said, even though the product he was selling was a good one, business suffered when low-priced competition entered the market. "I was going broke, trying to live on four hundred dollars a month," he said. "I decided I was deep enough in debt and decided I'd better go back to my real calling. I went to work for another leasing company."

Things went well in his new job. He was there three years and became the top salesman, but then he discovered what "employment-at-will" meant. The boss had two people for one position, and Black-wood admits he has never been someone who was easy to work with. The company reorganized and Blackwood was out of a job. Though he and his wife had planned for him to work another five years until he was fifty-five, he decided not to look for other work. Though headhunters would call him, he refused to pick up the phone. "I was tired," he said. "I was fifty years old. I didn't want a job where they could say, 'Can I see you in my office.' I had enough of putting up with that."

What Blackwood said he gave up in order to stop working was very little. Before they got married his wife had a condo in San Francisco and he had a house out in the country in western Marin County near Point Reyes. The two now own them debt-free and live in the city during the week and go out to the country on week-ends. "You get to a point and say, 'I don't need any more. I don't want a new car, a getaway home, a new house. I don't want a Jaguar. I don't want,'" he said. "When you don't want anything, you are pared back to your basic expenses." These days he studies French, is helping remodel the kitchen in his country home and takes walks around San Francisco for an hour or two a day. "You shouldn't be working at 50, if you have enough money not to work—unless you like working."

Downshifting experts say the biggest hurdles people who want to cut back on work face are not financial, but psychological. Leslie Godwin, founder of the management consulting firm Parent Support Service in Calabasas, California, works with employers and employees to help people strike a balance between their work and family lives. She tells the story of one professional couple, both of whom had interesting jobs. But with a ten-month-old child at home they had new stress in their lives and were concerned that their son wasn't getting the attention he needed from them. They wanted to know how they could simplify their lives. Ultimately, the woman decided to cut back on work, something that was hard for her to do because she had a good job and had always pictured herself doing it all. "The expectations we have for ourselves are probably the biggest problem: How much money we need to have. How many things we need to have. Once you get in a lifestyle you can get locked in to it," she said. "Once I start talking to people, I ask them to consider the possibility of working less. Once people allow themselves to imagine that what they need is more time, they find ways to do it."

13

Getting Gruntled

"Arbeit Macht Frei"
("Work brings freedom")

—Sign on the entrance to Auschwitz

At the Manhattan offices of Steelcase Inc., an office furniture–maker, workers and visitors are greeted in the lobby by a 6-by-4-foot ant farm. Though it is not the standard fare of murals, sculptures and fountains found in most office lobbies, it was chosen by the company to make a statement about work. In an article in the *Wall Street Journal* shortly after the installation of the ant farm, the company said it was looking for a metaphor to describe how people live and work. "Work is dramatically different than it used to be," Steelcase manager Dave Lathrop told the *Journal*. "For more people, work and nonwork are blending." He explained that the company liked that the ants were able to "silently represent that, simply by doing what they do."

While the company did indeed succeed in making a powerful statement about work, it was perhaps not the one intended. The *Journal* pointed out there was one little twist to the exhibit. The ants for the ant farm came from Uncle Milton Industries in Westlake Village, California. While the U.S. Department of Agriculture allows the company to ship the ants anywhere, it doesn't permit Uncle Milton to ship queen ants across state lines, for fear of potential environmental impacts caused by introducing a new species of ant in an area it doesn't belong. Without a queen, the colony would die in three to four months. The architects of the farm were hoping to find a queen for the colony in New York, but had no luck. The absence of success destined the ants to a very modern lifestyle. As *Journal* reporter Andrea Petersen wrote, "Alas, all these ants may ever do is work and die."

The ancient Greeks understood work. The word they used for it is derived from *ponos,* meaning "sorrow." Is it any wonder that when we think of civilization we think of the Greeks? Work was something for the slaves to do while Plato and the gang sat around drinking wine and laying out the foundation for thought in the western world. Somewhere along the way, though, we got lost. God, country and morality somehow became entangled with the notion that anything less than a love of hard work was sacrilegious, immoral and un-American.

A distaste for work is not unique. In America, though, the reality is obscured by a grotesque cultural outpouring of perverse notions of careers, happiness and success that bombards us at every turn so that those who see more to life than their daily grind feel they are one gripe away from a padded cell. But those who extol the virtues of work and happily push people's noses to the grindstone are either wealthy enough to not have to do it, profit from their preaching or are just too stupid to know any better.

What could be more American than engaging in leisure? Our great contributions to civilization all relate to leisure. Baseball, the great American pastime, was meant for lazy afternoons. (Employers thought up the insidious night game.) Hollywood did not craft its great works so people could borrow them from Blockbuster on the way home from work. They were made to be enjoyed on a big screen in a darkened theater, preferably during a sun-sheltering matinee with the air-conditioning blasting away. And the television, La-Z-Boy and six-pack were designed to be used when people still had enough energy to pop open a can, the strength to pull the recline lever and limber enough to stretch for the remote control without pulling a muscle.

Some people think that disgruntled employees are a recent phenomenon, a fallout from the massive corporate downsizings that began in the late 1980s. But before the AT&T layoffs, there were the IBM layoffs. Before IBM, there was Ronald Reagan throwing the air traffic controllers out on their asses. Before that, there was runaway inflation that eroded working wages. Before that, there were the armies of conformists in gray flannel suits living their lives of quiet desperation. And before that, we celebrated a rich heritage of sweatshops, life-threatening factories and worker-beating Pinkertons—not to mention the fact that before there were wage slaves driving our nation's economy there were simply those cotton-picking slaves.

Work has always sucked. The change is not that work has gotten crueler—that would be hard to do. But the places for shelter within the world of work, the so-called good jobs and good companies, are dissolving into the same stench-filled muck that more and more of us find ourselves wading in up to our elbows. The illusion that all anyone need do is their job— work hard and everything will be fine—now lies in the scrap heap next to the beliefs in a flat earth and spontaneous generation.

The rules of work have been rewritten, but

Long-Term Appreciation

I had a wonderful job for a short time. The pay was absolutely terrible. There were no benefits. The office was old, cold and outdated. The work was hard.

I wish I could afford to take that job again. My boss was a saint. Every day he thanked me for doing a good job. He only yelled once at me in six years. If he questioned me about my work, it was only about the work, never a personal attack.

It's amazing what a difference bosses make. I have never had, and will never again have a boss like him. He wanted me to have a life outside the office. He was concerned when I was sick. If I'm ever in a position to be boss, I'll definitely copy that page from his book.

JM

the laws meant to shield employees against the harsh and abusive elements of work have not. As a result, the people that these laws are meant to protect increasingly find themselves treading water in the moat rather than laboring safely behind the castle walls. We are a nation that prides itself on civil liberties, democracy and love of freedom, but at every turn we let them crumble in our workplaces. No indignity seems too great to suffer if it is part of what it takes to put food on the table.

For women at a Nabisco plant in Oxnard, California, that meant accepting their employer's rule that they could not go to the bathroom except at break times, even though men at the plant did not have to conform to the same rule. The restrictive policy led some women to take the degrading step of wearing diapers while at work. "It's humiliating to have to walk in there like a baby," fifty-nine-year-old Lydia Hernandez told the *Los Angeles Times*. "It was hell, a nightmare from the minute I got into work in the morning, not knowing whether I would be able to hold it." After twenty-five years on the job, Hernandez said, she was fired for fighting a supervisor over the policy. In 1995, workers filed a lawsuit against Nabisco, alleging sexual discrimination. But when Nabisco subsequently announced plans to sell the plant, coworkers blamed the women for the company's decision. Nabisco denied it had discriminated against the women and said its decision to sell the plant was for business reasons and was not retaliation over the lawsuit.

America continues to be a land of opportunity, a place that people throughout the world run, swim or crawl to because of the difference between work here and work in their homeland. Work can get rough here, but at least it is the good ol' U.S. of A., right? Workers from Thailand, wooed by the promise of making big money sewing—a sure fast lane onto the Forbes 400 list of wealthiest people—made their way to sunny California to work for a garment-maker who supplied clothes to major department stores on the East Coast, including Filene's, Hecht's, Macy's Northeast and Famous-Barr. After one worker escaped through an air-conditioning vent and reached authorities, officials raided the apartment complex that housed the operation. They found fifty-six workers in a prisonlike setting, some who worked seventeen-hour days and were only permitted to leave the barbed-wire enclosure once a year, on New Year's Day.

That sweatshops are a dark chapter from our nation's past is hardly the case. A 1994 study of sixty-nine garment factories in California cited by the Associated Press found that half failed to pay minimum wage, 68 percent did not pay overtime and 90 percent had health and safety violations. Most of us see this as alien to our experience, shake our heads and thank God that at least we have jobs good enough to allow us to shop in such places as Filene's, Hecht's, Macy's Northeast and Famous-Barr. Dressed neatly, we head off to our offices to become workers without names in cubicles without numbers.

It is easy enough to figure out that work sucks. The hard part is figuring out what to do about it. The more entrepreneurial among us might be able to free themselves from reliance on an employer, but for most people without a rich, dead uncle who was very fond of us, loaded in-laws or the six winning numbers in tonight's Super Lotto drawing, we have come to accept the reality that we are going to have to drag our sorry asses out of bed and toil to make our daily bread.

There are things that can be done to mitigate the harsher elements of work. The government can pass laws that protect the needs and rights of employees and reflect the dramatic changes in the way we work, such as our growing reliance on contingent workers—whose rights must be recognized as well. The government can give adequate resources

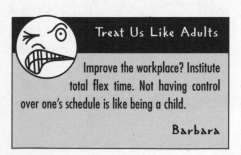

Treat Us Like Adults

Improve the workplace? Institute total flex time. Not having control over one's schedule is like being a child.

Barbara

to the Department of Labor, the Equal Employment Opportunity Commission and the Occupational Safety and Health Administration—all of which are significantly understaffed—to do the jobs that Congress has mandated them to do. It can use tax policy to encourage corporations to treat their workers well and share with them more of the fruit of their labor. The government can also revamp the tax code to stop penalizing workers who are trying to adapt to new ways of working in a world where employers don't want employees, but disposable contractors that can be tossed out when a project is done.

Unions can help too. They can reach beyond their shrinking ranks and speak not only to the needs of their members, but to a broader body of working people who share common needs and interests. Labor's greatest gains in the past have benefited not only union members, but all workers, whether it was a fight for shorter hours, wage standards or safer working conditions. Unions also need to reach out beyond their traditional membership and find new ways to bring together service sector workers who have not been traditionally organized and people working in nontraditional ways so that their voices can be heard not only in the workplace, but in the political arena.

Employers are in the position to have the most direct impact on improving the quality of life for working people, and stand to gain the most by doing so. They can begin by treating their employees with dignity and respect, by understanding that they have a life away from work, providing them with the necessary flexibility to address the needs of their families or other important aspects of their

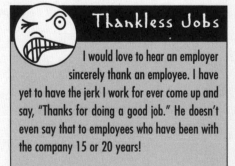

Thankless Jobs

I would love to hear an employer sincerely thank an employee. I have yet to have the jerk I work for ever come up and say, "Thanks for doing a good job." He doesn't even say that to employees who have been with the company 15 or 20 years!

D.J.

lives and by giving them salaries and benefits good enough that they don't have to work two jobs or depend on overtime to meet their living expenses. Instead of focusing on quarterly results, they can invest in their employees. In designing the work, they can reorganize it, keeping in mind the importance of making it as interesting as possible. They can communicate openly with their staffs about what's happening at the company, seek their employees' guidance and value their input. And instead of complaining that loyalty no longer exists, they can earn it by demonstrating it.

While there are plenty of things that the government, unions and employers can do to improve the lot of working people, anyone who continues to toil in a shitty job waiting for that to happen simply accepts their work today as it is. If you are not adequately paid, if the working conditions are bad or if the boss is a tyrannical madman, make the situation better any way you can. The challenge is to take as much control of your working life as possible and find ways to improve it. There is no single, simple solution. For some people it will

An Ill Wind

I just quit a job that was less than glamorous. My boss never took a bath, drank early in the morning, would not eat all day long and treated all employees like dirt except for one female in the office that he let get away with murder.

His body odor was so pronounced that when he was out of the office, his odor still lingered in the furniture. He'd put both arms over his greasy head while talking. The board of directors thought he could do no wrong and refused to take any action even though accounts started to drop off.

I finally asked myself why was I staying and punishing myself. I had no benefits, no retirement and poor working conditions that would never allow for advancement. So I left.

Now I am among those out pounding the pavement for work. But you know what? At least the air smells a lot better.

Saved at last.

KRC

mean cutting their work hours, for others quitting a job for a better one or starting a business and for others merely finding ways to reorganize the work they already do. But it must begin with a realistic understanding of the workplace.

Consider the lowly streptofaecalus bacteria that inhabit the deep recesses of the human bowel. Billions of them work hard night and day to break down the sludge traveling through the colon. This may not be fine dining at its best, but for these lowly bacteria that inhabit this twisted stinkfest, it's a living. Their work is critical to the functioning of the organism they inhabit and, in return, they get three squares and a roof over their head, so to speak. The bacteria are single-celled organisms that don't have a brain, but even if they did have one to go along with their microscopic bodies they would surely never be stupid enough to confuse this symbiotic marriage with love.

So too is it with work. Our employers may not be worthy objects for us to love, honor and obey, but that was never really part of the bargain, even if they seem to think it was. A day's work for a day's wages doesn't mean having to sacrifice life, liberty and the pursuit of happiness for the privilege of enriching our employers. Like a battered wife stuck in an abusive relationship from which she can't seem to free herself, some suffer the slings and arrows of outrageous misfortune and, rather than moving on, simply make excuses for their abusive bosses. "These

No Piece, No Justice

The only way to assure the long-term satisfaction of any employee is a stake in the company itself—and I'm not talking ESOPs where employees get tiny little pieces of the company with no real influence on the company's policy. An employee-owned workplace with ownership equally shared by all employees is the best answer.

As long as people are chained to the wage system, when managers can indiscriminately hire and fire, and corporate profits are channeled to a few, there's no justice in the workplace.

Sean G.

Good Question

The big question I always have for disgruntled people is why stick in a dead-end job working for shitty managers? I never stuck around in a bad situation, and now I work for myself. I'm not making quite as much money as I did before (although there is lots of potential), but I am a hell of a lot happier.

Dan

are difficult times," they will tell themselves. "My boss is under a lot of pressure right now," they say. "Everyone has to sacrifice a little now, but my loyalty will be recognized and rewarded." These honest, hardworking souls—the type P. T. Barnum noted were born every minute—think that with the right job they will be taken care of by a caring partner: their employer. If you go to the workplace in search of a nurturing parent, a life-mate or a best friend, you are looking for love in the wrong places. Get a dog.

That's not to say employers and employees can't get along or shouldn't, but any relationship works best when the two parties involved have a reasonable understanding of each other's expectations, needs and desires. Employers, for the most part, want their work to be done, properly and with as little distraction as possible. Employees, for the most part, want to be paid fairly for their labors, perform work that utilizes their talents and abilities and be treated with courtesy and respect. Tension will always exist between an employer's interests in maximizing profits and an employee's interest in having a life. That is inherent to the nature of work in our economy. Even when employer and employee get along, they are somewhat separated by their necessarily different perspectives.

While it may not be possible to change an employer's perspective, it is certainly possible for employees to change their own. That may mean undoing years of the schooling, parenting and cultural brainwashing that has shaped people to be good little worker bees. The cycle of anxiety in which someone's self-worth and identity become bound to a job begins when one is young. It starts with adults asking little children what they want to be when they grow up. It continues with an educational system that is more concerned with training people for the workforce than helping them acquire the skills to think critically and develop an appreciation of the things that humanize us, such as art, literature and music. And it leads right up to the books that tell the young graduate how to write a resume, interview for a job and be a success.

The assumption underlying all of this is that success is an absolute, that what makes one person happy should make all people happy. It's as if we should all want to call the man on the late-night infomercial who has operators standing by and tell him we want to drive the Mercedes convertible, take the big corner office and buy that multimillion-dollar home (preferably from a divorcing couple who are making a distress sale and using government grants and credit cards to finance the purchase). Of course, when we place the order for his home-study course, there's some mother of six sitting in a cubicle in the middle of a big room in Iowa with fifty other women at 2 A.M. to take the order. Is it really hard to see the absurdity of people's justifying working long, hard hours as the means to the end of someday not having to work? Success is not something measured quantitatively, but qualitatively and relatively. Before you can be successful you must first determine what success means to you.

It is bad enough to squander away precious life working; it is a tragedy to do so working at a job that you do not like, that is not rewarding and that offers no sense of accomplishment. The sad reality is that most of

Under Control

I finally got wise and gave up on trying to be a great manager. The owner couldn't have given a shit if I lived or died. I'm a menial administrative person now, and extremely happy to be a nobody. I do my job well, leave at 5:30 P.M. and don't have a worry or a care beyond which bus I need to take home.

Tyler

us not only have to work, but spend a third to a half of our adult waking life doing so. So it might as well be doing something we enjoy, in an environment that is nice, with people we like. If you are among those who are fortunate enough to enjoy their work and find fulfillment there, consider yourself lucky and hope you can sustain it. If not, find ways to improve work or move on.

This can be difficult, because the rules of work are tilted against the employee. The best way to change the rules is to be your own boss—something you can do mentally even if someone else employs you. Actively create the work situation you want. Find ways to re-create your work so it is more rewarding. If your company is engaging in illegal or unethical business practices, do what you can to call outside attention to it. If the company does not provide adequate breaks, find ways to create them within the work. If there are parts of your job you don't like, find ways to change them. Just remember, trying to change a workplace by yourself can be hazardous to your livelihood. One loudmouth is a nuisance who is disposed of easily. But a whole department of loudmouths is another story. Understand the common bonds you share with coworkers and seek them out to talk about work and about how to make the workplace a more inhabitable environment.

We live in a world of our own creation. If you want your boss to respect the fact that you have a life away from work, you have to begin by respecting that fact yourself. If you want your boss to compensate you fairly, don't work for substandard wages. And if you think you spend too much time working, find ways to work less. The ultimate leverage an employer has over an employee is the ability to fire him. If you develop a willingness to change jobs and acquire marketable and transferable skills—preferably at the expense of your employer—the employer's leverage is lessened and the chain around your ankle will loosen.

Ultimately, your relationship to work is a reflection of values. What work you do, how much time you spend doing it, the time you spend not doing other things, how you do the work, the conditions you are willing to subject yourself to and who you work for are all a reflection of your values. If you haven't given this thought and have just been sleepwalking through your life, it's time to wake up.

If this book frees just one person from the horrors of nine-to-five, it would have been worth it—assuming, of course, that person is me. If this book belongs to a library or friend or is still in a bookstore, please have the decency to purchase it. If I have done it right, I am now unemployable and can probably use the money. This book has been my effort to free myself from work. Now go free yourself.

Resources for Disgruntled Employees

CIVIL RIGHTS AND DISCRIMINATION

American Civil Liberties Union (ACLU)
http://www.aclu.org
125 Broad Street, 18th Floor
New York, NY 10004
(212) 549-2500

Center for Constitutional Rights
666 Broadway, 7th Floor
New York, NY 10012
(212) 614-6464

Center for Law and Social Policy
1751 N Street, NW
Washington, DC 20036
(202) 328-5140

Lawyers Committee for Civil Rights Under the Law
1450 G Street, NW
Suite 400
Washington, DC 20005
(202) 662-8600

EMPLOYMENT LAW

National Legal Aid and Defender Association
1625 K Street, NW
Suite 800
Washington, DC 20006
(202) 452-0620

Legal Services Corporation
http://www.lsc.gov
1st Street, NE
Washington, DC 20002
(202) 336-8800

The National Employment Lawyers Association
http://www.nela.org
600 Harrison Street
Suite 535
San Francisco, CA 94107-1370
(415) 227-4655

Southern Poverty Law Center
http://www.splcenter.org
400 Washington Avenue
Montgomery, AL 36104
(334) 264-0286

GENERAL INFORMATION FOR EMPLOYEES

National Employee Rights Institute
414 Walnut Street
Suite 911
Cincinnati, OH 45202
(800) HOW-NERI

Working Today
http://www.workingtoday.org
P.O. Box 681
Times Square Station
New York, NY 10108
(212) 840-6066

Employment Law Center
1663 Mission Street
Suite 400
San Francisco, CA 94103
(415) 864-8848

Language Rights Line
(800) 864-1664

Work and Family Line
(800) 880-8047

National Employment Law Project
55 John Street
New York, NY 10038
(212) 285-3025

GOVERNMENT

U.S. Equal Opportunity Commission
1801 L Street, NW
Washington, DC 20507
Phone: (202) 663-4900
TDD: (202) 663-4494

U.S. Department of Labor
http://www.dol.gov
200 Constitution Avenue, NW
Washington, DC 20210
(202) 219-6666

National Labor Relations Board
http://www.nlrb.gov
1099 14th Street, NW
Washington, DC 20570
(202) 273-1000

U.S. Occupational Health and Safety Administration
http://www.osha.gov
Room S-2315
200 Constitution Avenue, NW
Washington, DC 20210
(202) 219-0691

PENSION INFORMATION

American Association of Retired Persons
http://www.aarp.org
601 E Street, NW
Washington, DC 20049
(202) 434-2277

National Senior Citizens Law Center
1101 14th St, NW
Suite 400
Washington, DC 20005
(202) 289-6976

Older Women's League
666 11th Street, NW
Suite 700
Washington, DC 20001
(202) 783-6686

Pension Rights Center
918 16th Street, NW
Suite 704
Washington, DC 20006
(202) 296-3776

Pension Education Clearinghouse
P.O. Box 19821
Washington, DC 20036

National Alliance of Senior Citizens
1744 Riggs Place, NW
Washington, DC 20006
(202) 986-0117

RIGHTS OF RACIAL, ETHNIC AND OTHER GROUPS

Asian-American Legal Defense and Educational Fund
99 Hudson Street
12th Floor
New York, NY 10013
(212) 966-5932

Mexican-American Legal Defense and Education Fund
http://www.maldef.org
182 2nd Street, 2nd Floor
San Francisco, CA 94105
(415) 543-5598

NAACP Legal Defense Fund
99 Hudson Street
Suite 1600
New York, NY 10013
(212) 219-1900

National Conference of Black Lawyers
2 West 125th Street
New York, NY 10027
(212) 864-4000

National Veterans Legal Services Program
2001 S Street, NW
Suite 610
Washington, DC 20009
(202) 265-8305

Puerto Rican Legal Defense and Education Fund
99 Hudson Street
New York, NY 10013
(212) 219-3360

Native American Rights Fund
http://www.narf.org
1506 Broadway
Boulder, CO 80302
(303) 447-8760

American Association for Retired Persons Legal Advocacy Group
http://www.aarp.org
601 E Street, NW
Washington, DC 20049
(202) 434-2060

LAMBDA Legal Defense and Education Fund
http://www.lambdalegal.org
120 Wall Street
15th Floor
New York, NY 10005
(212) 809-8585

President's Committee on Employment of People with Disabilities
http://www.pcepd.gov
1331 F Street, NW
Suite 300
Washington, DC 20004
(202) 376-6200

Job Accommodation Network
http://janweb.icdi.wvu.edu
West Virginia University
918 Chesnut Ridge Road
Suite 1
P.O. Box 6080
Morgantown, WV 26506-6080
(800) 232-9675

National Association of Protection and Advocacy Systems
http://www.protectionandadvocacy.com
900 2nd Street, NE
Suite 211
Washington, DC 20002
(202) 408-9514

RIGHTS OF UNION MEMBERS

American Federation of Labor and Congress of Industrial Organizations (AFL-CIO)
http://www.aflcio.org
815 16th Street, NW
Washington, DC 20006
(202) 637-5000

Association for Union Democracy
http://www.igc.apc.org/laborlink/aud
500 State Street
Brooklyn, NY 11217
(718) 855-6650

SEX DISCRIMINATION, SEXUAL HARASSMENT AND WOMEN'S ISSUES

9 to 5, National Association of Working Women
614 Superior Avenue
Cleveland, OH 44113
(216) 566-9308
(800) 522-0925 (hotline)

NOW Legal Defense and Education Fund
http://www.nowldef.org
99 Hudson Street
12th Floor
New York, NY 10013
(212) 925-6635

Women's Legal Defense Fund
1875 Connecticut Avenue, NW
Suite 710
Washington, DC 20009
(202) 986-2600

U.S. Department of Labor Women's Bureau
200 Constitution Avenue, NW
Washington, DC 20210
(202) 219-8913

WHISTLE-BLOWING

Advocacy Institute
1707 L Street, NW
Suite 400
Washington, DC 20036
(202) 659-8475

Government Accountability Project
25 E Street, NW
Suite 700
Washington, DC 20001
(202) 347-0360

Public Citizen
www.citizen.org
1600 20th, NW
Washington, DC 20009
(202) 588-1000

*Thanks to the National Employees Rights Institute for its assistance
with this list.*

Disgruntled Links

THE INTERNET CAN be an employee's best friend. How else can someone waste time at work constructively while looking busy whenever the boss glances over?

There is a vast amount of useful information about work on the web, whether it's a matter of learning about your rights in the workplace, finding a job or discovering how to break free of one.

DISGRUNTLED maintains a growing links page on its website (http://www.disgruntled.com). Below is the twenty-five most useful, best or favorite websites on that list.

ACADEMICS

Cornell School of Industrial and Labor Relations
http://www.ilr.cornell.edu/
Features a vast amount of academic information about the workplace. Includes a site search engine to locate specific articles of interest.

Economic Policy Institute
http://epinet.org/
Stimulating information from a think tank that speaks clearly about the economic impact of public policy on working people. Excerpts of reports, studies and critiques of media coverage of economic news.

CONSUMER AND DOWNSHIFTING

The Bag Lady's Cart Full of Abe Pinching Tips
http://www.angelfire.com/ia/baglady/index.html
An extensive link page to websites with information for people who
want to live more frugally.

Frugal Corner
http://www.best.com/~piner/frugal.html
Originally inspired by the *Tightwad Gazette,* this site offers
information to people who want to minimize their spending and
consumption without feeling deprived.

The Leisure Party
http://freespace.virgin.net:82/sarah.peter.nelson/
Challenges readers to reexamine their belief systems regarding work
and to join the Leisure Party in its pursuit of sane alternatives to the
work ethic.

EXECUTIVE COMPENSATION

The Crystal Report
http://www.crystalreport.com/
Leading executive compensation expert Graef Crystal, whom the
New York Times called "the gadfly CEOs like to swat," draws from
his newsletter for this web page.

AFL-CIO Executive Pay Watch
http://aflcio.paywatch.org/ceopay/
A working person's guide to monitoring and curtailing the excessive
salaries, bonuses and perks in CEO compensation packages.

GOVERNMENT

Bereau of Labor Statistics
http://stats.bls.gov/blshome.html
The workplace by the numbers as compiled by the government.

U.S. Department of Labor
http://www.dol.gov/
Speeches, reports, press releases and other information centering on
the hot political issues revolving around work.

Equal Employment Opportunity Commission
http://www.eeoc.gov/
Features text of antidiscrimination laws, instructions on how to file
complaints and related information.

National Labor Relations Board
http://netsite.esa.doc.gov/nlrb/
Features text of recent NLRB decisions.

Occupational Safety and Health Administration
http://www.osha.gov/
Rich with information on health and safety issues in the workplace.

Securities and Exchange Commission's Edgar Database
http://www.sec.gov/edgarhp.htm
A good way to check out what your company is up to and how well
it is treating the head honchos.

LABOR

LaborNet
http://www.igc.org/igc/labornet/
Features labor news and information and an extensive links page of
related sites.

The WWW Virtual Library: Labor and Business History
http://www.iisg.nl/~w3vl/
This is a large collection of links to various sources of information about labor and business.

LEGAL

ACLU
http://www.aclu.org/
A good source of information about employee rights—or lack thereof—in the workplace.

National Employment Lawyers Association
http://www.nela.org/
Contains news about court decisions relating to employment law and other useful information.

POLITICAL

Corporate Watch
http://www.corpwatch.org/
Provides an array of tools to use to investigate and analyze corporate activity. Exposes corporate greed by documenting the social, political, economic and environmental impacts of these transnational giants.

WHISTLE-BLOWING

Courage Without Martyrdom: A Survival Guide for Whistleblowers
http://www.reporter.org/hillman/courage/index.html
This guide to whistle-blowing by Julie Stewart, Thomas Devine and Dina Rasor is an excellent beginning point for anyone considering taking the plunge.

Government Accountability Project

http://www.accessone.com/gap/

Information about ongoing whistle-blowing as well as general information and links from the granddaddy of whistle-blowing organizations.

WORKING

Working Today

http://www.workingtoday.org/

A organization advocating the rights of the new "independent workforce," including consultants, freelancers, temps, the self-employed and anyone else who "realizes a job doesn't last a lifetime."

WORKPLACE

About Work

http://www.aboutwork.com/

Advice-oriented site offers articles, experts and chat areas.

Ethan Winning Associates

http://www1.ewin.com/ewin/

Though geared to the employer, an excellent source of information on the rules and regulations regarding the workplace. Winning, who often helps Grunty out with advice for readers, mixes an encyclopedic knowledge of work rules with his unique brand of humor.

The Work Doctor

http://www.workdoctor.com

Workplace consultants with a pro-employee bent offer sharp commentary and sound advice about the workplace, particularly on the subject of bullying.

Society for Human Resource Management
http://www.shrm.org/
A good source for finding out about the workplace from an HR point of view and how HR people think.

Index